Student Activities Manual

HORIZONS

SIXTH EDITION

Joan H. Manley
University of Texas—El Paso

Stuart Smith
Austin Community College

John T. McMinn
Austin Community College

Marc A. Prévost
Austin Community College

CENGAGE
Learning·

Australia • Brazil • Japan • Korea • Mexico • Singapore • Spain • United Kingdom • United States

CENGAGE
Learning·

Horizons, Sixth Edition
Student Activities Manual
Manley | Smith | McMinn | Prévost

© 2015, 2012, 2009 Cengage Learning

For product information and technology assistance, contact us at
Cengage Learning Customer & Sales Support,
1-800-354-9706

For permission to use material from this text or product, submit all requests online at **www.cengage.com/permissions**
Further permissions questions can be emailed to
permissionrequest@cengage.com

ISBN-13: 978-1-285-43393-6
ISBN-10: 1-285-43393-9

Cengage Learning
5191 Natorp Boulevard
Mason, OH 45040
USA

Cengage Learning is a leading provider of customized learning solutions with office locations around the globe, including Singapore, the United Kingdom, Australia, Mexico, Brazil, and Japan. Locate your local office at:
www.cengage.com/global

Cengage Learning products are represented in Canada by Nelson Education, Ltd.

For your course and learning solutions, visit
www.cengage.com

Purchase any of our products at your local college store or at our preferred online store
www.cengagebrain.com

Printed in the United States of America
2 3 4 5 6   21 20 19 18 17

Table des matières

Préface

This *Student Activities Manual (SAM)* supports the **HORIZONS** textbook, and provides you an opportunity to develop the skills needed for effective communication in French. With the exception of the *Chapitre de révision,* there is a chapter in the *Student Activities Manual* with four *Compétences* corresponding to each chapter of the textbook. For each *Compétence* of the *Student Activities Manual,* there are four pages of writing activities followed by two pages of listening activities. These activities give you the opportunity to practice the grammatical structures, vocabulary and learning skills presented in the textbook. The two pages of listening activities at the end of each *Compétence* also give you the chance to improve your pronunciation and understanding of spoken French. You should always review all of the new words, phrases, grammar rules, and learning strategies presented in each *Compétence* in the **HORIZONS** textbook before beginning the corresponding section in the *Student Activities Manual.* Also remember that there are two sets of recordings that accompany **HORIZONS:** the **Text Audio** and the **SAM Audio.** The **Text Audio** contains activities marked with an audio symbol in the textbook. Be sure that you have the **SAM Audio** when working in the *Student Activities Manual.*

Writing the *Journal*

At the end of every other *Compétence* in the writing activities, you will write a journal entry. Each entry is a guided composition in which you combine all that you have learned in a global, communicative writing activity. As you begin each *Compétence* in class, look ahead in your workbook to see what you will be expected to communicate in written French after studying the vocabulary and the grammatical structures. This will help you stay focused on the real purpose of learning vocabulary and grammatical structures, which is communication. In class, note down expressions or sentences that you might need for your journal, and as you sit down to write your journal entry, reread the dialogues and readings in the chapter up to that point. This will give you examples of what to say. Try to be creative, but stick to what you know. Do not try to use vocabulary and structures that you have not yet studied in class, unless you feel confident that you understand them. If you do not have enough space to say all that you wish on the page in the workbook, you may write your journal entry on a separate sheet of paper.

Tips for success with the SAM Audio

It takes time, patience, and practice to understand French spoken at a normal conversational speed. Do not be surprised if at first you find it difficult to understand sections on the **SAM Audio** recordings. Relax and listen to passages more than once. You will understand a little more each time. Remember that you will not always understand everything, and that for particular activities, you are only expected to understand enough to answer specific questions. Read through listening exercises prior to listening to the recordings so that you know what you are listening for. If you find that you do not have enough time to process and respond to a question before the next one is asked, take advantage of the pause or stop button on your audio player to give yourself more time. Most importantly, stay patient and remember that you can always replay any section and listen again.

Practice, patience, and persistence pay!

On commence! Chapitre

 COMPÉTENCE 1

Greeting people

By the time you finish this *Compétence,* you should be able to introduce yourself, meet others, ask how they are, and say good-bye.

Partie écrite

A. Salutations formelles! Complete the following conversations logically by filling in the missing words. Base each conversation on the picture to the right.

— Bonjour, monsieur.

— Bonjour, _____ **(1)**.

— Comment _____ **(2)**?

— Je m'appelle Henri Prévost. Et _____**(3)**?

— Je _____ **(4)** Hélène Cauvin.

— Bonsoir, monsieur.

— _____**(5)**, madame.

— Comment _____ **(6)**?

— Je vais très _____ **(7)**, merci. Et vous?

— Assez _____ **(8)**.

B. Très bien, merci! How would each man answer the question «**Comment allez-vous?**»

1. _____ 2. _____ 3. _____

Line art on this page: © Cengage Learning

C. Conversation. Here is a conversation between two new business associates. Complete it as indicated, using formal French.

Mme Verdun: _____ **(1).**
                              (Good evening, sir)

                    _____ **(2)** allez-vous?
                              (How)

M. Prévost: _____ **(3)** très bien, merci.
                              (I'm doing)

                Et vous, _____ **(4)**?
                              (how are you)

Mme Verdun: _____ **(5)**, merci.
                              (Fairly well)

                    _____ **(6)** Caroline Verdun.
                              (My name is)

                Et vous, _____ **(7)**?
                              (what's your name)

M. Prévost: _____ **(8)** Lucas Prévost.
                              (I am)

D. Ça va? Complete the following informal (familiar) conversations logically by filling in the missing words. Base each conversation on the picture to the right.

— Bonjour, je m'appelle Rémy. Et _____ **(1)**?

  Tu _____ **(2)** comment?

— Je m'appelle Danielle.

— Salut, Nicolas.

— _____ **(3)**, Mélodie. _____ **(4)** va?

— _____ **(5)** va. Et _____ **(6)**? Comment ça va?

— _____ **(7)** mal.

E. Qu'est-ce qu'on dit? How might you say good-bye to …

1. your friends until tomorrow?

   _____

2. someone you will see later in the day?

   _____

3. a friend you will visit soon?

   _____

4. someone if you don't know when you'll see him/her again?

   _____

Line art on this page: © Cengage Learning

F. Bonjour! Decide if each of these expressions is appropriate for a formal relationship, for an informal relationship, or for either type of relationship. Put a check in the appropriate column. The first one has been done for you.

	Formal	Informal	Either
1. Bonjour, monsieur.	✓		
2. Comment vous appelez-vous?			
3. Tu t'appelles comment?			
4. Salut!			
5. Comment allez-vous?			
6. Comment ça va?			
7. Je vais très bien. Et vous?			
8. Au revoir!			
9. À demain!			

G. Les salutations familières. You might use the following phrases to talk to your instructor. What less formal expressions could you use to address the student who sits next to you?

EXEMPLE   Bonsoir, monsieur.   **Salut.**

1. Bonjour, madame. _____
2. Comment vous appelez-vous? _____
3. Comment allez-vous? _____
4. Je vais bien. Et vous? _____

H. Une autre conversation. Here is a conversation between two students on the first day of classes. Complete it as indicated, using informal (familiar) French.

ÉLODIE: Bonjour, _____ **(1)** Élodie.
          (my name is)

          Et toi, tu _____ **(2)**?
                     (what's your name)

AHMAD: _____ **(3)**! Je suis Ahmad. _____ **(4)**?
          (Hi)   *(How's it going)*

ÉLODIE: Ça va bien. _____ **(5)**?
                      (And you)

AHMAD: _____ **(6)**.
          (It's going fine)

ÉLODIE: _____ **(7)**!
          (Good-bye)

AHMAD: _____ **(8)**!
          (See you tomorrow)

I. Situations. What would you say in French in each of the following situations? Remember to use formal or informal (familiar) French as appropriate.

1. to greet your professor and ask his/her name

_____

2. to ask how he/she is

_____

3. to greet a classmate and ask his/her name

_____

4. to ask how he/she is doing

_____

*J. Réponses. Imagine that an older French woman says these things to you and give a logical response for each one. Use *formal* French.

1. Bonjour, monsieur/madame.

_____

2. Bonsoir, monsieur/madame.

_____

3. Comment vous appelez-vous?

_____

4. Comment allez-vous?

_____

5. Au revoir, monsieur/madame.

_____

Now imagine that a classmate, Juliette, says these things to you and write a logical response to each one. Use *informal (familiar)* French.

6. Salut!

_____

7. Tu t'appelles comment?

_____

8. Comment ça va?

_____

9. Au revoir! À demain!

_____

Partie auditive

A. Prononciation: Les consonnes muettes et la liaison. Pause the recording and review the *Prononciation* section on page 6 of the textbook. Then read the following list of words and indicate whether the final consonant of each word is pronounced or silent by underlining those that should be pronounced and crossing out those that should be silent. Turn on the recording and repeat as you hear each word, checking your decision about the final consonant.

EXEMPLES   YOU SEE: parc   YOU SEE: pas

      YOU MARK: par<u>c</u>   YOU MARK: pa~~s~~

      YOU HEAR AND REPEAT: par<u>c</u>   YOU HEAR AND REPEAT: pa~~s~~

1. Marc   **3.** très   **5.** mal   **7.** actif

2. salut   **4.** assez   **6.** bonjour   **8.** Luc

Now listen and repeat as you hear each of the sentences that follow pronounced. Then listen again and mark where the liaisons occur.

EXEMPLE   YOU SEE: Comment vous appelez-vous?

     YOU HEAR AND REPEAT: **Comment vous‿appelez-vous?**

     YOU MARK: **Comment vous‿appelez-vous?**

1. Comment allez-vous?

2. Je suis en cours.

3. Quelle heure est-il?

4. Il est trois heures.

5. Comment dit-on…?

6. À tout à l'heure!

B. Salutations. You will hear three short conversations in which people greet each other. Write the number of each conversation below the picture it matches.

© Cengage Learning

a. _____   **b.** _____   **c.** _____

Now you will hear a series of statements or questions. For each one, decide what would be the most logical response from the choices given. Write the letter of the most logical response next to the number of the statement you hear. One letter will be used more than once.

a. Je vais très bien, merci. Et vous?

b. Bonjour, madame. Comment allez-vous?

c. Je m'appelle Christian Laforge.

d. Ça va, et toi?

1. _____   **2.** _____   **3.** _____   **4.** _____   **5.** _____

Nom _____ Date _____

C. Prononciation: Les voyelles *a, e, é, i, o* et *u*.
Correct pronunciation of the basic vowels is essential to developing speaking and listening skills. Pause the recording and review the ***Prononciation*** section on page 8 of the textbook. Then turn on the recording and listen and repeat the following words.

a [a]	agréable	attitude	art	banane
e [ə]	me	le	regarde	que
é [e]	café	pâté	marié	divorcé
i [i]	quiche	idéaliste	ironie	agile
o [o]	kilo	nos	hôte	abricot
u [y]	université	usage	ultra	tube

Now listen to these words and fill in the missing vowels (**a, e, é, i, o, u**).

1. ___n___m___l
2. p___t___t
3. m___r
4. t___t___
5. n___
6. ___m___

7. qu___
8. t___m___de
9. m___n___
10. j___l___
11. j___pe
12. n___t___

D. Dictée.
You will hear a series of questions or statements. Write each one down. *Do not respond to what you hear, simply write it down* exactly *as you hear it.* Pause the recording to have sufficient time to respond.

1. _____
2. _____
3. _____
4. _____
5. _____

*Now you will hear more questions or remarks. This time, do *not* write what you hear. Instead, *respond* appropriately in French. Pause the recording during the pauses to have sufficient time to write.

1. _____
2. _____
3. _____
4. _____

COMPÉTENCE 2

Counting and describing your week

By the end of this **Compétence,** you should be able to count from zero to thirty, ask and tell what day of the week it is, and tell a little about your schedule.

Partie écrite

A. C'est quel nombre? Change these prices from words to numerals. The symbol **€** stands for **euros,** the currency used in France and most other countries in the European Union.

1. quatre euros = _____ €
2. cinq euros = _____ €
3. onze euros = _____ €
4. trente euros = _____ €
5. vingt-six euros = _____ €
6. dix-sept euros = _____ €

7. vingt-trois euros = _____ €
8. dix-neuf euros = _____ €
9. quinze euros = _____ €
10. dix euros = _____ €
11. deux euros = _____ €
12. treize euros = _____ €

13. seize euros = _____ €
14. douze euros = _____ €
15. dix-huit euros = _____ €
16. quatorze euros = _____ €
17. vingt-cinq euros = _____ €
18. vingt-neuf euros = _____ €

B. C'est combien? You are shopping in Quebec, where they use Canadian dollars. Give the price of the following items by spelling out the numbers *in words.*

1. Un sandwich, c'est _____ dollars.
2. Une calculatrice, c'est _____ dollars.
3. Un tee-shirt, c'est _____ dollars.

4. Une plante, c'est _____ dollars.
5. Un poster, c'est _____ dollars.
6. Un CD, c'est _____ dollars.

Nom _____ Date _____

C. Problèmes de maths. Complete the following math problems by filling in the missing numbers. Spell out the numbers in words.

1. 3 + 6 = 9

    — Combien font _____ et _____?

    — _____ et _____ font _____.

2. 10 + 5 = 15

    — Combien font _____ et _____?

    — _____ et _____ font _____.

3. 29 − 13 = 16

    — Combien font _____ moins _____?

    — _____ moins _____ font _____.

4. 20 − 17 = 3

    — Combien font _____ moins _____?

    — _____ moins _____ font _____.

5. 30 − 14 = 16

    — Combien font _____ moins _____?

    — _____ moins _____ font _____.

***D. Mon emploi du temps.** In French, fill in the days of the week in the left column on the following daily planner. The first one has been done as an example. Then, go back and indicate on the planner your typical weekly schedule. Use **Je travaille** to indicate when you work, **Je suis en cours** for when you are in class, and **Je suis à la maison** for when you are at home.

le jour	le matin	l'après-midi	le soir
le lundi			

*E. Quels jours? Complete the following sentences with the appropriate days. Remember to use **le** in numbers **3–8** to say that you do something on a particular day in general. If you do not work, leave numbers **4** and **5** blank.

1. Aujourd'hui, c'est _____.

2. Demain, c'est _____.

3. Je suis en cours de français _____.

4. Je travaille _____.

5. Je ne travaille pas _____.

6. Je ne suis pas en cours _____.

7. Je ne suis pas à la maison _____ matin.

8. Je suis à la maison _____ matin.

F. Conversation. Complete this conversation between two students, as indicated.

ROMAN: _____ **(1)** aujourd'hui?
        (What day is it)

CÉLINE: C'est _____ **(2)**.
        (Wednesday)

ROMAN: Tu es en cours _____ **(3)** ce semestre?
        (what days)

CÉLINE: _____ **(4)**, je suis en cours de français
        (In the morning)

        _____ **(5)**. Et
        (every day)

        _____ **(6)**,
        (from Monday to Thursday)

        je suis _____ **(7)** l'après-midi.
               (in another class)

ROMAN: Et _____ **(8)** tes *(your)* cours, tu es où *(where)*?
          (before)

CÉLINE: Avant mes *(my)* cours, je suis _____ **(9)**.
                                        (at home)

ROMAN: Tu travailles _____ **(10)**?
                      (too)

CÉLINE: _____ **(11)** le vendredi soir
        (Yes, I work)

        et _____ **(12)**. Et toi?
           (weekends)

ROMAN: Je travaille le soir _____ **(13)** mes cours.
                            (after)

        _____ **(14)**
        (I'm at home)

        le matin et _____ **(15)** l'après-midi.
                    (I'm in class)

*G. Questions. Imagine that a fellow student is asking you these questions and answer them *with complete sentences* in French. In numbers **6–9,** start with **oui** to say *yes* or **non** to say *no.*

1. Salut! Comment ça va?

    _____

2. Tu t'appelles comment?

    _____

3. C'est quel jour aujourd'hui?

    _____

4. Tu es en cours quels jours ce semestre?

    _____

5. Tu es en cours de français le matin, l'après-midi ou *(or)* le soir?

    _____

6. Tu es en cours de français du lundi au vendredi?

    _____

7. Tu es à la maison avant le cours de français?

    _____

8. Après le cours de français, tu es dans un autre cours?

    _____

9. Tu travailles aussi?

    _____

At the end of the second and fourth *Compétences* of a chapter, you will be asked to write a journal entry. The journal allows you to combine all that you have studied to communicate your own thoughts.

* Journal. Write a paragraph about your typical week. Tell when you are at home, when you are in class, and when you work (or that you don't work).

_____

_____

_____

_____

_____

_____

_____

_____

_____

Partie auditive

A. Comptez de un à trente! Repeat each number after the speaker. Notice that the final consonants of some numbers are pronounced, whereas others are silent. Some consonants in the middle of the word are also silent. Repeat this exercise until you feel comfortable counting from 1 to 30 by yourself.

___ 1 un	___ 7 sept	___ 13 treize	___ 19 dix-neuf	___ 25 vingt-cinq
___ 2 deux	___ 8 huit	___ 14 quatorze	___ 20 vingt	___ 26 vingt-six
___ 3 trois	___ 9 neuf	___ 15 quinze	___ 21 vingt et un	___ 27 vingt-sept
___ 4 quatre	___ 10 dix	___ 16 seize	___ 22 vingt-deux	___ 28 vingt-huit
___ 5 cinq	___ 11 onze	___ 17 dix-sept	___ 23 vingt-trois	___ 29 vingt-neuf
___ 6 six	___ 12 douze	___ 18 dix-huit	___ 24 vingt-quatre	___ 30 trente

Now you will hear twelve numbers between 1 and 30 in random order. As you hear each one, place a check mark next to it in the preceding list of numbers.

B. Calculs. You will hear some simple math problems. Pause the recording after each one in order to fill in the numbers and solve the problem. All the problems and answers will be repeated at the end. Listen and verify your responses.

EXEMPLE	YOU HEAR:	Deux et deux font…
	YOU WRITE:	**2 + 2 = 4**
	AT THE END YOU HEAR:	Deux et deux font quatre.

1. ____ + ____ = ____   3. ____ + ____ = ____   5. ____ + ____ = ____

2. ____ + ____ = ____   4. ____ + ____ = ____   6. ____ + ____ = ____

C. Prononciation: Les voyelles nasales. Pause the recording and review the ***Prononciation*** section on page 10 of the textbook. Then turn on the recording and repeat these nasal sounds and the model words and phrases that contain them after the speaker. (Notice that, although a final **c** is often pronounced, it is silent at the end of **blanc**.)

$[\tilde{a}]$:	**an / am**	blanc	avant	dans	chambre
	en / em	trente	enfant	vendredi	temps
$[\tilde{\varepsilon}]$:	**in / im**	cinq	quinze	fin	impossible
	un / um	un	lundi	brun	parfum
	ain / aim	demain	américain	prochain	faim
$[\tilde{o}]$:	**on / om**	onze	bonsoir	réponse	nom
$[j\tilde{\varepsilon}]$:	**ien**	bien	bientôt	combien	lien
$[w\tilde{\varepsilon}]$:	**oin**	moins	loin	coin	point

un vin / un vin blanc / un bon vin blanc / un bon vin blanc américain

C'est un bon vin blanc américain, Henri.

Now listen to these pairs of words. Fill in the missing letters in both words of the pair with the *same* choice from the two choices given.

EXEMPLE	YOU SEE:	en / in	v____	qu___ze
	YOU HEAR:	en / in	vin	quinze
	YOU WRITE:	en / in	v**in**	qu**in**ze

1. an / on   mais_____   citr_____   **5.** ien/oin   l_____   c_____

2. an / in   vois_____   chem_____   **6.** un / en   br_____   comm_____

3. en / on   c_____tre   r_____trer   **7.** an / on   dev_____t   rom_____

4. en / un   g_____til   souv_____t

D. Les jours de la semaine. Listen and repeat the names of the days of the week.

1-9

lundi   mardi   mercredi   jeudi   vendredi   samedi   dimanche

Now you will hear the start of a sentence about what day comes *before* or *after* another. Fill in the blank with the day of the week you hear, then complete the sentence logically. After a pause for you to respond, you will hear the correct answer. Pause the recording if you need more time.

EXEMPLE	VOUS ENTENDEZ *(YOU HEAR)*:	Avant lundi, c'est…
	VOUS ÉCRIVEZ *(YOU WRITE)*:	Avant **lundi**, c'est **dimanche.**
	VOUS ENTENDEZ *(YOU HEAR)*:	Avant lundi, c'est dimanche.

1. Avant _____, c'est _____.

2. Avant _____, c'est _____.

3. Avant _____, c'est _____.

4. Après _____, c'est _____.

5. Après _____, c'est _____.

6. Après _____, c'est _____.

E. Mon emploi du temps. You will hear a student describe his schedule. The first time, just listen to what he says. It will then be repeated more slowly with pauses for you to fill in the missing words. Pause the recording and play this section again as needed.

1-10

_____ **(1),** je suis à la maison

_____ **(2)** avant mes *(my)* cours. Le lundi et

_____ **(3),** je suis en cours de français

_____ **(4).** Après le cours de français, je suis

_____ **(5).** Je travaille le soir

_____ **(6).**

Nom _____ Date _____

 **COMPÉTENCE 3**

Talking about yourself and your schedule

By the end of this *Compétence,* you should be able to tell a little about yourself and describe your schedule.

Partie écrite

*A. Moi, je... A French student is talking about herself. Rewrite her sentences to make them true for you.

1. Je suis étudiante à l'université de Paris.

Moi, je _____.

2. Je suis française.

Moi, je _____.

3. Je suis de Paris.

Moi, je _____.

4. J'habite à Paris avec ma famille.

Moi, je/j' _____.

5. Je ne travaille pas.

Moi, je _____.

6. Je parle français, anglais et un peu espagnol.

Moi, je _____.

7. Je pense que le français est très facile et assez cool.

Moi, je _____.

*B. Qui suis-je? Using the French actor Jean Dujardin's description of himself as an example, tell how three famous Americans, Canadians, or French people would describe themselves. Have them say their name, their nationality, what city they are from, and in what city they live now.

EXEMPLE   **Je m'appelle Jean Dujardin. Je suis français. Je suis de Rueil-Malmaison et j'habite à Paris maintenant.**

1. _____

_____

_____

2. _____

_____

_____

3. _____

_____

_____

C. Conversation. Two people meet at a conference in Montreal. Complete their conversation, as indicated.

LAURIE NGUYEN: Vous _____ **(1)** canadien, monsieur?
                          (are)

RENAUD GARNIER: Non, _____ **(2)** Paris. Mais _____ **(3)**
                          (I am from)   *(I live)*

ici maintenant _____ **(4)** je travaille ici. J'habite
                  (because)

_____ **(5).** Et vous, vous êtes _____ **(6)**?
        (with my family)   *(from here)*

LAURIE NGUYEN: Non, je suis _____ **(7).**
                                  (American)

RENAUD GARNIER: _____ **(8)** vous parlez _____ **(9)** français.
                      (But)   *(very well)*

Vous habitez ici _____ **(10)**?
                      (now)

LAURIE NGUYEN: Oui, j'habite ici _____ **(11).**
                                      (with a [female] friend)

Je suis _____ **(12).**
            (professor at the university)

D. Quelle heure est-il? Tell the time for each clock *in complete sentences,* spelling out all numbers.

EXEMPLE   **Il est une heure.**

1. _____

2. _____

3. _____

4. _____

5. _____

6. _____

7. _____

Line art on this page: © Cengage Learning

E. À la télé. Here are some of the programs on some French TV stations. What time do the indicated programs start this morning and this afternoon?

EXEMPLE *30 millions d'amis:* Ça *(That)* commence **à six heures et quart.**

6:15	30 millions d'amis	10:15	Un gars, une fille
6:45	Info	11:35	Les z'amours
8:30	Téléshopping	12:05	Vous les femmes
9:20	Allô quiz		

1. *Info:* Ça commence _____.

2. *Téléshopping:* Ça commence _____.

3. *Allô quiz:* Ça commence _____.

4. *Un gars, une fille:* Ça commence _____.

5. *Les z'amours:* Ça commence _____.

6. *Vous les femmes:* Ça commence _____.

F. Le lundi. Here is a friend's typical schedule on Mondays. How would he say the following things in French? *Include the French expressions equivalent to* A.M. *and* P.M. *with the times and spell out the numbers.*

1. I am at home before ten A.M.

   _____

2. I am in class from ten A.M. to one P.M. My class (**Mon cours**) starts at ten A.M. and ends at one P.M.

   _____

   _____

3. I work from two to four P.M.

   _____

4. I am at home after five P.M.

   _____

G. Des excursions. While visiting France, you are taking some day trips **(excursions)** listed in your tourist guidebook. Complete the responses to the questions with the appropriate days or times. Spell out all numbers.

M Malmaison 27 €
Excursion accompagnée par un **guide-interprète diplômé.**
❺ DÉPART: 9 h 30, mercredi et vendredi.
DURÉE: 3 h environ.

1. Il y a *(There are)* des excursions pour Malmaison quels jours?

   Il y a des excursions pour Malmaison le _____ et le _____.

2. L'excursion pour Malmaison commence à quelle heure?

   L'excursion commence à _____ et _____.

3. Il y a des excursions pour Cheverny quels jours?

   Il y a des excursions pour Cheverny

   le _____ , le _____,

   le _____ et le _____.

4. L'excursion pour Cheverny commence à quelle heure?

   L'excursion commence à _____

   et _____.

CL1 Cheverny (journée entière) ▶99 €
Excursion accompagnée par un **guide-interprète diplômé.**
DÉPART: 7 h 15, mardi, jeudi, samedi, dimanche. Déjeuner compris.
RETOUR: vers 19 h 30.

*H. Une interview. Answer the following questions *with complete sentences* in French.

1. Vous êtes américain(e)? Vous êtes de quelle ville *(from what city)*?

   _____

   _____

2. Vous habitez ici maintenant? Vous habitez seul(e)?

   _____

   _____

3. Vous travaillez quels jours? De quelle heure à quelle heure? Vous travaillez beaucoup?

   _____

   _____

4. Vous parlez un peu français? Le français est difficile ou assez facile?

   _____

   _____

5. Vous êtes en cours quels jours et de quelle heure à quelle heure?

   _____

   _____

6. Vous êtes en cours de français quels jours? Le cours de français commence à quelle heure et finit à quelle heure?

   _____

   _____

Partie auditive

🔊 **A. Masculin ou féminin?** When the masculine form of an adjective ends in a consonant other than **c, r, f,** or **l,** the final consonant is usually silent. Since the feminine form of an adjective usually ends in **-e,** this consonant is no longer final and is pronounced. You will hear several pairs of words. Repeat each pair after the speaker.

Masculine	Feminine	Masculine	Feminine
1. _____ américain	_____ américaine	4. _____ anglais	_____ anglaise
2. _____ français	_____ française	5. _____ canadien	_____ canadienne
3. _____ intéressant	_____ intéressante	6. _____ étudiant	_____ étudiante

Now you will hear either the masculine or feminine form from each pair. Listen and place a check mark next to the form you hear.

🔊 **B. Un étudiant.** Listen as a student talks about himself. Repeat each pair of sentences after he says them and fill in the missing words.

1. Je ne suis pas _____. Je suis _____.

2. Je ne suis pas _____. Je suis _____.

3. Je ne suis pas d' _____. Je suis _____ Portland.

4. Je n'habite pas avec _____. J'habite _____.

5. Je ne _____ pas. Je suis _____.

6. Je ne parle pas _____. Je parle _____ et un peu _____.

7. Je pense que le français est _____ difficile mais _____.

🔊 **C. Autoportraits.** You will hear two people give a short description of themselves. The first time, just listen to each one. Then, as you hear them a second time, write in the missing words from each description. Play this section again as needed.

1. MARIE:

   Je _____ (1) Marie et je suis _____ (2),

   mais _____ (3) à Paris avec _____ (4).

   Je suis _____ (5) où j'étudie les langues.

   Je _____ (6) anglais, espagnol… et français, bien sûr!

2. MARC:

   Je _____ (1) Marc et je _____ (2)

   français. J'habite à Paris _____ (3), mais ma _____ (4)

   est de Lyon. J'habite _____ (5) et je _____ (6).

   Je suis _____ (7) d'espagnol _____ (8).

Nom _____ Date _____

1-14

D. Prononciation: L'heure et la liaison. Pause the recording and review the *Prononciation* section on page 18 of the textbook. Remember that the pronunciation of some of the numbers changes in liaison with the word **heures.** Listen and repeat as you hear each time pronounced. Then listen again, marking where you hear liaison occur.

EXEMPLE   VOUS LISEZ *(YOU READ):*   Il est dix heures.
           VOUS ÉCOUTEZ ET RÉPÉTEZ *(YOU LISTEN AND REPEAT):*   **Il est dix heures.**
           VOUS MARQUEZ *(YOU MARK):*   **Il est dix‿heures.**

1. Il est deux heures dix.
2. Il est trois heures et quart.
3. Il est cinq heures et quart.

4. Il est six heures et demie.
5. Il est huit heures moins le quart.
6. Il est neuf heures moins vingt.

1-15

E. Quelle heure est-il? Write the number of each item under the clock showing the time you hear. The first one has been done as an example.

EXEMPLE   VOUS ENTENDEZ *(YOU HEAR):*   **1.** — Quelle heure est-il?
                                        — Il est cinq heures dix.
           VOUS ÉCRIVEZ *(YOU WRITE):*

_____   _____   _____

_____   _____1   _____

_____   _____

1-16

F. L'heure. You will hear the time announced. Write down the time you hear for each announcement. Pause the recording after each announcement to allow enough time to respond.

EXEMPLE   VOUS ENTENDEZ *(YOU HEAR):*   Il est trois heures et quart du matin.
           VOUS ÉCRIVEZ *(YOU WRITE):*   **3:15 A.M.**

1. _____   3. _____   5. _____   7. _____   9. _____

2. _____   4. _____   6. _____   8. _____   10. _____

COMPÉTENCE 4

Communicating in class

By the end of this *Compétence,* you should be able to follow instructions in class and ask your professor for clarification.

Partie écrite

A. Les instructions en classe. What did the professor say to these students? Write the appropriate phrase from the list in the blank corresponding to the matching illustration.

Allez au tableau.
Écoutez la question.
Répondez à la question.
Écrivez la réponse avec une phrase complète.

Ouvrez votre livre à la page 23.
Prenez une feuille de papier et un stylo.
Donnez-moi votre feuille de papier.
Fermez votre livre.

1

2

3

4

1. _____
2. _____
3. _____
4. _____

5

6

7

8

5. _____
6. _____
7. _____
8. _____

Nom _____ Date _____

B. Des instructions logiques. Using vocabulary you have learned, list at least three things that logically complete the following commands. (With **Ouvrez…** and **Faites,** list only two things.)

1. Écoutez…
_____
_____
_____

2. Lisez…
_____
_____
_____

3. Ouvrez…
_____
_____

4. Prenez…
_____
_____
_____

5. Écrivez…
_____
_____

6. Faites…
_____
_____

C. Les accents. In French, accents do not indicate stress. They may indicate how a word is pronounced, and sometimes the presence or absence of an accent changes a word's meaning entirely. For example, the word **ou** means *or*, whereas the accented word **où** means *where*. You will find accents only on vowels.

a. An **accent circonflexe (â, ê, î, ô, û)** frequently indicates that an **s** has been dropped from the spelling of a word. Knowing this will help you recognize the meaning of more words. Can you guess what the following words mean in English by inserting an *s* after the vowel with the **accent circonflexe**? Write the English words in the blanks.

1. hôpital: _____
2. hôtesse: _____
3. forêt: _____
4. hâte: _____
5. honnête: _____
6. île: _____
7. ancêtre: _____
8. quête: _____

b. When writing in French, pay close attention to accents. With practice, you will learn to determine where the accents should go on a word. In the meantime, learn accents and the **cédille (ç)** as part of the spelling of words. To get started, recopy the following words, making sure to place the accents and **cédille** where they belong.

1. À bientôt.   _____
2. répétez   _____
3. le français   _____
4. Noël   _____
5. Ça s'écrit…   _____

20   *Horizons,* Sixth Edition • **Student Activities Manual**

© 2015 Cengage Learning. All Rights Reserved. May not be scanned, copied or duplicated, or posted to a publicly accessible website, in whole or in part.

D. Vous parlez anglais? Someone asks or says the following things to you. Complete the reponses to each question in French.

1. Vous parlez anglais?

   Oui, _____ anglais.

2. Comment dit-on **exercice** en anglais?

   En anglais, on _____.

3. *Exercise* s'écrit avec un *c* ou avec un *s* en anglais?

   En anglais, *exercise,* ça _____.

4. Je ne comprends pas le mot **prochain.** Qu'est-ce que ça veut dire en anglais?

   En anglais, ça _____.

5. Vous comprenez les mots **ouvrez** et **fermez**?

   Oui, je _____ les mots **ouvrez** et **fermez. Ouvrez** veut dire _____
   et **fermez** veut dire _____.

6. Qu'est-ce que ça veut dire: **Fermez votre livre**?

   Ça _____ en anglais.

7. Merci bien.

   De _____.

E. Ça s'écrit comment? Explain to a student from France how to spell the English equivalents of the following French words by filling in the missing words.

EXEMPLES   hôpital
En anglais, *hospital,* ça s'écrit **sans** accent circonflexe et **avec** un *s.*

biologie
En anglais, *biology,* **ça s'écrit** avec un *y.*

1. philosophie

   En anglais, *philosophy,* ça s'écrit _____ un *y.*

2. mariage

   En anglais, *marriage,* _____ avec deux *r.*

3. forêt

   En anglais, *forest,* ça s'écrit _____ accent circonflexe et _____ un *s.*

4. intellectuel

   En anglais, *intellectual,* _____ avec un *a.*

5. adresse

   En anglais, *address,* ça s'écrit _____ deux *d* et _____ *e.*

F. Comment? Using phrases learned in *Compétence 4,* tell or ask your professor the following.

1. Ask him/her how to say *book* in French.

_____

2. Ask him/her to repeat something.

_____

3. Tell him/her that you don't understand.

_____

4. Ask him/her what the word **prenez** means.

_____

5. Ask him/her how **prenez** is written.

_____

6. Tell him/her that you don't know the answer.

_____

7. Thank him/her.

_____

---

*Journal. Write two paragraphs introducing yourself. Include the following information.

In paragraph 1, tell your name, where you are from originally, where you live now, and with whom you live.

In paragraph 2, tell which days you are in class and from what time to what time. Then say whether you work, where, which days, and from what time to what time.

_____

_____

_____

_____

_____

_____

_____

_____

_____

_____

_____

_____

_____

Partie auditive

 A. Qu'est-ce qu'on fait? You will hear a series of classroom commands. Write the number of each
1-17 command under the picture that best represents it.

a. _____   **b.** _____   **c.** _____   **d.** _____

e. _____   **f.** _____   **g.** _____   **h.** _____

 B. Prononciation: Les voyelles groupées. Pause the recording and review the **Prononciation** section
1-18 on page 21 of the textbook. Then turn on the recording and repeat each of the words that follow after the
speaker, paying attention to the pronunciation of the vowel combinations. Repeat this exercise as needed.

EXEMPLE   VOUS ENTENDEZ *(YOU HEAR):*   seize
              VOUS RÉPÉTEZ *(YOU REPEAT):*   **seize**

au, eau [o]:	au	aussi	beaucoup	tableau
eu [ø]:	deux	peu	jeudi	monsieur
eu [œ]:	heure	neuf	professeur	seul(e)
ou [u]:	vous	douze	jour	pour
ai [ɛ]:	français	je vais	je sais	vrai
ei [ɛ]:	treize	seize	beige	neige
oi [wa]:	moi	toi	trois	au revoir
ui [ɥi]:	huit	minuit	aujourd'hui	suis

Line art on this page: © Cengage Learning

Nom _____ Date _____

Now repeat these pairs of words after the speaker.

1. _____ cuisine   _____ cousine   5. _____ poire   _____ peur
2. _____ fou   _____ feu   6. _____ suivant   _____ souvent
3. _____ saison   _____ Soisson   7. _____ toile   _____ tuile
4. _____ chou   _____ chaud   8. _____ lait   _____ loup

Now you will hear one word pronounced from each of the preceding pairs. Place a check mark next to the one you hear.

C. À vous maintenant! You will hear a series of words. Complete each one with the correct missing vowel combination from the two choices given.

1-19

EXEMPLE   VOUS VOYEZ *(YOU SEE)*:   eu / oi   coul___r
              VOUS ENTENDEZ *(YOU HEAR)*: couloir
              VOUS ÉCRIVEZ *(YOU WRITE)*: coul**oi**r

1. au / ai   f_____t   5. au / eu   chev_____x
2. ui / ou   c_____vre   6. ai / ou   v_____s
3. eu / au   chev_____x   7. eu / ou   d_____x
4. eu / oi   cr_____x   8. ui / ou   c_____r

D. L'alphabet. Say each letter of the alphabet after the speaker. Repeat this exercise until you feel comfortable reciting the alphabet by yourself.

1-20

a b c d e f g h i j k l m n o p q r s t u v w x y z

Now fill in the blanks with the words you hear spelled out. You have not seen all of these words before.

EXEMPLE   VOUS ENTENDEZ *(YOU HEAR)*: b-e-a-u-c-o-u-p
              VOUS ÉCRIVEZ *(YOU WRITE)*: **beaucoup**

1. _____   5. _____
2. _____   6. _____
3. _____   7. _____
4. _____   8. _____

E. En cours. You will hear a series of statements and questions. For each one, decide in which of these situations it would be used. Put the number of the statement or question you hear next to the situation to which it corresponds.

1-21

_____ **a.** You need something repeated.
_____ **b.** You want to know how a word is spelled.
_____ **c.** You want to know what a word means.
_____ **d.** You need to excuse yourself.
_____ **e.** You want to thank someone.
_____ **f.** You want to know how to say *zero* in French.
_____ **g.** You don't understand what was said.

À l'université Chapitre 1

COMPÉTENCE 1

Identifying people and describing appearance

By the time you finish this **Compétence,** you should be able to identify friends and classmates and tell a little about them.

Partie écrite

A. David et Léa. In the left-hand column below, write new sentences about David using the *opposite* of each of the words in boldface. Then, in the right-hand column, say the same things about Léa, by rewriting the sentences about David. Remember to use the feminine form of the adjective.

EXEMPLE Il n'est pas **gros.**
Il est mince.

EXEMPLE Elle n'est pas **grosse.**
Elle est mince.

1. Il n'est pas **vieux.**

    _____

2. Il n'est pas **grand.**

    _____

3. Il n'est pas **marié.**

    _____

4. Il n'est pas **laid.**

    _____

1. Elle n'est pas _____.

    _____.

2. Elle n'est pas _____.

    _____.

3. Elle n'est pas _____.

    _____.

4. Elle n'est pas _____.

    _____.

B. Conversation. Reread the conversation between David and Léa on page 33 of your textbook. Then, complete this conversation between two other students with the indicated words.

Noah et Chloé se rencontrent *(meet)* la _____ **(1)** des cours.
                                                     (first week)

NOAH: Salut! Je suis Noah Leclerc. _____ **(2)** dans le _____ **(3)** cours de maths, non?
                                                     (We are)   *(same)*

CHLOÉ: Oui, c'est ça. _____ **(4)**, bonjour. Moi, _____ **(5)** Chloé Dubonnet.
                          (So)   *(my name is)*

        Tu es _____ **(6)**?
              (from here)

Noah: Oui, je suis d'ici. Et toi? Tu es _____ (7)?
(from where)

Chloé: Je suis _____ (8) Nîmes.
(from)

C. C'est ou il/elle est?

In the left-hand column below, complete the sentences about David. Remember to use **c'est** if you are identifying him with *a noun* and **il est** if you are describing him with *an adjective*. Next, in the right-hand column, change the sentences so that they describe Léa.

DAVID
EXEMPLE   Il est français.

LÉA
EXEMPLE   Elle est américaine.

1. _____ un ami.
2. _____ David.
3. _____ petit.
4. _____ beau.
5. _____ jeune.

1. _____ .
2. _____ .
3. _____ .
4. _____ .
5. _____ .

Now use **ce sont** and **ils sont** to complete the sentences about David and Jean in the left column below. Then, in the right column, rewrite the same sentences to talk about Léa and Lisa.

DAVID ET JEAN
EXEMPLE   Ils sont français.

LÉA ET LISA
EXEMPLE   Elles sont américaines.

1. _____ mes amis.
2. _____ David et Jean.
3. _____ célibataires.
4. _____ beaux.

1. _____ .
2. _____ .
3. _____ .
4. _____ .

D. Comment sont-ils?

Complete these descriptions with the appropriate form (masculine, feminine, singular, plural) of the indicated adjective. The first one has been done as an example.

Léa et Lisa sont sœurs _____jumelles_____. Elles ne sont pas
(twin)

_____ (1); elles sont _____ (2).
(Canadian)   (American)

Elles sont assez _____ (3), _____ (4) et _____ (5).
(short)   (young)   (beautiful)

Elles ne sont pas _____ (6). Elles sont _____ (7).
(married)   (single)

David n'est pas très _____ (8); il est assez _____ (9). Il est
(tall)   (short)

_____ (10) et il est très _____ (11). Il est _____ (12)
(thin)   (handsome)   (French)

et il habite avec son *(his)* frère, Jean. Jean et David ne sont pas frères _____ (13).
(twin)

Jean est moins *(less)* _____ **(14)**, mais il n'est pas _____ **(15)**. Il est
    (young)   *(old)*

plus *(more)* _____ **(16)** et un peu plus _____ **(17)** que *(than)* David.
    (tall)   *(fat)*

Jean et David sont tous les deux *(both)* _____ **(18)** et _____ **(19)**!
                                          (handsome)   *(single)*

E. Pour mieux lire: *Using cognates and familiar words to read for the gist.* Guess the
meaning of each boldfaced cognate, writing your answer in the blank. The first one has been done as an
example.

1. Je comprends **généralement**.   *generally* _____

2. **Normalement,** le cours de français est facile.   _____

3. Les examens sont **probablement** difficiles.   _____

4. Je suis **frustré(e)**.   _____

5. Je suis **fatigué(e)**.   _____

F. Mots apparentés. Scan this list of courses for foreigners at a French university and *identify at least 20
cognates.* (The first one has been done as an example.) Then, read the list and answer the questions that follow.
Let the cognates guide you as you read and don't worry about understanding every word.

⬭SESSION⬭DE PRINTEMPS
Du 10 mai au 19 juin

Les étudiants et étudiantes doivent s'inscrire à un minimum de 6 crédits jusqu'à un maximum de 12 crédits.
Les cours de trois crédits suivants (en français ou en anglais selon le cas) sont offerts:

Archéologie de la Méditerranée

Histoire de l'art: La Renaissance; L'art français
  du XXe siècle

Commerce (6 crédits): Le commerce international

Écrivains anglais de la Méditerranée

Arts: Le dessin; L'histoire du cinéma français

Français: Le roman français moderne

Géographie: L'Union européenne

Histoire du monde méditerranéen moderne

**Introduction interdisciplinaire à la culture
  européenne de la période suivant la Renaissance**

Musique et culture populaires

Science politique: L'Union européenne

Français semi-intensif: S'adresse aux étudiants
  qui désirent le suivre de concert avec un ou
  plusieurs cours offerts lors de la session de
  printemps.

© Cengage Learning

---

1. What is the minimum number of credits a student can take? _____ The maximum? _____

2. What courses could you recommend for …

   a. someone interested in history?

      _____

   b. someone interested in art?

      _____

   c. someone interested in music?

      _____

G. Qui est-ce? Reread the story *Qui est-ce?* on pages 36–37 of the textbook. Then complete the paragraph, using the following choices. The first one has been done as an example.

Léa / suis / Vous ne comprenez pas / arrive /
la situation / elle ne parle pas / pense / sœurs jumelles / sauvée / comprend

David ___*arrive*___ **(1)** au musée des Beaux-Arts et il voit Lisa. Il dit: «Salut, Léa» parce qu'il

_____ **(2)** que c'est son amie Léa. Lisa répond avec difficulté parce

qu' _____ **(3)** très bien français. Elle dit:

«_____ **(4)**. Je ne suis pas Léa.

Je _____ **(5)** Lisa.» David ne _____ **(6)** pas. Finalement,

_____ **(7)** arrive et Lisa est _____ **(8)**. David comprend

_____ **(9)**. Léa et Lisa sont _____ **(10)**.

*H. Un autre étudiant. You run into a student from your French class. Answer his questions *with complete sentences* about yourself.

1. Tu t'appelles comment?

   _____

2. Tu es d'où?

   _____

3. Tu es étudiant(e) à l'université, non?

   _____

4. Tu es en cours de français quels jours *(which days)*?

   _____

5. Tu es en cours de français de quelle heure à quelle heure?

   _____

6. Nous sommes dans le même cours de français, non?

   _____

7. Tu es marié(e) ou célibataire?

   _____

Nom _____ Date _____

Partie auditive

2-2

A. C'est qui? You will hear a series of sentences. Decide if each is about a male (**Marc**), a female (**Sophie**), or a group (**des amis** *[some friends]*) and indicate the number of the sentence you hear in the appropriate column. The first one has been done as an example. Listen for **c'est** versus **ce sont** and for **il est** versus **elle est** or **ils sont**.

EXEMPLE   VOUS ENTENDEZ: **1.** C'est un jeune homme.

VOUS MARQUEZ:

Marc	Sophie	des amis
1		

Shutterstock.com, © wavebreakmedia / *Shutterstock.com, © Andresr* / *Shutterstock.com, © Monkey Business Images*

2-3

B. Prononciation: *Il est* + adjectif / *Elle est* + adjectif. Pause the recording and review the *Prononciation* section on page 35 of the textbook. Then turn on the recording, listen, and repeat the sentences you hear. Be careful to differentiate between the masculine and feminine forms of the pronouns and some of the adjectives. Remember some adjectives sound the same in the masculine and feminine forms.

Il est français. / Elle est française.

Ils sont américains. / Elles sont américaines.

Il est petit. / Elle est petite.

Ils sont grands. / Elles sont grandes.

Il n'est pas laid. / Elle n'est pas laide.

Il est jeune. / Elle est jeune.

Ils sont mariés. / Elles sont mariées.

Il est espagnol. / Elle est espagnole.

Ils sont célibataires. / Elles sont célibataires.

2-4

C. On parle de qui? You will hear a series of sentences. For each one, decide who is being described: **David, Léa, Léa et Lisa,** or **tous les trois** *(all three)*. Mark the appropriate column. Listen for **il est** versus **elle est** and for **ils sont** versus **elles sont**.

EXEMPLE   VOUS ENTENDEZ: Il est français.

VOUS ÉCRIVEZ:

	David	Léa	Léa et Lisa	tous les trois
	✓			
1.				
2.				
3.				
4.				
5.				
6.				

D. Première rencontre. Listen as two people meet for the first time. Then pause the recording and complete the statements about them by choosing the words in italics that are appropriate.

1. Ils sont dans le même cours *de français / d'anglais / d'espagnol.*

2. Le jeune homme s'appelle *Alex / Daniel / Jean-Luc / Alain.*

3. La jeune femme s'appelle *Marie / Sophie / Alice / Catherine.*

4. Elle est de *Paris / Montréal / Nice / Marseille.*

5. Elle est à Nice pour *étudier / voir la France.*

6. Il habite *seul / avec sa* (his) *famille / à l'université.*

E. Lecture: *Qui est-ce?* Pause the recording and reread the story ***Qui est-ce?*** on pages 36–37 of the textbook. Then turn on the recording. You will hear three excerpts based on the encounter between Lisa and David. Listen to each one and decide which illustration depicts what is happening. Fill in the number of the excerpt in the blank below the appropriate picture.

a. _____   b. _____   c. _____

© Cengage Learning

F. Dictée. You will hear a friend talking about Jean-Marc and his sister Marion. The first time, just listen to what she says at normal speed. Then fill in the missing words as it is repeated more slowly. Pause the recording as needed to allow enough time to fill in the words.

_____ (1) Jean-Marc, un _____ (2) français.

_____ (3) étudiant. Jean-Marc est _____ (4),

_____ (5) et _____ (6). Jean-

Marc et moi, _____

(7) de littérature. C'est Marion, _____ (8) de Jean-Marc.

_____ (9) étudiante. Elle

_____ (10). Marion est _____ (11) et elle est

_____ (12). Jean-Marc et Marion

_____ (13).

COMPÉTENCE 2

Describing personality

By the time you finish this **Compétence,** you should be able to describe a person's personality and compare two individuals.

Partie écrite

A. Qui est-ce? Decide who from each pair of drawings is best described by each of the following adjectives. Then translate each adjective into French and write a sentence.

Louis ou Raphaël?

Louis

> **EXEMPLES** *(very active)* **Raphaël est très dynamique.**
> *(unpleasant)* **Louis est désagréable.**

1. *(lazy)* _____
2. *(fun)* _____
3. *(a little boring)* _____
4. *(athletic)* _____
5. *(rather pessimistic)* _____

Raphaël

Emma ou Isabelle?

> **EXEMPLE** *(very young)* **Emma est très jeune.**

6. *(nice)* _____
7. *(very shy)* _____
8. *(divorced)* _____
9. *(little)* _____
10. *(fairly tall)* _____

Emma

Isabelle

André et Rosalie ou Léa et Lisa?

> **EXEMPLE** *(American)* **Léa et Lisa sont américaines.**

11. *(young)* _____
12. *(old)* _____
13. *(married)* _____
14. *(single)* _____
15. *(beautiful)* _____

André et Rosalie

Léa et Lisa

Line art on this page: © Cengage Learning

B. Comparaisons. First impressions can be misleading, but what impressions do these pictures give you of Jean, David, Léa, and Lisa? Complete the following comparisons. Use **plus... que, moins... que,** or **aussi... que.**

David et Jean

Léa et Lisa

EXEMPLES (grand) David est **moins grand que** Jean.
(sympa) Léa est **aussi sympa que** Lisa.

1. (gros) Jean est _____ David.

2. (mince) Jean est _____ David.

3. (petit) David est _____ Jean.

4. (grande) Léa est _____ Lisa.

5. (belle) Léa est _____ Lisa.

6. (marrantes) Léa et Lisa sont _____ David et Jean.

C. Conversation. Reread the conversation between David and Nadia on page 38 of your textbook. Then, complete this conversation between two other students with the indicated words.

PAUL: Tes amis et toi, vous êtes étudiants, _____ **(1)**?
(right)

ANNE: Mes amis _____ **(2)**, mais moi,
(are students)

les études, _____ **(3)**.
(that's not my thing)

_____ **(4)** intellectuelle. Mais je suis
(I am not at all)

_____ **(5)**.
(rather athletic)

PAUL: Alors, _____ **(6)** le sport?
(you like)

ANNE: Oui, _____ **(7)** beaucoup _____ **(8)**
(I like) *(soccer)*

et _____ **(9)**. Et toi?
(football)

PAUL: J'aime bien _____ **(10)**, mais _____ **(11)** beaucoup
(tennis) *(I don't like)*

le football. En fait *(In fact)*, je suis _____ **(12)**.
(more intellectual than athletic)

D. Quel pronom? Léa is talking to a new friend. Complete what she says with the logical subject pronoun: **je, tu, il, elle, nous, vous, ils,** or **elles.** The first one has been done as an example.

1. Ma famille et moi, __nous__ sommes de Californie. Et ta *(your)* famille et toi, _____ êtes d'où? Ma sœur Lisa est ici pour voir la France mais _____ ne parle pas très bien français. Moi, _____ parle très bien français! Mes parents ne sont pas ici en France. _____ sont à Los Angeles.

2. C'est mon ami David. _____ est étudiant. Et toi? _____ es étudiante aussi? Les amies de Lisa ne sont pas étudiantes. _____ travaillent.

E. Des présentations. David is introducing his friends. Complete their conversation with the correct form of **être.** The first one has been done as an example.

DAVID: Léa, Lisa, c' ___est___ **(1)** mon ami Thomas. Il _____ **(2)** aussi étudiant à l'université de Nice. Nous _____ **(3)** dans le même cours de maths. Thomas, ce _____ **(4)** mes amies Léa et Lisa. Elles _____ **(5)** de Californie.

THOMAS: Bonjour, Léa! Bonjour, Lisa! Vous _____ **(6)** américaines, alors?

LÉA: Oui, nous _____ **(7)** de Los Angeles. Moi, je _____ **(8)** à Nice pour étudier. Lisa n' _____ **(9)** pas étudiante. Et toi? Tu _____ **(10)** d'où?

THOMAS: Je _____ **(11)** d'ici.

F. Questions. A classmate is asking Léa questions. In the first blank, rephrase her classmate's question, using **est-ce que.** Then, complete Léa's answers by filling in the missing subject pronoun and the correct form of the verb **être** in the affirmative or negative.

> **EXEMPLE**   Tu es étudiante?
> — **Est-ce que tu es étudiante?**
> — Oui, **je suis** étudiante.

1. Lisa est étudiante?

   — _____

   — Non, _____ étudiante.

2. Vous êtes d'ici, Lisa et toi?

   — _____

   — Non, _____ d'ici.

3. Tu es américaine?

   — _____

   — Oui, _____ américaine.

4. David et Thomas sont américains?

   — _____

   — Non, _____ américains.

G. Encore des questions. A new friend is asking Lisa questions. Based on the answers she gives, supply her friend's questions. Use **est-ce que.**

EXEMPLE   — **Est-ce que tu es intellectuelle?**
                    — Non, je ne suis pas très intellectuelle.

1. — _____

    — Oui, je suis sportive.

2. — _____

    — Oui, j'aime le sport.

3. — _____

    — Oui, Léa est assez sportive aussi.

4. — _____

    — Oui, Léa est étudiante.

5. — Et Léa et toi? _____

    — Léa et moi? Non, nous ne sommes pas canadiennes.

6. — _____

    — Oui, nous sommes célibataires.

7. — _____

    — Oui, David et Jean sont d'ici.

---

*Journal. Below, write an e-mail message to a new French pen pal. Tell her your name and where you are from. Then write three sentences describing yourself. Finally, ask her questions to find out: her name, if she is from Paris, and if she is married or single.

_____

_____

_____

_____

_____

_____

_____

_____

_____

_____

_____

_____

Partie auditive

A. Jean-Marc et Marion. You will hear a friend talking about Jean-Marc and Marion. Complete what he says.

2-8

1. Jean-Marc n'est pas _____.

   Il est un peu _____.

2. Marion est _____, mais Jean-Marc

   n'est pas _____.

3. Jean-Marc et Marion sont _____.

   Ils ne sont pas _____.

4. Marion n'est pas _____.

   Elle est _____. Jean-Marc est _____

   aussi. Il n'est pas _____ non plus *(either)*.

B. Les adjectifs. As you have learned, adjectives agree in number and gender with the noun they describe. Mark the form of the adjective that has the correct agreement for the sentence you hear.

2-9

EXEMPLE VOUS VOYEZ: petit ____ petits ____ petite ____ petites ____
VOUS ENTENDEZ: Elles sont assez petites.
VOUS INDIQUEZ: petit ____ petits ____ petite ____ petites ✓

1. ennuyeux _____   ennuyeux _____   ennuyeuse _____   ennuyeuses _____

2. américain _____   américains _____   américaine _____   américaines _____

3. sportif _____   sportifs _____   sportive _____   sportives _____

4. marié _____   mariés _____   mariée _____   mariées _____

5. intelligent _____   intelligents _____   intelligente _____   intelligentes _____

C. Prononciation: Les pronoms sujets et le verbe *être*.
Listen and repeat the subject pronouns and the verb **être**, paying particular attention to the pronunciation. Then complete the sentences you see with the correct form of the verb **être** as you hear the narrator read them. Stop the recording as needed.

être	
je suis	nous sommes
tu es	vous êtes
il est	ils sont
elle est	elles sont

1. Moi, je _____ David Cauvin.

2. Nathan, c' _____ mon ami.

3. Il _____ de Marseille.

4. Nathan et Eva _____ très sympathiques.

5. Nous _____ dans le même cours d'espagnol.

6. Et toi, tu _____ étudiante aussi?

7. Lisa et toi, vous _____ américaines, non?

*D. Toujours des questions.
You will hear a series of questions about your French class. Answer them in complete sentences. Pause the recording as needed.

EXEMPLE   VOUS ENTENDEZ: Est-ce que vous êtes en cours maintenant?
   VOUS ÉCRIVEZ: **Oui, je suis en cours maintenant.**
   Non, je ne suis pas en cours maintenant.

1. _____

2. _____

3. _____

4. _____

5. _____

6. _____

COMPÉTENCE 3

Describing the university area

By the time you finish this **Compétence,** you should be able to describe your campus and tell what's in the surrounding neighborhood.

Partie écrite

A. Qu'est-ce que c'est? Identify the following places or things. Remember to use **c'est** or **ce sont** when identifying something with a noun.

EXEMPLE C'est un cinéma.

 1

 2

 3

 4

 5

 6

 7

 8

 9

 10

1. _____
2. _____
3. _____
4. _____
5. _____

6. _____
7. _____
8. _____
9. _____
10. _____

B. Conversation. Reread the conversation on page 45 of the textbook. Then, complete this conversation between two friends.

PAUL: _____ **(1)** à ton université là-bas en Californie?
(*What's the campus like*)

MATHÉO: Il est trop (*too*) _____ **(2)** et il n'est pas _____ **(3)**. Il y a
(*big*) (*very pretty*)

_____ **(4)** avec des _____ **(5)**
(*lots of buildings*) (*classrooms*)

et des _____ **(6)** et il n'y a pas _____ **(7)**.
(*offices*) (*enough trees*)

PAUL: Qu'est-ce qu'il y a _____ **(8)**?
(*in the university neighborhood*)

MATHÉO: _____ **(9)**, il y a une librairie et un
(*Near the university*)

_____ **(10)** où on passe des films étrangers. Il y a aussi
(*movie theater*)

_____ **(11)**, mais il n'y a pas de _____ **(12)**.
(*a lot of fast-food restaurants*) (*good restaurants*)

C. Près de l'université. According to these individuals' preferences, what sort of place might they ask about? Compose logical questions for them to ask. For each, use one of the items named in **A. Qu'est-ce que c'est?** on the preceding page.

> **EXEMPLE** J'aime beaucoup les matchs de football américain.
> **Est-ce qu'il y a un stade** près de l'université?

1. J'aime beaucoup les films étrangers.

_____ près de l'université?

2. J'aime beaucoup les cours d'aérobic.

_____ près de l'université?

3. J'aime beaucoup les livres.

_____ près de l'université?

4. J'aime beaucoup le cappuccino.

_____ près de l'université?

D. À l'université. Indicate whether each of these things is found on your campus. Be sure to use the correct form of the indefinite article (**un, une, des**) and remember that after **ne… pas, un, une,** and **des** become **de (d')**.

> **EXEMPLE** (*rock concerts*) Sur le campus, **il y a des concerts de rock /**
> **il n'y a pas de concerts de rock.**

1. (*a nightclub*) Sur le campus, _____.

2. (*lecture halls*) Sur le campus, _____.

3. (*dorms*) Sur le campus, _____.

4. (*houses*) Sur le campus, _____.

Nom _____ Date _____

E. Votre université. Complete these sentences with the correct indefinite article (**un, une, des**). Remember that these articles change to **de (d')** after **ne... pas** or after quantity expressions such as **beaucoup** or **assez,** and also directly before plural adjectives. Then indicate if each sentence describes your university by checking **vrai** or **faux.**

EXEMPLE   Il y a beaucoup __**de**__ vieux bâtiments dans le quartier.   ✔ vrai _____ faux

1. Il y a _____ grands bâtiments dans le quartier.   _____ vrai _____ faux

2. Il y a _____ salles de cours modernes sur le campus.   _____ vrai _____ faux

3. Il y a _____ théâtre sur le campus.   _____ vrai _____ faux

4. Il y a _____ bibliothèque avec Wi-Fi.   _____ vrai _____ faux

5. Il y a _____ résidences sur le campus.   _____ vrai _____ faux

6. Il n'y a pas _____ boîte de nuit sur le campus.   _____ vrai _____ faux

7. Il y a assez _____ parkings sur le campus.   _____ vrai _____ faux

8. Il y a beaucoup _____ librairies dans le quartier.   _____ vrai _____ faux

F. Descriptions. Choose the adjective that best describes each noun and write it in the blank before or after the noun. Remember that most adjectives are placed after the noun in French, but review the fifteen adjectives that are generally placed before the noun and the special forms **bel, nouvel,** and **vieil** on page 48 of the textbook before you begin.

EXEMPLES

C'est une _____ ville **intéressante**.
(ennuyeuse, intéressante)

C'est une ____**jolie**____ville _____.
(jolie, laide)

1. C'est une _____ ville _____.
   (grande, petite)

   C'est une _____ ville _____.
   (américaine, canadienne)

2. C'est un _____ quartier _____.
   (vieux/vieil, moderne)

   C'est un _____ quartier _____.
   (agréable, désagréable)

3. C'est un _____ bâtiment _____.
   (vieux/vieil, nouveau/nouvel)

   C'est un _____ bâtiment _____.
   (beau/bel, laid)

4. C'est un _____ homme _____.
   (jeune, vieux/vieil)

   C'est un _____ homme _____.
   (antipathique, sympa)

Line art on this page: © Cengage Learning

G. Optimiste! Léa is always positive and enjoys everything. Complete what she would say by writing the French equivalent of the adjective given in English in the correct position in the sentence. Pay attention to the form of the adjective (masculine, feminine, singular, plural).

EXEMPLE C'est une _____*jolie*_____ maison _____. *(pretty)*

1. David est un _____ homme _____. *(handsome)*

2. C'est un _____ ami _____. *(nice)*

3. C'est un _____ homme _____. *(optimistic)*

4. Jean est un _____ homme _____. *(intelligent)*

5. Ce sont des _____ amis _____. *(interesting)*

6. Lisa est une _____ femme _____. *(beautiful)*

7. C'est une _____ femme _____. *(athletic)*

8. Il y a un _____ restaurant _____ près d'ici. *(good)*

9. Il y a un _____ parc _____ près d'ici. *(pretty)*

10. Il y a un _____ parking _____ à l'université. *(large)*

*H. Comment est l'université? A friend is asking you about your university. Answer his questions *in complete sentences.*

1. Est-ce que tu aimes le campus? Comment est le campus?

   _____

   _____

2. Est-ce qu'il y a plus de *(more)* vieux bâtiments ou plus de nouveaux bâtiments sur le campus?

   _____

3. Est-ce qu'il y a beaucoup d'arbres sur le campus? Est-ce qu'il y a assez de parkings?

   _____

   _____

4. Est-ce qu'il y a un restaurant sur le campus? Si oui *(If so)*, est-ce que c'est un bon restaurant?

   _____

   _____

5. Qu'est-ce qu'il y a sur le campus? (Nommez au moins trois choses. *[Name at least three things.]*)

   _____

6. Comment est le quartier universitaire?

   _____

7. Qu'est-ce qu'il y a près de l'université? (Nommez au moins trois choses. *[Name at least three things.]*)

   _____

Partie auditive

 A. Identification. You will hear the following places identified. Fill in the number of each sentence you
2-12 hear under the picture it identifies.

> **EXEMPLE**   VOUS ENTENDEZ: C'est un cinéma.
> VOUS ÉCRIVEZ:

   a. _____   b. _____   c. *Exemple*   d. _____

   e. _____   f. _____   g. _____   h. _____

 B. Ici il y a... You will hear a student say whether or not each of the places depicted in *A. Identification*
2-13 is located on campus or in the university neighborhood. List each place that is found there. Do not write
anything for the places that are not on campus or in the neighborhood.

> **EXEMPLE**   VOUS ENTENDEZ: Il y a un cinéma dans le quartier universitaire.
> VOUS ÉCRIVEZ:

Il y a *un cinéma,* _____

_____.

 C. Prononciation: L'article indéfini. Pause the recording and review the *Prononciation* section on
2-14 page 46 of the textbook. Then turn on the recording and fill in the form of the indefinite article, **un** or **une,**
that you hear with each noun.

_____ cours	_____ classe	_____ bibliothèque	_____ bâtiment
_____ salle de gym	_____ boîte de nuit	_____ ami	_____ amie
_____ résidence	_____ laboratoire	_____ quartier	_____ librairie

🔊 **D. Quelle forme?** You will hear a series of questions about your university. Indicate the form of the
2-15 indefinite article you hear in each one.

1. un ____   une ____   des ____   4. un ____   une ____   des ____

2. un ____   une ____   des ____   5. un ____   une ____   des ____

3. un ____   une ____   des ____   6. un ____   une ____   des ____

*Now play this section again and *answer* the questions about your university with complete sentences in
French. Remember that **un, une,** and **des** *will change to* **de (d')** after a negative expression.

1. _____

2. _____

3. _____

4. _____

5. _____

6. _____

🔊 **E. L'université.** Listen as two students talk about one of their courses. Then pause the recording and
2-16 complete each sentence logically.

1. Les étudiants sont dans le même cours _____.

2. Ils sont en cours le mardi et _____.

3. Le cours est à _____ heure _____.

4. Le professeur est _____.

🔊 **F. Dictée.** You will hear a student talking about his university. The first time, just listen to what he says at
2-17 normal speed. Then fill in the missing words as it is repeated more slowly.

1. Sur le campus, il y a _____.

2. Il y a _____

   et _____ pour les profs.

3. _____ l'université,

   il y a _____

   et _____.

4. Dans le _____, il y a

   _____

5. _____, il y a _____.

Nom _____ Date _____

Talking about your studies

By the time you finish this **Compétence,** you should be able to talk about the activities and courses at your university and say what you are studying.

Partie écrite

A. Préférences. Fill in the name of each of these courses in the logical category.

le marketing / l'histoire / le théâtre / la chimie / l'anglais / la psychologie / l'espagnol / la musique / l'informatique / la biologie / les sciences politiques / le français / la physique / l'allemand / la comptabilité / les mathématiques

LES LANGUES	LES SCIENCES	LES SCIENCES HUMAINES
_____	_____	_____
_____	_____	_____
_____	_____	_____
_____		

LES ARTS	LE COMMERCE	LES TECHNOLOGIES
_____	_____	_____
_____	_____	_____

*Now complete these sentences about your studies.

1. Ce semestre, j'étudie _____.

2. Je n'étudie pas _____.

3. Je comprends bien _____.

4. Je ne comprends pas très bien _____.

5. J'aime le cours de _____ parce qu'il est _____.

*Now express your feelings about these courses, activities, and places at your university by writing each of them in the appropriate category.

la philosophie / la littérature / les fêtes / les devoirs / les examens / les matchs de basket / la salle d'informatique / la bibliothèque / les cours en ligne

J'aime beaucoup…	J'aime assez…	Je n'aime pas…
_____	_____	_____
_____	_____	_____
_____	_____	_____
_____	_____	_____
_____	_____	_____

B. Comparaisons. Thomas loves all math and science classes, but he finds all other courses difficult and boring. How would he compare the following courses for the quality indicated in parentheses? Use the expressions **plus… que** and **moins… que** and remember to use the correct form of the adjective (masculine, feminine, singular, plural).

> **EXEMPLE** physics / German (interesting)
> **La physique est plus intéressante que l'allemand.**

1. chemistry / philosophy (easy)

_____

2. psychology / math (interesting)

_____

3. biology / history (difficult)

_____

4. literature / chemistry (boring)

_____

C. Conversation. Reread the conversation on page 50 of the textbook. Two friends are talking about their studies. Complete their conversation.

ISABELLE: _____ **(1)** ce semestre?
(What are you studying)

RACHID: _____ **(2)** l'anglais, _____ **(3)**,
(I'm studying)   *(history)*

_____ **(4)**, _____ **(5)** et
(computer science)   *(chemistry)*

_____ **(6)**.
(accounting)

ISABELLE: _____ **(7)**?
(How are your classes)

RACHID: _____ **(8)** mon cours d'histoire
(I prefer)

_____ **(9)** le prof est _____ **(10)**.
(because)   *(very interesting)*

Et toi? _____ **(11)** tes cours?
(Do you like)

ISABELLE: Comme toi, _____ **(12)** beaucoup mon cours d'histoire.
(I like)

D. Mon université. A friend is asking about life at your school. Complete her questions by filling in the correct form of the definite article: **Le, La, L', or Les.**

1. _____ université est grande?   4. _____ étudiantes sont sympas?

2. _____ cours sont faciles?   5. _____ campus est agréable?

3. _____ professeurs sont sympathiques?   6. _____ bibliothèque est moderne?

*Now answer each of her questions, *using the appropriate pronoun, **il, elle, ils,** or **elles,** to replace the subject.* The first one has been done as an example.

1. **Oui, elle est grande. / Non, elle n'est pas grande. / Non, elle est petite.**
2. _____
3. _____
4. _____
5. _____
6. _____

*E. Quel article? Complete a friend's questions with the correct form of the definite article (**le, la, l', les**), the indefinite article (**un, une, des**), or **de (d')**. Then answer each question *with a complete sentence.* The first one has been done as an example.

1. Comment est _____*le*_____ cours de français?
   <u>Il est intéressant.</u> _____

2. Est-ce que _____ langues sont faciles pour toi?
   _____

3. Combien _____ étudiants est-ce qu'il y a dans le cours?
   _____

4. Est-ce qu'il y a _____ étudiants étrangers dans le cours?
   _____

5. Est-ce qu'il y a _____ cinéma dans le quartier universitaire?
   _____

6. Est-ce que tu aimes _____ films étrangers?
   _____

F. Qui est-ce? Complete these sentences using **c'est, ce sont, il/elle est,** or **ils/elles sont.** The first blank has been completed as an example.

1. _____*Ce sont*_____ mes amis.
   _____ à la maison.
   _____ américains.
   _____ sympas.

2. _____ une femme.
   _____ étudiante.
   _____ en cours.
   _____ timide.

3. _____ David et Lisa.

_____ à Nice.

_____ mes amis.

_____ sympas.

---

*Journal. Write a message to a new French-speaking pen pal.

In the first paragraph, tell her:
• your name, where you are a student, and what you are studying

In the second paragraph, tell her:
• whether or not you like the university and why
• three things there are on campus and one thing there is not

In the third paragraph, ask her:
• if she is a student
• if she is married or single

_____

_____

_____

_____

_____

_____

_____

_____

_____

_____

_____

_____

_____

_____

_____

_____

_____

_____

_____

_____

_____

_____

_____

Partie auditive

2-18

A. Les cours. You will hear the names of various courses. For each one, indicate the field to which it belongs.

EXEMPLE   VOUS ENTENDEZ: l'anglais
VOUS SÉLECTIONNEZ: C'est une langue. ✓   C'est une science. _____

   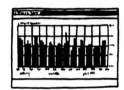   

© Cengage Learning

1. C'est une langue. _____   C'est une science. _____
2. C'est une science humaine. _____   C'est un cours de technologie. _____
3. C'est une science. _____   C'est une science humaine. _____
4. C'est une langue. _____   C'est une science. _____
5. C'est un cours de technologie. _____   C'est un cours de commerce. _____
6. C'est un cours de commerce. _____   C'est une langue. _____
7. C'est une science humaine. _____   C'est un cours de technologie. _____
8. C'est un cours de technologie. _____   C'est une science humaine. _____

2-19

B. Quels cours? Listen as two students talk about their classes. Then complete the following statements according to the conversation.

1. Le cours d'informatique de la jeune femme est à _____ heures.
2. Elle pense que le cours d'informatique est un peu _____.
3. Le prof de théâtre du jeune homme est très _____.
4. La sœur du jeune homme étudie la _____.

2-20

C. Prononciation: L'article défini. Pause the recording and review the *Prononciation* section on page 52 of the textbook. Then turn on the recording and practice pronouncing the forms of the definite article by repeating these words after the speaker.

le campus   la bibliothèque   l'université   les cours   les activités

le français   la comptabilité   l'informatique   les langues   les arts

2-21

D. Préférences. You will hear the names of places or activities common to university life. Fill in the form of the definite article (**le, la, l', les**) that you hear for each one. Pause the recording between items to allow enough time to respond.

1. _____   2. _____   3. _____   4. _____   5. _____   6. _____   7. _____

*Now play this recording again and, as you hear each one, decide how much you like it and write it under the appropriate column. Stop the recording to have enough time to respond.

EXEMPLE   VOUS ENTENDEZ: les fêtes
           VOUS ÉCRIVEZ:

J'aime beaucoup...	J'aime assez...	Je n'aime pas du tout...
les fêtes		

*E. Colocataires. The following people are looking for housemates. Listen to each description. Then pause the recording and indicate the names of two students who, in your opinion, would make good housemates. Finally, explain your choice in English.

2-22

Daniel / Ahmad / Philippe / Pierre / Léa / Hyemi

_____

_____

Now play this section again. Then complete the statement you see, explaining which person you would prefer to live with and why.

Je préférerais *(would prefer)* habiter avec _____ parce que (qu') _____

_____.

*F. Vos cours. A friend is asking about your courses this semester. Answer her *with complete sentences* in French.

2-23

1. _____
2. _____
3. _____
4. _____
5. _____

Après les cours Chapitre 2

 COMPÉTENCE 1

Saying what you like to do

By the time you finish this *Compétence,* you should be able to tell how you spend your free time and invite a friend to do something.

Partie écrite

A. Est-ce que vous aimez… ? David finds certain activities fun or interesting and others boring. Does he say that he likes to do each pictured activity? Start each sentence with **J'aime…** or **Je n'aime pas…** based on whether he says the activity is fun/interesting or boring.

> **EXEMPLES** **J'aime aller au cinéma.** C'est amusant.
> **Je n'aime pas faire du jogging.** C'est ennuyeux.

1. _____. C'est ennuyeux.

2. _____. C'est amusant.

3. _____. C'est ennuyeux.

4. _____. C'est amusant.

5. _____. C'est intéressant.

6. _____. C'est ennuyeux.

7. _____. C'est intéressant.

B. Quel verbe? Fill in each blank on the left with a logical infinitive. Then indicate whether you generally go out with friends or to the park or stay at home to do the activity.

	A	B
	SORTIR AVEC DES AMIS OU AU PARC	RESTER À LA MAISON

EXEMPLE **dîner** au restaurant   X ____ ____

1. _____ au cinéma   ____ ____
2. _____ un verre avec des amis   ____ ____
3. _____ un texto   ____ ____
4. _____ la radio   ____ ____
5. _____ au tennis   ____ ____
6. _____ de la guitare   ____ ____
7. _____ du vélo   ____ ____
8. _____ au téléphone   ____ ____
9. _____ sur l'ordinateur   ____ ____
10. _____ des mails   ____ ____

C. Conversation. Reread the conversation between David and Léa on p. 69 of your textbook. Then, complete this conversation between two other students with the indicated words.

ADRIEN: Est-ce que tu voudrais _____ (1)
                                              (to do something)

     avec moi cet *(this)* après-midi?

LUCILE: _____ (2) cet après-midi. Ça te dit de
              (I'm not free)

    _____ (3) ce soir?
         (to go out)

ADRIEN: Ce soir? Oui! Tu aimes la musique classique? Il y a un concert à l'université.

LUCILE: _____ (4). Je préfère aller au concert de rock
        (No, not really)

     au stade en ville à huit heures.

ADRIEN: Bon, _____ (5).
            (okay)

LUCILE: On va dîner _____ (6)?
             (before)

ADRIEN: _____ (7). _____ (8)
      (Okay)   *(I would like to go)*

     au restaurant Beauchamps.

LUCILE: Bon. Alors, _____ (9) au restaurant Beauchamps.
             (around six thirty)

ADRIEN: Oui. À _____ (10).
          (later)

D. Trop fatiguée. Léa is very tired and wants to put off doing the more demanding activities until later, and do those that take less energy now. Complete her statements with the logical indicated activities.

> **EXEMPLE** Je préfère **aller danser en boîte** demain soir. Je voudrais **rester à la maison** ce soir. (rester à la maison / aller danser en boîte)

1. Je préfère _____ ce week-end, mais cet (*this*) après-midi

   je voudrais _____. (jouer au tennis /

   regarder un match à la télé)

2. Je préfère _____ demain matin.

   Je voudrais _____ aujourd'hui après les cours. (dormir /

   faire mes devoirs)

3. Je préfère _____ plus tard. Je voudrais

   _____ maintenant. (faire du jogging / lire)

4. Je préfère _____ demain et

   _____ ce soir. (rester à la maison / dîner au restaurant)

5. Je préfère _____ vendredi soir, mais aujourd'hui je voudrais

   _____. (regarder un DVD à la maison /

   aller au cinéma)

6. Je préfère _____ samedi. Aujourd'hui,

   je voudrais _____. (inviter des amis à la maison / être seule)

E. Pourquoi? Léa is explaining why she likes to go to different places. Which words in parentheses go in which blanks? Remember that **pour** means *in order to*, rather than *for*, when it is used before infinitives.

> **EXEMPLE** J'aime **aller au cinéma Gaumont** pour **voir des films.** (voir des films, aller au cinéma Gaumont)

1. J'aime _____ pour _____

   _____. (prendre un verre avec des amis, aller au café Hugo)

2. Je préfère _____ pour _____

   _____. (dîner avec des amis, aller au restaurant Roma)

3. Je n'aime pas beaucoup _____ pour

   _____. (sortir en boîte, danser)

4. Le samedi, j'aime _____ pour

   _____. (aller à la bibliothèque, lire des magazines)

5. J'aime _____ pour _____

   _____. (jouer au volley, aller au parc)

6. Quelquefois, j'aime _____ pour

   _____. (rester à la maison, dormir)

*F. Projets. Choose two activities you would like to do during your free time this week. Indicate with whom, on what day, and at what time you want to do each.

Activité	Avec qui *(whom)*?	Quel jour?	À quelle heure?
EXEMPLE aller au cinéma	avec Kim	samedi soir	à 8h
_____	_____	_____	_____
_____	_____	_____	_____

*G. On sort? Write a conversation in which you invite one of the people listed in *F. Projets* to do the suggested activity.

    EXEMPLE   aller au cinéma   avec Kim   samedi soir   à 8h

— **Kim, tu es libre samedi soir? Tu voudrais aller au cinéma avec moi?**
— **Oui, d'accord. Vers quelle heure?**
— **Vers huit heures?**
— **À huit heures? Ça va. Alors, à samedi.**
— **Au revoir!**

_____

_____

_____

_____

_____

*H. Et vous? A friend is making plans with you for this weekend. Answer his/her questions *with complete sentences.*

1. Est-ce que tu préfères sortir vendredi soir ou samedi soir?

_____

2. Tu préfères aller au cinéma ou en boîte?

_____

3. Vers quelle heure est-ce que tu voudrais sortir?

_____

4. Tu voudrais dîner au restaurant avant?

_____

5. Est-ce que tu es libre dimanche après-midi?

_____

6. Qu'est-ce que tu aimes faire le dimanche?

_____

Partie auditive

 A. Loisirs. You will hear expressions for several leisure activities. Repeat each phrase after the speaker. Then, write both the number of the item and the verb under the corresponding picture. The first one has been done as an example.

EXEMPLE	VOUS ENTENDEZ: **1.** lire un livre
	VOUS RÉPÉTEZ: **lire un livre**
	VOUS ÉCRIVEZ: **1. lire** *under k*

a. _____

b. _____

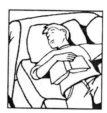

c. _____

d. _____

e. _____

f. _____

g. _____

h. _____

i. _____

j. _____

k. **1. lire**

l. _____

m. _____

n. _____

o. _____

B. Prononciation: La consonne *r* et l'infinitif. Pause the recording and review the *Prononciation* section on page 70 of the textbook. Then turn on the recording and repeat these infinitives after the speaker. Place a check mark under the verbs where you hear the boldfaced **r** in the infinitive ending pronounced.

manger *(to eat)* invite**r** surfe**r** reste**r** alle**r** sorti**r** dormi**r** voi**r** fai**r**e écri**r**e prend**r**e êt**r**e

___   ___   ___   ___   ___   ___   ___   ___   ___   ___   ___   ___

Now, stop the recording and complete the following questions between two friends with the logical infinitives from the preceding list. Use each infinitive only once. Then turn on the recording and check your work, repeating after the speaker. The first blank has been completed as an example.

1. Tu préfères __sortir__ avec des amis le week-end ou _____ des amis à la maison?

2. Tu préfères _____ au cinéma ou _____ un DVD à la maison?

3. Tu voudrais _____ un verre ou _____ un sandwich?

4. Tu préfères _____ des mails ou _____ sur Internet?

5. Tu aimes _____ le dimanche matin ou tu n'aimes pas _____ au lit *(in bed)*?

6. Tu voudrais _____ quelque chose avec moi ou tu préfères _____ seule?

🔊 3-4 **C. Pour mieux comprendre:** *Listening for specific information.* Listen to three conversations in which people are making plans. For each one, select the correct option from the list given to indicate what they decide to do, where, what day, and at what time.

ACTIVITÉ: jouer au foot / regarder la télé / aller au café / dîner / regarder un match de foot

OÙ: à la maison / au café / au stade / au parc / au restaurant

LE JOUR: mercredi soir / jeudi / aujourd'hui / samedi / mardi soir

L'HEURE: vers sept heures / à quatre heures et demie / à deux heures / à midi / à cinq heures et quart

CONVERSATION A: Activité: _____ Où: _____

Le jour: _____ L'heure: _____

CONVERSATION B: Activité: _____ Où: _____

Le jour: _____ L'heure: _____

CONVERSATION C: Activité: _____ Où: _____

Le jour: _____ L'heure: _____

🔊 3-5 **D. On fait quelque chose?** Listen to a conversation in which David invites Léa and Lisa to do something tomorrow, and complete these statements with the appropriate activities from the following list.

aller au cinéma   faire du jogging   jouer au tennis

1. David aime _____, mais Lisa préfère _____

et Léa préfère _____.

2. David voudrait _____ avec Lisa demain matin et

_____ avec Lisa et Léa demain après-midi.

🔊 3-6 ***E. Une invitation.** A friend is inviting you to do something. Answer in *complete sentences in French.*

1. _____

2. _____

3. _____

4. _____

5. _____

6. _____

 COMPÉTENCE 2

Saying how you spend your free time

By the time you finish this **Compétence,** you should be able to tell what you and those around you do regularly and how often and how well you do it.

Partie écrite

A. Talents et connaissances. Complete the sentences saying whether or not you often do these things on Saturday.

> **EXEMPLE** Je **joue** souvent au football le samedi matin.
> Je **ne joue pas** souvent au football le samedi matin.

1. Je _____ souvent au lit jusqu'à dix heures.

2. Je _____ souvent mes cours le samedi après-midi.

3. Le samedi soir, je _____ souvent au cinéma.

Now say whether you do the following things well.

> **EXEMPLE** Je **joue** bien au hockey.
> Je **ne joue pas** bien au hockey.

4. Je _____ bien.

5. Je _____ bien au tennis.

6. Je _____ bien.

B. Adverbes. Number the adverbs in the left column from 1 (most often) to 5 (least often), according to how often they indicate that people do something. Then number the adverbs in the right column from 1 (best) to 4 (worst), according to how well someone does something. The first one has already been numbered as an example.

HOW OFTEN
____ rarement
____ ne... jamais
____ quelquefois
__1__ presque toujours
____ souvent

HOW WELL
____ assez mal
____ très mal
__1__ très bien
____ assez bien

Line art on this page: © Cengage Learning

C. Conversation. Reread the conversation between David and Léa on page 75 of your textbook. Then, complete this conversation between two other students with the indicated words.

ÉRIC: _____ (1) d'habitude le samedi?
(What do you do)

SOPHIE: Le samedi matin, _____ (2) au parc pour faire du jogging ou pour jouer au tennis.
_(I go)_

L'après-midi, _____ (3) et le soir j'aime sortir avec des amis.
(I stay home)

ÉRIC: Tu voudrais _____ (4) avec moi ce week-end?
(to play tennis)

SOPHIE: Oui, d'accord. _____ (5) vers dix heures généralement.
(I play)

ÉRIC: Je _____ (6) vers neuf heures et demie?
(pass by your house)

SOPHIE: D'accord! Tu voudrais _____ (7)?
(to eat something afterward)

ÉRIC: Oui, ça te dit d'aller au café Rousseau?

SOPHIE: Oui, j'aime bien le café Rousseau. Alors, à samedi!

ÉRIC: Au revoir. À samedi.

D. Une fille dynamique. If _Lisa leaves home early, spends a lot of time with friends, and usually only returns home to sleep,_ which adverb in parentheses goes with which sentence? Rewrite the sentences inserting the logical adverb.

EXEMPLE   Elle aime sortir avant neuf heures du matin. / Elle reste au lit après huit heures.
(ne… jamais, toujours)
**Elle aime toujours sortir avant neuf heures du matin. Elle ne reste
jamais au lit après huit heures.**

1. Elle reste à la maison. / Elle préfère sortir avec des amis. (ne… presque jamais, presque toujours)

   _____

   _____

2. Elle préfère voir des films au cinéma. / Elle regarde des DVD à la maison. (rarement, toujours)

   _____

   _____

3. Elle bricole le week-end. / Elle joue au tennis avec des amis. (ne… jamais, quelquefois)

   _____

   _____

4. Elle mange à la maison le week-end. / Elle dîne au restaurant avec des amis. (presque toujours, rarement)

   _____

   _____

E. La famille de Léa. Léa is talking to a new friend about her family. Complete her statements with the correct conjugated form of the verb in parentheses. The first one has been done as an example.

Ma famille __habite__ (1) (habiter) à Los Angeles. Mes parents _____ (2) (être) à la retraite *(retired)*. Ils ne _____ (3) (travailler) pas. Mon père *(father)* _____ (4) (rester) souvent à la maison. Il _____ (5) (regarder) la télé et il _____ (6) (bricoler). Ma mère *(mother)* préfère sortir et elle _____ (7) (inviter) souvent des amies à la maison. Elles _____ (8) (parler) et elles _____ (9) (jouer) au bridge. Ma mère _____ (10) (aimer) la musique. Elle _____ (11) (danser) et elle _____ (12) (chanter) très bien. Ma sœur Lisa _____ (13) (travailler) dans une salle de gym. Elle _____ (14) (aimer) beaucoup le sport et elle _____ (15) (jouer) très bien au tennis.

Moi, j'_____ (16) (habiter) à Nice maintenant, parce que j'_____ (17) (étudier) à l'Université de Nice. Lisa _____ (18) (être) ici à Nice maintenant. Nous _____ (19) (aimer) passer beaucoup de temps ensemble *(together)*. Le soir, nous _____ (20) (dîner) ensemble et après nous _____ (21) (inviter) des amis à sortir.

F. Chacun ses goûts. Léa is talking about what people prefer to do in their free time. Review the spelling change verbs on page 80 of the textbook. Then, complete each sentence with a conjugated form of **préférer** and the logical infinitive from the list.

   voir   faire   écrire   jouer   lire   prendre   surfer   dîner   aller   danser

EXEMPLE   Moi, je **préfère lire** des magazines.

1. Mes amis _____ au foot au parc.

2. Moi, je _____ un film au cinéma.

3. Mon meilleur ami _____ sur Internet.

4. Mes amis et moi, nous _____ au restaurant le week-end.

5. Lisa _____ des mails à des amis le soir.

6. David et Jean _____ un verre au café.

7. Quelquefois, mes amis et moi _____ en boîte.

8. Et toi, qu'est-ce que tu _____ avec tes amis?

*G. Mes amis et moi. Say how often the following people do the indicated things. Remember to conjugate the verb and to place the adverb in the correct position in the sentence. The verbs in **2, 5, 6,** and **7** have spelling changes, as explained on page 80 of the textbook.

toujours / souvent / quelquefois / rarement / ne… jamais

EXEMPLE   moi, je / jouer au golf le week-end
Moi, je joue rarement au golf le week-end.

1. mes amis / regarder la télévision le week-end

_____

2. moi, je (j') / envoyer un texto à un(e) ami(e)

_____

3. ma meilleure amie / inviter des amis à la maison le week-end

_____

4. les étudiants de l'université / étudier le week-end

_____

5. en cours de français, les étudiants / répéter après le prof

_____

6. en cours de français, nous / commencer à l'heure *(on time)*

_____

7. nous / manger en cours

_____

---

*Journal. Write a paragraph describing how you typically spend your time on the weekend. If you want to use the verb **aller,** or verbs that do not end in **-er,** such as **dormir** or **sortir,** see the *Note de grammaire* in the margin on page 76 of your textbook.

EXEMPLE   **Le vendredi soir, je reste souvent à la maison parce que je suis fatigué(e) *(tired).***
Quelquefois, je préfère sortir avec des amis. Le samedi matin, je reste au lit jusqu'à…

_____

_____

_____

_____

_____

_____

_____

_____

_____

_____

Partie auditive

 A. Le week-end. Listen and repeat as a woman says how often she does different things on weekends. Pause the recording and write the adverb saying how often under the corresponding illustration.

EXEMPLE VOUS ENTENDEZ: D'habitude, je rentre à la maison à 4h00 le vendredi.
VOUS RÉPÉTEZ: **D'habitude, je rentre à la maison à 4h00 le vendredi.**
VOUS ÉCRIVEZ:

 a. _____

 b. _____

 c. *d'habitude*

 d. _____

 e. _____

 f. _____

 g. _____

 h. _____

B. Prononciation: Les verbes en -er. Pause the recording and review the ***Prononciation*** section on page 77 of the textbook. Then read the following sentences and cross out the boldfaced verb endings that are not pronounced. Finally, turn on the recording and repeat the sentences after the speaker, checking your work. The first one has been done as an example.

_____ Léa et Lisa préfèr~~ent~~ le restaurant *Le Lion d'Or.*

_____ Où est-ce que vous mang**ez?**

___1___ Tu rest**es** à la maison ce soir?

_____ Léa aim**e** passer beaucoup de temps avec toi, non?

___6___ Oui, je pass**e** beaucoup de temps avec elle.

_____ Non, Léa, Lisa et moi dîn**ons** au restaurant.

Now stop the recording and reorder the preceding sentences to create a logical conversation between David and his brother Jean by numbering them from **1** to **6.** The first one and the last one have been done for you. Then turn on the recording and listen to their conversation to check your work.

Nom _____ Date _____

C. Prononciation: Les verbes à changements orthographiques.
3-9 Pause the recording and review the *Prononciation* section on page 80 of the textbook. Then turn on the recording and repeat these verb forms after the speaker.

je préfère   nous préférons   tu répètes   vous répétez

Pause the recording, look at the following words, and decide how the underlined **c** or **g** is pronounced. Where **c** is pronounced like **s,** write an **s** in the blank. Where **g** is pronounced like **j,** write **j.** If the indicated **c** or **g** has a hard sound, leave the blank empty. Finally, turn on the recording and check your work, repeating each word after the speaker.

_____ café   _____ culture   _____ gare   _____ guitare

_____ célèbre   _____ créole   _____ général   _____ gosse

_____ ici   _____ commençons   _____ gré   _____ voyageons

_____ cocorico   _____ gitane

D. Le week-end.
3-10 Pause the recording and review the verbs with spelling changes on page 80 of the textbook. Then turn on the recording and listen as David's friends, Thomas and Elsa, say what they do. The first time, just listen to their conversation at normal speed. Then listen as it is repeated in short phrases at a slower speed, with pauses for you to fill in the missing words.

THOMAS: Qu'est-ce que tu fais _____ (1) le week-end?

ELSA: Le samedi après-midi je _____ (2), mais le samedi soir j'aime

_____ (3).

Nous _____ (4) souvent ensemble au

restaurant et nous _____ (5) beaucoup.

Et toi, Thomas, tu _____ (6) beaucoup de

temps à la maison ou tu _____ (7) sortir?

THOMAS: Moi, je _____ (8) inviter des amis à la maison. Beaucoup

de mes amis _____ (9) de la musique. Nous _____ (10)

et nous _____ (11). Et toi, tu _____ (12),

non? Tu es libre samedi? Tu voudrais jouer avec nous?

ELSA: Oui, je veux bien, mais je _____ (13)!

Je _____ (14) chez toi à quelle heure?

THOMAS: Nous _____ (15) à jouer vers huit heures généralement.

*E. Et toi?
3-11 Listen as a friend asks you questions about what you do on the weekend. Answer each question *with a complete sentence.*

1. _____

2. _____

3. _____

4. _____

5. _____

 **COMPÉTENCE 3**

Asking about someone's day

By the time you finish this **Compétence,** you should be able to ask how people typically spend their day and tell how you spend yours.

Partie écrite

A. Ma journée. Write each possible answer from the list after the logical question word. The first one has been done as an example.

avec mon copain (ma copine) / tous les jours / parce que c'est amusant / toute la journée /
parce que j'aime ça / chez moi / dans un fast-food / avec mon mari (ma femme) / pour déjeuner /
à la bibliothèque / le matin / seul(e) / de deux heures à quatre heures

Quand? _____

_____

Où? _____

_____

Avec qui? _avec mon copain (ma copine),_ _____

_____

Pourquoi? _____

_____

B. Conversation. Reread the conversation between Jean and Léa on page 82 of your textbook. Then, complete this conversation between two other friends with the indicated words.

ABDUL: _____ **(1)** est-ce que tu travailles?
　　　　　　　　　　　(When)

YANN: Je travaille _____ **(2)** le week-end.
　　　　　　　　　　　　　(every day, except)

ABDUL: Tu travailles _____ **(3)**?
　　　　　　　　　　　　　(all day long)

YANN: Oui, _____ **(4)** huit heures _____ **(5)** cinq heures, mais _____ **(6)** à la
　　　　(from)　　　　　　　　*(to)*　　　　　　　　　　　*(I return)*

maison à midi pour _____ **(7)**.
　　　　　　　　　　　　(to have lunch)

ABDUL: Et le soir, qu'est-ce que tu fais _____ **(8)**?
　　　　　　　　　　　　　　　　　(in general)

YANN: _____ **(9)** à la maison vers cinq heures et demie.
　　　　(I return)

_____ **(10)** un peu avant de dîner.
　　　　(Sometimes, I sleep)

ABDUL: Et après?

YANN: Je parle au téléphone _____ **(11)** ou
　　　　　　　　　　　　　　(with my girlfriend)

_____ **(12)**.
　　　　(I surf the Net)

Nom _____ Date _____

C. Une lettre. Léa is writing to her former French teacher in California about her new experiences in Nice. Complete her statements with the correct form of the indicated verb. Pay attention to the verbs with spelling changes. The first one has been done as an example.

Chère Madame Filloux,

Je _____ **suis** _____ (1) (être) très contente ici à Nice.

J' _____ (2) (aimer) beaucoup mes cours et l'université. Les

étudiants _____ (3) (être) sympas et les cours _____ (4)

(être) intéressants. Je _____ (5) (être) à l'université

tous les jours sauf le week-end. Le matin, je _____ (6)

(réviser) mes cours à la bibliothèque. Je _____ (7) (préférer)

étudier avec une amie. Nous _____ (8) (commencer)

à travailler vers neuf heures et l'après-midi, je _____ (9)

(être) en cours. Je ne _____ (10) (passer) pas tout mon

temps (all my time) à l'université, bien sûr (of course). J' _____ (11)

(aimer) sortir avec des amis. Nous _____ (12) (aimer) aller

au cinéma et nous _____ (13) (manger) souvent ensemble.

Quelquefois, nous _____ (14) (déjeuner) ensemble dans un fast-

food et d'autres fois (other times) nous _____ (15) (dîner) ensemble au

restaurant. J' _____ (16) (aimer) mieux aller au restaurant! Lisa

_____ (17) (être) ici et nous _____ (18) (passer)

beaucoup de temps ensemble. Elle _____ (19) (être) très

sportive et elle _____ (20) (aimer) beaucoup jouer au tennis.

Moi, je n' _____ (21) (aimer) pas beaucoup jouer avec elle

parce qu'elle _____ (22) (gagner) toujours. Quelquefois, nous

_____ (23) (voyager) le week-end pour voir un peu la France.

Amitiés,
Léa Clark

Now complete the following questions by translating the question words in parentheses. Then complete the missing words in each response according to what Léa says in the preceding letter.

1. *(How)* _____ sont les étudiants et les cours?

   Les étudiants sont _____ et les cours sont _____.

2. *(What days)* _____ est-ce que Léa est à l'université?

   Elle est à l'université _____ les jours _____ le week-end.

3. *(With whom)* _____ est-ce que Léa aime sortir?

   Elle aime sortir avec des _____.

4. *(What)* _____ est-ce qu'ils aiment faire ensemble?

   Ils aiment aller au _____ et ils _____ souvent ensemble.

5. *(Where)* _____ est-ce que Léa aime mieux manger?

Elle aime mieux manger au _____.

6. *(Why)* _____ est-ce que Léa n'aime pas jouer au tennis avec Lisa?

Elle n'aime pas jouer au tennis avec Lisa parce que Lisa _____ toujours.

7. *(When)* _____ est-ce que Léa et Lisa voyagent?

Elles voyagent quelquefois _____.

D. Projets. Two friends are talking about plans for the evening. Complete their conversation with the logical question words.

à quelle heure / pourquoi / qui / que (qu') / où / comment

— _____ **(1)** est-ce que tu voudrais faire ce soir? Ça te dit de faire quelque chose ensemble?

— Pas ce soir. Je vais chez mon amie Florence.

— _____ **(2)** est-ce que tu vas *(are going)* chez elle?

— Parce qu'il y a une fête pour son anniversaire *(birthday)*.

— _____ **(3)** est-ce qu'elle habite?

— Elle habite près de l'université.

— _____ **(4)** est-ce que la fête commence?

— À sept heures.

— _____ **(5)** est-ce que tu vas chez Florence?

— Une amie passe chez moi vers six heures et demie.

— _____ **(6)** est-ce?

— Une autre amie, Yasmine.

E. Beaucoup de questions. Léa is answering a friend's questions. Based on the italicized part of each of Léa's answers, provide the question her friend asked. Use **est-ce que** to form the questions.

> **EXEMPLE** — **Quels jours est-ce que tu es à l'université?**
> — Je suis à l'université *tous les jours sauf le week-end.*

1. _____?

Je suis à l'université *de neuf heures à trois heures.*

2. _____?

Je déjeune *avec Lisa.*

3. _____?

Nous aimons manger *au café Le Trapèze.*

4. _____?

Nous mangeons *vers une heure et demie* d'habitude.

5. _____?

Je rentre *à trois heures et demie.*

6. _____?

Je révise les cours *avec une amie.*

7. _____?

Elle préfère étudier *à la bibliothèque.*

8. _____?

Le soir, j'aime faire *quelque chose avec mes amis.*

F. Mon meilleur ami. Using inversion, rewrite the following questions about you and your best male friend.

EXEMPLE Est-ce que ton meilleur ami habite ici ou dans une autre ville?
Ton meilleur ami habite-t-il ici ou dans une autre ville?

1. Est-ce que ton meilleur ami travaille le week-end?

_____

2. Est-ce que vous aimez sortir le week-end?

_____

3. Quel jour est-ce que vous préférez sortir?

_____

4. Est-ce que ton ami préfère aller danser ou aller au cinéma?

_____

5. Est-ce qu'il danse bien?

_____

6. Est-ce que vous mangez souvent ensemble au restaurant?

_____

7. Est-ce que tu préfères déjeuner ou dîner au restaurant?

_____

*G. Mon meilleur ami et moi. Answer the questions about you and your best male friend from **F. Mon meilleur ami** with complete sentences.

EXEMPLE Ton meilleur ami habite-t-il ici ou dans une autre ville?
Il habite ici. / Il habite à San Juan.

1. _____

2. _____

3. _____

4. _____

5. _____

6. _____

7. _____

Partie auditive

3-12

A. C'est logique? For each item, you will hear two questions. Repeat the question that would logically elicit the response shown. Indicate whether it was the first or second option by selecting **1ᵉ** or **2ᵉ** and write out the question word used. Finally, check your work as you hear the correct answer.

EXEMPLE VOUS VOYEZ: tous les jours   1ᵉ____ 2ᵉ____ _____
VOUS ENTENDEZ: Quand est-ce que vous êtes à l'université?
Pourquoi est-ce que vous êtes à l'université?
VOUS DITES: **Quand est-ce que vous êtes à l'université?**
VOUS INDIQUEZ: tous les jours   1ᵉ ✓   2ᵉ____   **quand**
VOUS ENTENDEZ: Quand est-ce que vous êtes à l'université?

1. au café du quartier   1ᵉ____ 2ᵉ____ _____
2. avec une amie   1ᵉ____ 2ᵉ____ _____
3. un sandwich   1ᵉ____ 2ᵉ____ _____
4. vers quatre heures   1ᵉ____ 2ᵉ____ _____
5. chez moi   1ᵉ____ 2ᵉ____ _____
6. avec mon copain (ma copine)   1ᵉ____ 2ᵉ____ _____
7. jouer au tennis   1ᵉ____ 2ᵉ____ _____

3-13

B. Prononciation: Les lettres *qu*. Pause the recording and review the ***Prononciation*** section on page 84 of the textbook. Then turn on the recording and repeat these questions after the speaker. When you have finished, turn off the recording and match the questions to their logical responses by writing the letter of the logical response in the blank next to the corresponding question.

____ 1. Est-ce que tu travailles?
____ 2. Où est-ce que tu travailles?
____ 3. Quand est-ce que tu travailles?
____ 4. Avec qui est-ce que tu travailles?
____ 5. Qu'est-ce que tu aimes faire le week-end?
____ 6. Pourquoi?

a. À l'université.
b. Avec Ali.
c. Parce que j'aime le sport.
d. Tous les jours sauf le week-end.
e. J'aime jouer au foot.
f. Oui, je travaille beaucoup.

3-14

C. Prononciation: L'inversion et la liaison. Pause the recording and review the ***Prononciation*** section on page 86 of the textbook. Decide whether the boldfaced final consonants *of the verbs* in the following questions should be pronounced. Cross out those that are silent and mark those that are pronounced in liaison with a link mark [‿]. Then turn on the recording and repeat the sentences after the speaker, checking your pronunciation.

EXEMPLE   Le café es**t‿il** près d'ici?

1. Voudrai**s‿**tu aller au café?
2. Lisa et Léa son**t‿**elles au café?
3. David voudrai**t‿il** aller prendre un verre?
4. Aimen**t‿**ils aller au café?

D. Quelle est la question? You are eavesdropping on your friend Jean-Luc, who is talking on the phone about what he likes to do on the weekend. You cannot hear the questions of the person on the other end of the line, but you figure them out from Jean-Luc's answers. Complete the questions asked by the other person by writing the logical question word from the following list.

À quelle heure / Quand / Avec qui / Que (Qu') / Où / Pourquoi

EXEMPLE VOUS ENTENDEZ: J'aime aller danser le samedi soir.
VOUS ÉCRIVEZ: **Qu'**est-ce que tu aimes faire le samedi soir?

1. _____ est-ce que tu préfères sortir?

2. _____ est-ce que tu aimes aller danser?

3. _____ aimes-tu sortir avec elle?

4. _____ est-ce que tu dînes d'habitude?

5. _____ est-ce que tu étudies?

E. À l'université. Listen as Léa asks a friend, Bruno, about his day and indicate all of the items that complete the following sentences according to what he says. You may need to select more than one.

1. Bruno est à l'université...

_____ du lundi au vendredi _____ seulement le lundi, le mercredi et le vendredi

2. Il révise ses cours...

_____ le matin _____ l'après-midi _____ le soir _____ le week-end

3. D'habitude, il travaille...

_____ à la maison _____ chez un ami _____ au café

4. Après les cours, il aime...

_____ aller au café _____ faire du jogging _____ jouer au tennis

*F. Et vous? Answer the following questions about your typical day with complete sentences.

1. _____

2. _____

3. _____

4. _____

5. _____

Nom _____ Date _____

Going to the café

By the time you finish this *Compétence,* you should be able to say what you like to eat and drink at a café.

Partie écrite

A. Je voudrais un/une/des... Some people are discussing food and drinks and ordering at a café. Complete their sentences with the name of the pictured item. Remember to use **un, une,** or **des.**

EXEMPLE   Je voudrais **un café.**

    1   2   3   4   5   6   7

1. Je voudrais _____.

2 Pour moi, _____.

3. Pour mon ami, _____.

4. David voudrait _____.

5. Je vais prendre _____.

6. Je voudrais _____.

7. Pour Lisa, _____.

B. Préférences. Some people are discussing their eating habits or ordering at a café. Complete their sentences with the logical noun in parentheses, including the appropriate article. Remember to use **un, une,** or **des** to say *a* or *some,* but use **le, la, l',** or **les** after verbs indicating likes or preferences. (**J'aime le café. Je préfère le thé.**)

   EXEMPLE   Je mange souvent **des frites,** mais je n'aime pas **les sandwichs au jambon.** Je suis végétarien.
   (sandwichs au jambon, frites)

1. Le matin, je préfère _____. Je n'aime pas

   _____ parce que je n'aime pas prendre de boissons avec de la caféine.

   (café, jus de fruit)

2. J'ai soif. Je voudrais _____. J'ai faim aussi, alors je vais prendre

   _____ avec ça. (sandwich au fromage, eau minérale)

3. Je n'aime pas beaucoup _____ parce que je n'aime pas l'alcool. Je

   préfère _____. (bière, coca)

4. _____ pour mon ami. Moi, je préfère quelque chose de chaud, alors je

vais prendre _____. (demi, thé au citron)

5. Je mange souvent _____ avec un hamburger et je commande

_____ comme boisson d'habitude. (Orangina, frites)

6. Au café, je commande _____ d'habitude. Je voudrais prendre

_____ quelquefois, mais l'alcool n'est pas bon pour moi parce que je

suis diabétique. (verre de vin, eau minérale)

*C. Et vous? Do you like to go to cafés? Complete the following questions with the logical question words, according to the answers suggested in parentheses. Then answer each question about yourself. One of the words will be used twice.

où / que (qu') / comment / qui / pourquoi / quand / quelle / combien

EXEMPLE **Combien** de temps est-ce que vous passez au café? (beaucoup de temps, peu de temps)
Je passe beaucoup de temps au café.

1. Avec _____ est-ce que vous aimez aller au café? (avec mes amis, avec mon copain,

avec ma copine, seul[e], ???)

_____

2. _____ est-ce que vous préférez aller? (à Starbucks, au café Java, à Seattle's Best, au

café Spider House, ???)

_____

3. _____ est-ce que vous aimez ce *(that)* café? (parce que le café est très bon, parce que

la clientèle est intéressante, parce qu'il est près de l'université, ???)

_____

4. _____ est le service dans ce café? (toujours très bon, quelquefois mauvais, ???)

_____

5. _____ est-ce que vous préférez aller au café? (le matin, l'après-midi, le soir)

_____

6. À _____ heure est-ce que ce café ferme? (à minuit, à neuf heures du soir, ???)

_____

7. _____ est-ce que vous aimez prendre au café? (un café, un coca, un thé, ???)

_____

8. _____ est-ce que vous aimez faire au café? (lire, parler avec des amis, écouter de la

musique, surfer sur Internet, faire les devoirs, écrire des mails, ???)

_____

D. Conversation. Reread the conversation in which David and Léa order at a café on pages 88–89 of your textbook. Then, complete the following conversation in which Léa is at the café with another friend.

LÉA: _____ **(1)** et _____ **(2)**. Et toi?
                        (I'm very hungry)   *(I'm thirsty too)*

ELSA: _____ **(3)**.
                        (Me too)

LÉA: Monsieur, _____ **(4)**.
                                          (please)

LE SERVEUR: Bonjour, mesdames. Vous désirez?

LÉA: _____ **(5)** un coca et _____ **(6)**.
                        (I would like)   *(some fries)*

ELSA: _____ **(7)**.
                        (For me, a glass of white wine and a ham sandwich)

LE SERVEUR: Très bien.

Après, Léa et Elsa _____ **(8)**.
                                  (pay)

LÉA: _____ **(9)**, monsieur?
                        (That makes how much)

LE SERVEUR: _____ **(10)** vingt euros _____ **(11)**.
                        (That makes)   *(fifty)*

LÉA: _____ **(12)** trente euros.
                        (Here are)

LE SERVEUR: Et _____ **(13)**. Merci bien.
                        (here is your change)

E. Les prix. Write the following prices in numerals.

    EXEMPLE   quarante-huit euros **48 €**

  1. soixante-quatre euros _____ €

  2. soixante-quatorze euros _____ €

  3. quatre-vingt-un euros _____ €

  4. cinquante-quatre euros _____ €

  5. cinquante-sept euros _____ €

  6. quarante-deux euros _____ €

  7. quatre-vingt-dix-neuf euros _____ €

  8. soixante-quinze euros _____ €

  9. quatre-vingt-huit euros _____ €

10. cent euros _____ €

F. C'est combien? Léa is writing some checks. Write out these amounts as they would appear on her checks.

EXEMPLE   84 €   **quatre-vingt-quatre** euros

36 € _____ euros   100 € _____ euros

92 € _____ euros   83 € _____ euros

76 € _____ euros   95 € _____ euros

88 € _____ euros   55 € _____ euros

47 € _____ euros   89 € _____ euros

65 € _____ euros   41 € _____ euros

71 € _____ euros   74 € _____ euros

---

*Journal. Write a paragraph describing your activities the days you go to school. Include the following information. You may change the order as needed to fit your day.

- what days you are at the university
- what time you are at the university on one of those days
- where, at what time, and with whom you have lunch that day
- what you like to do after class
- how often you go to a café, with whom, what you order, and what you like to do there
- what time you return home
- what you do in the evenings usually

EXEMPLE   **Je suis à l'université tous les jours sauf le week-end. Le lundi, je suis à l'université toute la journée, de neuf heures à cinq heures…**

_____

_____

_____

_____

_____

_____

_____

_____

_____

_____

_____

_____

_____

_____

_____

_____

Partie auditive

A. Au café. Order each of these items by repeating the order after the speaker.

3-18

un expresso

un jus de fruit

un demi

un Orangina

un café au lait

_____ _____ _____ _____ _____

un coca

un sandwich
au jambon

un thé au citron

un verre de vin rouge
et un verre de vin blanc

_____ _____ _____ _____

un sandwich
au fromage

une eau minérale

une bière

des frites

_____ _____ _____ _____

B. Je voudrais… You will hear a conversation in which a family is ordering at a café. As they order, check
off the items they ask for in the illustrations in **A. Au café.**

3-19

C. Comptons! Listen to the numbers and repeat after the speaker.

3-20

30… 40… 50… 60… 70… 80… 90… 100

D. Prononciation: Les nombres. Pause the recording and review the **Prononciation** section on page 90
of the textbook. Decide whether the final consonants of these numbers should be pronounced. Cross out those
that are silent and mark those that are pronounced in liaison with a link mark [‿] as in the first item, which
has been done as an example. Then turn on the recording and repeat after the speaker, checking your answers.

3-21

1. un / un‿étudiant / un livre

2. deux / deux étudiants / deux livres

3. trois / trois étudiants / trois livres

4. six / six étudiants / six livres

5. huit / huit étudiants / huit livres

6. dix / dix étudiants / dix livres

E. Prix moyens. You will hear the average price for beverages at cafés in France. Write the name of the beverage and the price.

EXEMPLE VOUS ENTENDEZ ET VOUS ÉCRIVEZ: Une bouteille *(bottle)* de **bière**, c'est **3,50 €.**

1. Un _____, c'est _____ €.

2. Un _____, c'est _____ €.

3. Un _____, c'est _____ €.

4. Un _____, c'est _____ €.

5. Un _____, c'est _____ €.

F. Les numéros de téléphone. French phone numbers are read in pairs. You will hear the phone numbers for several business advertisements. Complete each ad by filling in the number in the space provided.

EXEMPLE VOUS ENTENDEZ: Le numéro de téléphone des Jardins La Fayette est le 04.42.78.71.34.
VOUS ÉCRIVEZ:

LES JARDINS LA FAYETTE FLEURISTE *Fleurs et plantes* *artificielles et naturelles* Entretien - Location de plantes Mariages - Deuils 89, rue La Fayette Tél: _04.42.78.71.34_	**AUTOAUDIO** crédit immédiat Autoradios & Systèmes d'alarme 88, boulevard Victor Hugo Tél: _____	**DATATEC INFORMATIQUE** Analyse – conseil 95, rue Provence Logiciels – Formation Tél: _____	**CLINIQUE VÉTÉRINAIRE FARELL** 71, avenue Versailles Tél: _____

© Cengage Learning

G. On va au café? Listen to a conversation in which two students who just met in class at the **Université de Nice** are making plans to go to a café together. Fill in the missing numbers *using numerals.*

— On va prendre quelque chose au café?

— D'abord, je voudrais rentrer rapidement chez moi, mais peut-être dans _____ **(a)** minutes.

— Où est-ce que tu habites?

— Dans la résidence Jean Médecin.

— Moi aussi! J'ai *(I have)* la chambre _____ **(b)**.

— Moi, je suis dans la chambre _____ **(c)**. Quel est ton numéro de téléphone?

— C'est le 06. _____._____._____._____ **(d)**.

— Mon téléphone, c'est le 06. _____._____._____. _____ **(e)**.

— Alors, je passe chez toi dans _____ **(f)** minutes?

— D'accord.

H. Au café. Review the dialogue on pages 88–89 of the textbook, in which David and Léa order something at the café. Then listen as they order at the café another time and complete the following sentences.

1. _____ voudrait manger, mais _____ n'a pas faim.

2. David commande _____ et _____
_____. Léa commande _____.

3. Ils paient _____ € _____.

Un nouvel appartement

Chapitre 3

COMPÉTENCE 1

Talking about where you live

By the time you finish this **Compétence,** you should be able to describe where you live in French.

Partie écrite

*A. Chez Thomas. Read about where Thomas lives, then say what is true for you by completing the following statements.

> **EXEMPLE** Thomas est étudiant à l'université Laval.
> Moi, je suis **étudiant(e) à l'université...**

1. Thomas habite dans un appartement avec un colocataire.

   Moi, j'habite _____.

2. Thomas habite en centre-ville. Sa *(His)* famille habite en banlieue. Son *(His)* meilleur ami habite à la campagne.

   Moi, j'habite _____.

   Ma famille habite _____.

   Mon meilleur ami (Ma meilleure amie) habite _____.

3. L'appartement de Thomas n'est pas trop loin de l'université. C'est très pratique.

   Mon appartement / Ma maison / Ma chambre _____

   _____.

4. L'appartement de Thomas est grand et il n'est pas trop cher. Le loyer est de 825$ par mois.

   Mon appartement / Ma maison / Ma chambre _____

   _____

   _____.

B. Une maison. Tell what rooms there are in this house by filling in each blank to identify the room. Use the indefinite article **un, une,** or **des.**

Dans cette *(this)* maison, il y a six pièces:

> **EXEMPLE** **une chambre**

1. _____

2. _____

3. _____

4. _____

5. _____

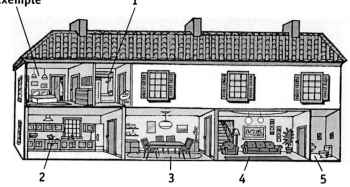

C. L'immeuble de Thomas. Change these cardinal numbers to their ordinal equivalents.

EXEMPLE deux → **deuxième**

1. un → _____

2. trois → _____

3. quatre → _____

4. cinq → _____

5. neuf → _____

6. dix → _____

Now, identify parts of Thomas's apartment building by filling in items **1–8** below.

EXEMPLE **l'ascenseur**

1. la _____

2. la _____

3. l' _____

4. le _____ étage

5. le _____ étage

6. le _____ étage

7. le _____

8. le _____

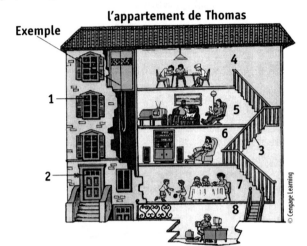

l'appartement de Thomas

© Cengage Learning

Now, complete the statements that follow to say what is going on in the building. In the first blank, identify the floor. In the second blank, say what the indicated person is doing by writing the correct form of the logical verb from the list. Remember to use **au** to say *on the* or *in the* with a floor.

réviser	jouer	manger	travailler	écouter	regarder

EXEMPLE **Au troisième étage,** trois étudiants **révisent** les cours.

1. _____, Thomas et son ami _____

   la télévision.

2. _____, une jeune femme _____

   de la musique.

3. _____, la mère et deux de ses enfants _____.

   Les deux autres enfants _____ au ballon *(ball)*.

4. _____, un vieux monsieur _____

   sur l'ordinateur.

D. Une conversation. Reread the conversation between Robert and Thomas on page 109 of your textbook. Then, complete this conversation in which Robert asks Thomas about his apartment.

ROBERT: _____ **(1)** est ton appartement?
(On what floor)

THOMAS: J'habite _____ **(2)**
(on the second floor [U.S. third floor])

d'un _____ **(3)**.
(large apartment building)

ROBERT: Tu habites _____ **(4)** l'université?
(near)

THOMAS: Mon appartement n'est pas _____ **(5)** l'université
(too far from)

et il y a _____ **(6)** tout près.
(a bus stop)

ROBERT: Qu'est-ce qu'il y a comme _____ **(7)** dans ton appartement?
(rooms)

THOMAS: Il y a trois _____ **(8)**, _____ **(9)**,
(bedrooms) *(a modern kitchen)*

_____ **(10)** et _____ **(11)**.
(a living room) *(a small dining room)*

E. En quelle année? Fill in the following important years from Quebec's history in numerals.

EXEMPLE **1534** Jacques Cartier prend *(takes)* possession du Canada pour la France
en **mille cinq cent trente-quatre.**

_____ **1.** La ville de Québec est fondée *(founded)* en **mille six cent huit.**

_____ **2.** La France cède ses territoires canadiens aux Anglais en **mille sept cent soixante-trois.**

_____ **3.** Pendant les années soixante *(During the sixties)*, un mouvement pour la reconnaissance *(the recognition)* de l'identité francophone québécoise et pour les réformes sociales et économiques, appelé la Révolution tranquille, commence. Et en **mille neuf cent soixante-huit,** le Parti québécois est fondé.

_____ **4.** Presque *(Nearly)* cinquante pour cent des Québécois votent pour un Québec libre en **mille neuf cent quatre-vingt-seize.**

_____ **5.** En **deux mille trois,** les provinces canadiennes créent *(create)* le Conseil de la fédération.

_____ **6.** En **deux mille dix,** le Québec commémore le 50ᵉ anniversaire de la Révolution tranquille.

F. C'est combien? People are writing checks for the amounts shown. Write the amounts.

EXEMPLE 210$ = **deux cent dix** dollars

1. 845$ = _____ dollars

2. 492$ = _____ dollars

3. 1 512$ = _____ dollars

4. 3 925$ = _____ dollars

5. 1 718 000$ = _____ dollars

6. 2 685 050$ = _____ dollars

*G. Pour mieux lire: *Guessing meaning from context.* Use what you know and context to guess the meaning of the **boldfaced** words below. The verbs are all in the *present* tense.

Robert **ouvre** la lettre de Thomas et **vérifie** l'adresse. Il **lit:** «*Mon appartement **se trouve** 38, rue Dauphine. J'habite au deuxième étage.*» «Oui, c'est bien là», pense-t-il. Il **descend de** la voiture, **entre** dans l'immeuble et **monte** l'escalier.

EXEMPLE   ouvre = **opens**

1. vérifie = _____

2. lit = _____

3. se trouve = _____

4. descend de = _____

5. entre = _____

6. monte = _____

*H. Un nouvel appartement. Reread the story *Un nouvel appartement* on page 113 of your textbook. Then answer the following questions with *short answers in English.*

1. What floor does Thomas live on? What floor does Robert first go to?

_____

2. Who is the Gabrielle Robert speaks to? Who does Robert think she is?

_____

_____

3. What *two* things was Robert confused about? Why?

_____

_____

_____

*I. Et vous? Answer the following questions about your living situation with complete sentences.

1. Est-ce que vous habitez dans un appartement, dans une maison ou dans une chambre à la résidence universitaire?

_____

2. Est-ce que vous aimez l'appartement / la maison / la résidence où vous habitez? Pourquoi ou pourquoi pas?

_____

_____

3. Est-ce qu'il/elle est en centre-ville, en ville, en banlieue ou à la campagne? Il/Elle est près de l'université ou loin de l'université?

_____

_____

4. À quel étage est-ce que vous préférez habiter? Il y a un ascenseur ou un escalier chez vous?

_____

_____

5. Qu'est-ce qu'il y a comme pièces chez vous? (Si vous habitez dans une résidence universitaire, qu'est-ce qu'il y a comme pièces chez vos parents)? (To say *at my parents' house,* use **chez mes parents.**)

_____

_____

Partie auditive

A. Qu'est-ce que c'est? Identify the places and things in this house as in the example. After a pause for you to respond, you will hear the correct answer. Verify your response and your pronunciation.

EXEMPLE VOUS ENTENDEZ: C'est une chambre ou une salle de bains?
VOUS DITES: **C'est une chambre.**
VOUS ENTENDEZ: C'est une chambre.

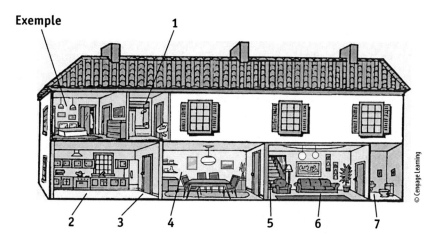

B. Où habitent-ils? Pause the recording and review the expressions used to talk about where you live on page 108 and in the dialogue between Robert and Thomas on page 109 of the textbook. Then turn on the recording and listen as three students, Didier, Sophie, and Caroline, talk about their living arrangements. The first time, just listen to what they say. Then listen again, stop the recording, and complete these statements by indicating the correct expressions in italics.

1. Didier habite *en ville / en banlieue / à la campagne.*

2. Il habite *au rez-de-chaussée / au premier étage / au deuxième étage / au troisième étage.*

3. Il habite *dans une vieille maison / dans un vieil immeuble / dans une résidence universitaire.*

4. Son *(His)* appartement est *tout près de l'université / assez loin de l'université.*

5. Sophie habite *dans un appartement / dans une maison / dans une chambre à la résidence.*

6. Sa *(Her)* chambre est *grande et moderne / petite et moderne / petite et vieille.*

7. Le loyer est de *plus de / moins de* cinq cents dollars par mois.

8. Caroline habite *seule / avec sa famille / avec une amie.*

9. Elle habite *en centre-ville / en ville / en banlieue / à la campagne.*

10. Sa maison est *petite / vieille / moderne.*

C. Les nombres. Listen and repeat these numbers after the speaker, paying careful attention to your pronunciation.

105 _____	454 _____	700 _____	1 000 _____	1 000 000 _____
220 _____	500 _____	800 _____	2 150 _____	1 304 570 _____
310 _____	670 _____	999 _____	5 322 _____	1 800 000 _____

Now you will hear some of the numbers above. Indicate the numbers that you hear.

D. Encore des nombres. Fill in the number you hear, using numerals, not words.

> **EXEMPLE** VOUS ENTENDEZ: mille sept cent cinquante-huit
> VOUS ÉCRIVEZ: **1 758**

a. _____   e. _____

b. _____   f. _____

c. _____   g. _____

d. _____   h. _____

E. Dictée. You will hear a student talk about where she lives. The first time, just listen to what she says at normal speed. Then fill in the missing words as it is repeated more slowly. Pause the recording as needed to allow enough time to fill in the words.

Moi, j'habite dans un appartement _____ **(1).**

Mon appartement est _____ **(2)** d'un grand

_____ **(3).** Il y a _____ **(4)** et

_____ **(5).** Mon appartement n'est pas

_____ **(6)** l'université et il n'est pas

_____ **(7).** C'est très _____ **(8).**

Ma chambre est _____ **(9)** et elle est

_____ **(10)** la salle de bains. Ma sœur habite dans une

maison _____ **(11),** mais mon frère préfère habiter

_____ **(12).**

*F. Et vous? Answer the following questions about where you live. Pause the recording between questions to allow enough time to respond.

1. _____

2. _____

3. _____

4. _____

5. _____

Nom _____ Date _____

Talking about your possessions

By the time you finish this *Compétence,* you should be able to talk about your belongings in French and tell where they are.

Partie écrite

A. Qu'est-ce que vous avez? Look at the illustration of the living room. Say if you have each of the pictured items in your home. Use **un, une,** or **des** with the noun, or change them to **de (d')** if the verb is negated.

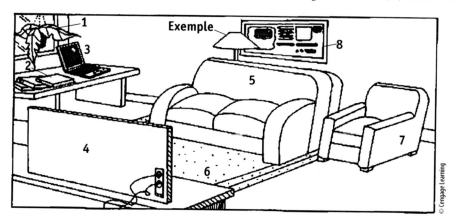

EXEMPLE **J'ai une lampe / J'ai des lampes / Je n'ai pas de lampe** chez moi.

1. _____ chez moi.
2. _____ chez moi.
3. _____ chez moi.
4. _____ chez moi.
5. _____ chez moi.
6. _____ chez moi.
7. _____ chez moi.
8. _____ chez moi.

B. Dans le salon. Look at the living room pictured in *A. Qu'est-ce que vous avez?* Choose the correct word or expression in parentheses to complete the sentences.

EXEMPLE La lampe est **derrière** le canapé. (derrière / devant)

1. La table est _____. (près de la porte / dans le coin)

2. Le portable est _____ la table. (sur / sous)

3. Les livres sont _____ l'ordinateur. (à gauche de / à droite de)

4. La télé est _____ canapé. (en face du / à côté du)

5. Le canapé est _____ le fauteuil et la table. (entre / devant)

6. Le tapis est _____ le canapé. (sous / sur)

Nom _____ Date _____

C. Une conversation. Reread the telephone conversation between Robert and Thomas on page 115 of your textbook. Then, complete this conversation between two friends who are thinking of sharing a house.

CLARA: Tu _____ **(1)** un appartement ici? Écoute, moi, j'ai
(are looking for)

une maison avec deux _____ **(2).** Elle est assez
(bedrooms)

_____ **(3)** l'université et elle n'est pas _____ **(4).**
(near) (expensive)

Tu voudrais _____ **(5)** la maison avec moi?
(to share)

KARIMA: _____ **(6).** Tu aimes _____ **(7)?**
(Maybe) (animals)

J'ai _____ **(8)** et _____ **(9).**
(a cat) (a dog)

Ils sont un peu _____ **(10).** Ils aiment dormir
(annoying)

_____ **(11)** ou _____ **(12).**
(on the chairs) (on the couch)

CLARA: _____ **(13).** J'aime beaucoup les animaux. Est-ce que tu
(No problem)

_____ **(14)?** Parce que moi, _____ **(15).**
(smoke) (I don't smoke)

KARIMA: _____ **(16).** Alors, ça va.
(Me neither)

D. Possessions. Robert is talking to Thomas about what they have. Complete the following statements with the verb **avoir** and the pictured noun.

Exemple   **1**   **2**   **3**   **4**

5   **6**   **7**

EXEMPLE   Moi, j'ai un iPod.

1. Nous _____ .   5. Moi, j' _____ .
2. Gabriel _____ .   6. Gabriel et toi, vous _____ ?
3. Thomas, tu _____ ?   7. Les étudiants au quatrième étage _____
4. Gabriel _____ .   _____ .

Line art on this page: © Cengage Learning

80 *Horizons,* Sixth Edition • **Student Activities Manual**

© 2015 Cengage Learning. All Rights Reserved. May not be scanned, copied or duplicated, or posted to a publicly accessible website, in whole or in part.

E. C'est où? First, complete each of the phrases that follow with the correct form of **de** (**du, de la, de l', des**). Remember that **de + le = du** and **de + les = des.** Then, indicate whether the first or second italicized choice is the most logical completion for each sentence by selecting **1** or **2.**

EXEMPLE   Les livres sont *à côté* **de l'***ordinateur* / *à côté* **de la** *voiture.*   1. ✓   2. ___

1. La chaise est *en face* _____ *bureau* / *en face* _____ *voiture.*   1. ___ 2. ___

2. L'ordinateur est *à gauche* _____ *vélo* / *à gauche* _____ *imprimante* (printer).   1. ___ 2. ___

3. Le lecteur Blu-ray est *à côté* _____ *télé* / *à côté* _____ *tapis.*   1. ___ 2. ___

4. Les CD sont *à droite* _____ *lecteur CD* / *à droite* _____ *lecteur Blu-ray.*   1. ___ 2. ___

5. La télé est *en face* _____ *tableaux* / *en face* _____ *canapé.*   1. ___ 2. ___

F. Où? Look at the illustration of Thomas's friend Emma's living room. Complete the paragraph with the appropriate prepositions (**sous, sur,** etc.). Imagine that you have just entered the room through the door and you are standing in the doorway, facing the table. The first one has been done as an example.

Dans ce salon, l'ordinateur est **sur** la table et les livres

sont _____ **(1)**

l'ordinateur. Il y a des plantes _____ **(2)** la table.

Le fauteuil est _____ **(3)** la télé. Le chien est

_____ **(4)** le fauteuil, _____ **(5)**

le fauteuil et la télé. Les plantes sont _____ **(6)** la télé. L'escalier est

_____ **(7)** les deux tableaux.

— Vous êtes ici

© Cengage Learning

Look back at the picture of Emma's living room and create sentences in French telling where these objects are with respect to each other in the room. You are still standing in the doorway. Remember **de + le = du** and **de + les = des.**

EXEMPLE   the computer / the table   **L'ordinateur est sur la table.**

1. the laptop / the books

_____

2. the stairway / the door

_____

3. the lamp / the armchair

_____

4. the TV / the plants

_____

5. the cat / the table

_____

*G. Colocataires. You and a new friend are thinking about sharing a house and he/she wants to know more about you. Answer the questions he/she asks.

1. Tu as beaucoup de choses?

_____

2. Quels meubles *(furniture)* as-tu pour le salon?

_____

3. Tu passes beaucoup de temps dans le salon?

_____

4. Quels appareils électroniques *(electronics)* est-ce que tu as? Tu écoutes souvent de la musique? Tu regardes souvent la télé?

_____

_____

5. Tu fumes?

_____

6. Tu aimes les animaux? Tu as des animaux?

_____

_____

---

*Journal. Create a paragraph describing where you live. Tell:
- whether you live in a house, an apartment, or a dorm room.
- whether it is downtown, in town, in the suburbs, or in the country; and if it is near, far from, or on campus.
- if you like your house / apartment / dorm room, and why or why not.
- what there is in the living room (**Dans le salon, il y a…**) and where each item is located (**La télé est en face du fauteuil…**). *[Note: If you live in a dorm room, talk about the living room at your parents' house. (Dans le salon chez mes parents…)]*

_____

_____

_____

_____

_____

_____

_____

_____

_____

_____

_____

Partie auditive

4-8

A. Dans le salon de Thomas. You will hear sentences saying where some of the items in Thomas's living room are located. Decide if each one is true or false according to the illustration and indicate **vrai** or **faux** as appropriate.

EXEMPLE   VOUS ENTENDEZ: La table est dans le coin.
               VOUS MARQUEZ: vrai ✓ faux ____

1. vrai ____   faux ____   **3.** vrai ____   faux ____   **5.** vrai ____   faux ____   **7.** vrai ____   faux ____

2. vrai ____   faux ____   **4.** vrai ____   faux ____   **6.** vrai ____   faux ____   **8.** vrai ____   faux ____

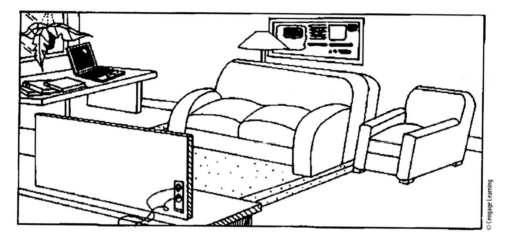

© Cengage Learning

4-9

B. Prononciation: *Avoir* et *être*. Pause the recording and review the ***Prononciation*** section on page 116 of the textbook. Then turn on the recording and repeat these forms of **avoir** and **être,** paying attention to how they are different.

ÊTRE: tu es   il est   elle est   ils sont   elles sont

AVOIR: tu as   il a   elle a   ils ᶻont   elles ᶻont

Now you will hear questions about Thomas's living room. Fill in the verb form you hear in the question under the correct column and indicate **oui** or **non** to answer the question according to the illustration in *A. Dans le salon de Thomas.* Pause the recording as needed to allow enough time to respond.

EXEMPLE   VOUS ENTENDEZ: Thomas, il a un grand salon?
               VOUS ÉCRIVEZ:

	AVOIR	ÊTRE		
EXEMPLE	a		oui _____	non ✓

	AVOIR	ÊTRE		
1.	_____	_____	oui _____	non _____
2.	_____	_____	oui _____	non _____
3.	_____	_____	oui _____	non _____
4.	_____	_____	oui _____	non _____
5.	_____	_____	oui _____	non _____
6.	_____	_____	oui _____	non _____

🔊 **C. Prononciation: *De, du, des.*** Pause the recording and review the *Prononciation* section on page 118
4-10 of the textbook. Then turn on the recording and listen to the sentences, completing them with the form of the preposition **de** you hear. Afterwards, look at the illustration in ***A. Dans le salon de Thomas*** and indicate if each sentence is true (**vrai**) or false (**faux**).

EXEMPLE   VOUS ENTENDEZ: La table est près de la fenêtre.
          VOUS COMPLÉTEZ: La table est près **de la** fenêtre.   vrai ✓_____   faux _____

1. La table est dans le coin _____ salon.   vrai _____   faux _____

2. Le fauteuil est à côté _____ table.   vrai _____   faux _____

3. L'ordinateur est à côté _____ livres.   vrai _____   faux _____

4. La télé est en face _____ canapé.   vrai _____   faux _____

5. La plante est à gauche _____ ordinateur.   vrai _____   faux _____

🔊 **D. Un appartement.** You will hear a conversation between two prospective roommates. The first time,
4-11 just listen to it at normal speed. Then fill in the missing words as it is repeated more slowly.

— Tu cherches un appartement _____ **(1)**?

  Je _____ **(2)** un nouveau colocataire. Tu voudrais

  _____ **(3)** mon appartement avec moi?

— Je ne sais pas. _____ **(4)** ton appartement?

— Il n'est pas très grand, mais _____ **(5)** beaucoup de choses.

— Tu _____ **(6)** ou un chat? _____ **(7)**

  beaucoup d'allergies.

— Non, je n'ai pas _____ **(8)**. Et _____ **(9)**

  non plus. Est-ce que tu voudrais _____ **(10)** cet après-midi

  pour voir l'appartement?

— Oui, j'ai cours jusqu'à deux heures, alors _____ **(11)**?

— Oui, c'est parfait!

🔊 ***E. Et vous?*** Now imagine that you are considering moving in with a classmate. How would you answer
4-12 these questions? Answer each one with a complete sentence. Pause the recording between items in order to respond.

1. _____

2. _____

3. _____

4. _____

5. _____

COMPÉTENCE 3

Describing your room

By the time you finish this *Compétence,* you should be able to describe your room in French.

Partie écrite

A. Une chambre. Label the objects in this student's bedroom. Include the indefinite article (**un, une, des**) with the noun. The first one has been done as an example.

1. *une fenêtre* _____
2. _____
3. _____
4. _____
5. _____
6. _____
7. _____

*Now answer the following questions about the bedroom above with complete sentences.

1. La chambre est en ordre ou en désordre? Tout est à sa place? La chambre est propre ou un peu sale?

_____

_____

2. Où sont les vêtements? L'étudiante laisse ses vêtements par terre?

_____

_____

3. Qu'est-ce qu'il y a devant la fenêtre? Qu'est-ce qu'il y a derrière la plante?

_____

_____

*B. Couleurs. Complete the following sentences with the name of a color. Remember that colors agree (masculine/feminine, singular/plural) with the noun they describe. If you live in a dormitory, describe where you live when not at the university. If you do not have one of the items mentioned, imagine what color you would like this item to be if you had one.

EXEMPLE Dans ma chambre, les rideaux sont **bleus.**

1. Dans ma chambre, la porte est _____ et les murs sont

_____. Le tapis est _____ et les rideaux sont

_____. Ma couverture est _____.

2. Dans le salon, la porte est _____ et les murs sont

_____. Le tapis est _____

et les rideaux sont _____. Le canapé est

_____. Le fauteuil est _____.

C. Une conversation. Reread the conversation between Robert and Thomas on page 121 of your textbook. Then, complete this conversation in which a student is visiting a friend's new apartment.

SOPHIE: C'est ta chambre là, _____ (1)?
         (at the end of the hallway)

HAHN: Non, ça c'est _____ (2).
         (Anne's bedroom)

         _____ (3). Sa chambre est toujours un peu
         (Come see)

         _____ (4) et _____ (5).
         (dirty)   *(in disorder)*

         Elle _____ (6) tout _____ (7).
              (leaves)   *(on the floor)*

         _____ (8)! Voilà ma chambre.
         (What a mess)

         _____ (9), chez moi,
         (As you see)

         _____ (10) est _____ (11).
         (each thing)   *(in its place)*

SOPHIE: Tu as _____ (12). J'aime beaucoup ta chambre.
               (a beautiful view)

D. C'est-à-dire... Sometimes you may need to rephrase what you want to say. Here are several ideas, each expressed two ways. Complete the first sentence with the correct form of **avoir** and the second one with the appropriate possessive adjective (**mon/ma/mes, ton/ta/tes, son/sa/ses, notre/nos, votre/vos, leur/leurs**).

EXEMPLES   J'**ai** un beau chien. **Mon** chien est beau.
               Vous **avez** une très belle maison. **Votre** maison est très belle.

1. J' _____ un grand lit. _____ lit est grand.

2. J' _____ une couverture bleue. _____ couverture est bleue.

3. J' _____ une nouvelle étagère. _____ étagère est nouvelle.

4. J' _____ de jolis rideaux. _____ rideaux sont jolis.

5. Tu _____ une belle chambre. _____ chambre est belle.

6. Tu _____ un grand bureau. _____ bureau est grand.

7. Tu _____ des meubles bizarres. _____ meubles sont bizarres.

8. Marie _____ un beau tapis. _____ tapis est beau.

9. Thomas _____ une belle voiture. _____ voiture est belle.

10. Il _____ une grande étagère. _____ étagère est grande.

11. Il _____ des amis bizarres. _____ amis sont bizarres.

12. Nous _____ de grands placards. _____ placards sont grands.

13. Nous _____ une belle vue. _____ vue est belle.

14. Vous _____ des murs blancs? _____ murs sont blancs?

15. Vous _____ une belle chambre? _____ chambre est belle?

16. Mes amis _____ une belle maison. _____ maison est belle.

17. Ils _____ de beaux chiens. _____ chiens sont beaux.

E. Je préfère mes affaires.

Everyone likes his or her *own* things. Complete these sentences with the correct form of the possessive adjective (**mon, ma, mes, ton, ta, tes, son, sa, ses, notre, nos, votre, vos, leur,** or **leurs**). *(I like my . . . , you like your . . . , he likes his . . . , etc.).*

EXEMPLE Moi, j'aime **mon** portable.

Ma sœur aime mieux **son** portable.

1. Tu aimes _____ table et _____ chaises.

Robert aime mieux _____ table et _____ chaises.

2. Nous aimons _____ chaîne hi-fi et _____ CD.

Vous aimez mieux _____ chaîne hi-fi et _____ CD?

3. Mes amis aiment _____ vêtements.

Moi, j'aime mieux _____ vêtements.

4. Nous aimons _____ maison.

Nos voisins *(neighbors)* aiment mieux _____ maison.

5. J'aime _____ fauteuil.

Ma sœur aime mieux _____ fauteuil.

*F. Et toi?

A friend is asking you about your bedroom. Complete each question with **ton, ta,** or **tes.** Then answer the question, using **mon, ma,** or **mes.**

EXEMPLE — Quelle est **ta** couleur préférée?

— **Ma couleur préférée, c'est le rouge.**

1. — Comment est _____ chambre?

— _____

2. — De quelle couleur sont _____ murs? Et _____ rideaux? De quelle couleur est _____

couverture? Et _____ tapis?

— _____

_____

_____

3. — _____ chambre est en ordre ou en désordre en général? Tu laisses _____ vêtements partout?

— _____

_____

4. — Tu mets *(put)* _____ livres sur une étagère? Tu mets _____ vêtements dans un placard
   ou dans une commode? *(Answer with* **Je mets...** *or* **Je ne mets pas...**)

   — _____

5. — Est-ce que _____ lit est près de la fenêtre?

   — _____

6. — Tu aimes faire _____ devoirs dans _____ chambre?

   — _____

G. Les adjectifs possessifs. Complete the following conversation logically with **son, sa, ses,** or **leur, leurs.** The first one has been done as an example.

— L'appartement de Thomas, Robert et Gabriel est super, non?

— Oui, il est super. **Leur (1)** salon est très confortable et _____ **(2)** chambres sont assez grandes.

— Oui, mais la chambre de Gabriel est un désastre. Il laisse tous _____ **(3)** vêtements par terre!
   _____ **(4)** chien aime dormir sur _____ **(5)** lit et _____ **(6)** chat aime dormir sur l'étagère.

— Pourtant, dans les chambres de Thomas et de Robert, c'est le contraire. _____ **(7)** chambres sont
   presque toujours en ordre. _____ **(8)** vêtements sont dans le placard, _____ **(9)** livres sont sur
   l'étagère et _____ **(10)** lits sont toujours faits *(made)*.

*H. Et vous? Answer the following questions about your room with complete sentences.

1. Est-ce que vous aimez votre chambre? Pourquoi ou pourquoi pas?

   _____

   _____

2. Votre chambre est à quel étage?

   _____

   _____

3. Qu'est-ce qu'il y a dans votre chambre? Qu'est-ce que vous voudriez acheter *(to buy)* pour votre chambre?

   _____

   _____

4. Quelle est votre couleur préférée? Qu'est-ce que vous avez de cette *(this)* couleur chez vous?

   _____

   _____

5. Est-ce que vous passez beaucoup de temps dans votre chambre?

   _____

   _____

6. Qu'est-ce que vous aimez faire dans votre chambre?

   _____

   _____

Partie auditive

4-13

A. Dans la chambre. Stop the recording, look at the illustration of the bedroom, and complete the sentences that follow. When you have finished, start the recording and verify your responses. Repeat each sentence after the speaker, paying attention to your pronunciation.

EXEMPLE   VOUS COMPLÉTEZ: Il y a un chien sous **le lit.**
             VOUS ENTENDEZ: Il y a un chien sous le lit.
             VOUS RÉPÉTEZ: **Il y a un chien sous le lit.**

1. Il y a une plante devant _____.

2. Par terre, derrière la plante, il y a _____.

3. Il y a une couverture sur _____.

4. Entre la fenêtre et le lit, il y a _____.

5. Les vêtements sont dans _____.

6. _____ est à droite de la porte.

7. Par terre, il y a _____.

4-14

B. C'est à moi! A friend is asking if these items are yours. Identify them as yours, as in the example. After a pause for you to respond, you will hear the correct answer. Verify your response and your pronunciation and indicate the form of the possessive adjective that is used.

EXEMPLE   VOUS ENTENDEZ: C'est ta chambre?
             VOUS DITES: **Oui, c'est ma chambre.**
             VOUS ENTENDEZ: Oui, c'est ma chambre.

EXEMPLE   mon _____ ma ____✓____ mes _____

1. mon _____ ma _____ mes _____   5. mon _____ ma _____ mes _____

2. mon _____ ma _____ mes _____   6. mon _____ ma _____ mes _____

3. mon _____ ma _____ mes _____   7. mon _____ ma _____ mes _____

4. mon _____ ma _____ mes _____

Line art on this page: © Cengage Learning

C. Chez Thomas. Thomas exaggerates everything. How does he answer a friend's questions? Use the appropriate possessive adjective (**mon, ma, mes, ton, ta, tes, son, sa, ses, notre, nos, votre, vos, leur, leurs**) in the response. Pause the recording between items in order to respond.

EXEMPLES	VOUS ENTENDEZ:	La chambre de Gabriel est agréable?
	VOUS ÉCRIVEZ:	Oui, **sa** chambre est très agréable.
	VOUS ENTENDEZ:	Votre appartement est grand?
	VOUS ÉCRIVEZ:	Oui, **notre** appartement est très grand.

1. Oui, _____ chambre est très agréable.

2. Oui, _____ lit est très confortable.

3. Oui, _____ colocataires sont très sympas.

4. Oui, _____ chambre est très agréable.

5. Oui, _____ chat est très beau.

6. Oui, _____ animaux sont quelquefois très embêtants.

7. Non, _____ appartement n'est pas très cher.

8. Oui, _____ pièces sont très spacieuses *(spacious)*.

9. Oui, _____ cuisine est très moderne.

10. Oui, _____ livres sont super intéressants.

D. On sort? Robert and his friend Didier are going out to dinner, and Didier has arranged to pick up Robert at his apartment. Listen to their conversation, pause the recording, and answer the questions *in English*. You may need to listen more than once.

1. Name two things Didier particularly admires about Robert's apartment.

   _____

2. What is one of the things Didier likes about where he lives?

   _____

3. What are two inconveniences he mentions about where he lives?

   _____

4. Why does Thomas decline Didier's invitation to the restaurant?

   _____

5. What is the street number on **rue Caroline** of the restaurant Robert and Didier are going to?

   _____

*E. Comment est ta chambre? A friend is asking you questions about your room. Answer each one with a complete sentence in French. Pause the recording between items in order to respond.

1. _____

2. _____

3. _____

4. _____

Nom _____ Date _____

Giving your address and phone number

By the time you finish this **Compétence,** you should be able to give personal information about yourself, such as your address and telephone number, in French.

Partie écrite

A. Des renseignements personnels. You are
working at the **Hôtel Vieux Québec.** A newly-arrived guest gives you the following information. Complete what she says.

EXEMPLE **Mon nom de famille,** c'est Smith.

1. _____, c'est Jane.

2. _____,
c'est le 700 Unicorn Way.

3. _____, c'est Austin et
_____, c'est le Texas.

4. Le 78701, c'est _____.

5. Les États-Unis, c'est _____.

6. Le (512) 826-7660, c'est _____.

7. _____, c'est jmcs123@airmail.net.

> **HÔTEL VIEUX QUÉBEC**
> Fiche d'inscription pour voyageurs étrangers.
> Nom de famille:
> _____
> Prénom(s):
> _____
> Adresse:
> _____
> _____
> _____
> Numéro de téléphone: _____
> Nationalité: _____

© Cengage Learning

B. Une conversation. Reread the conversation between Robert and Alex on page 126 of your textbook.
Then, complete this conversation between two friends.

LOLA: Tu habites dans _____ (1)?
_____ *(a new apartment)*

JULES: Oui, je _____ (2) un appartement _____ (3)
_____ *(share)* _____ *(near)*

l'université avec un ami.

LOLA: Il te plaît?

JULES: Oui, beaucoup. Il y a _____ (4) tout près
_____ *(a bus stop)*

et l'appartement n'est pas _____ (5).
_____ *(too expensive)*

LOLA: C'est combien, _____ (6)?
_____ *(the rent)*

JULES: C'est 700 dollars _____ (7), _____ (8)
_____ *(per month)* _____ *(shared between)*

nous deux. Alors pour moi, ça fait 350 dollars.

C. Un immeuble. Complete these questions with
ce, cet, cette, or **ces**, as appropriate.

Exemple

EXEMPLE **Cet** immeuble a combien d'étages?

1. Est-ce que _____ étudiants révisent les
cours ou est-ce qu'ils jouent au foot maintenant?

2. Qu'est-ce qu'il y a dans le salon
de _____ appartement?

3. Qu'est-ce que _____ jeunes hommes
aiment faire?

4. Qu'est-ce que _____ jeune femme aime
faire?

5. Combien d'enfants est-ce qu'il y a dans _____ famille?

6. _____ homme est paresseux ou travailleur *(hard-working)*?

*Now answer the preceding questions according to the illustration.

EXEMPLE **Il a un sous-sol, un rez-de-chaussée et trois étages.**

1. _____
2. _____
3. _____
4. _____
5. _____
6. _____

D. Où est-ce que je mets ça? A friend is helping you move in. Tell your friend to put these items in
the logical room: **la chambre, le salon** or **la salle à manger.** Use **ce, cet, cette, ces** in your answers, as in the
example.

Exemple **1** **2** **3**

EXEMPLE Mets *(Put)* **cette table dans la salle à manger.**

1. Mets _____ .

2. Mets _____ .

3. Mets _____ .

4   **5**   **6**   **7**

4. Mets _____.

5. Mets _____.

6. Mets _____.

7. Mets _____.

E. Quel est... ? Complete these questions that a hotel clerk would ask a newly-arrived guest with the correct form of **quel (quel, quelle, quels, quelles).**

    EXEMPLE   **Quel** est votre nom de famille?

1. _____ est votre prénom?

2. _____ est votre adresse?

3. Vous habitez dans _____ ville?

4. C'est dans _____ état?

5. _____ est votre code postal?

6. _____ est votre numéro de téléphone?

7. _____ est votre adresse mail?

8. Vous êtes de _____ nationalité?

*F. Quel mot? Both **quel** and **qu'est-ce que** can mean *what*. Use a form of **quel** directly before a noun or before the verb forms **est** and **sont**. In other cases, use **qu'est-ce que**. Complete the following questions with **qu'est-ce que** or a form of **quel**. Then answer each question with a complete sentence.

1. _____ est votre adresse?

    _____

2. Votre chambre est à _____ étage?

    _____

3. _____ vous avez dans votre chambre?

    _____

4. Chez vous, dans _____ pièces est-ce que vous préférez passer votre temps?

    _____

5. _____ vous aimez faire dans le salon?

_____

6. _____ sont vos loisirs préférés?

_____

7. _____ vos amis préfèrent faire le week-end?

_____

8. _____ vous voudriez faire aujourd'hui après les cours?

_____

---

*Journal. Describe your bedroom. Include the following information:

- whether or not you like your bedroom and why or why not
- what furniture there is and where it is placed
- what color the walls, rug, bed cover, and curtains are
- what floor your bedroom is on and, if it's not on the ground floor, whether there is a stairway or an elevator
- if you spend a lot of time in your room
- whether or not you smoke in your room

_____

_____

_____

_____

_____

_____

_____

_____

_____

_____

_____

_____

_____

_____

_____

_____

_____

_____

Partie auditive

4-18 ***A. L'inscription à l'université.** You are enrolling at a Canadian university. Complete the questions you hear. Then provide the information requested. *You do not need to answer in complete sentences.* Pause the recording as needed to allow enough time to write.

1. Quel est votre _____ ?
   _____

2. Quel est votre _____ ?
   _____

3. Quelle est votre _____ ?
   _____

4. Vous habitez dans quelle _____ ?
   _____

5. Vous habitez dans quel _____ ?
   _____

6. Quel est votre _____ ?
   _____

7. Quelle est votre _____ ?
   _____

8. Quelle est votre _____ ?
   _____

4-19 **B. Prononciation: La voyelle e de *ce, cet, cette, ces*.** Pause the recording and review the *Prononciation* section on page 128 of the textbook. Then turn on the recording, listen, and repeat these words.

ce	de	je	ne	que	le	me
ces	des	mes	tes	les	aller	danser
cet	cette	quel	elle	cher	frère	mère

4-20 **C. Quel appartement?** You are talking about an apartment where you are considering rooming with someone. Describe it by filling in the missing words you hear. Pause the recording as needed to allow enough time to fill in the words.

EXEMPLE VOUS ENTENDEZ: Cet appartement est loin de l'université.
VOUS COMPLÉTEZ: **Cet appartement** est loin de l'université.

1. La vue de _____ est laide.

2. _____ est près du centre-ville.

3. _____ est agréable.

4. _____ sont très grandes.

5. La couleur de _____ est jolie.

6. _____ est nouveau.

7. _____ est sale.

8. _____ fume.

🔊 **D. Mes préférences.** A friend is asking about your preferences. Listen to his questions and indicate the
4-21   form of **quel** that would be used in each one, based on the gender and number of the noun that follows.

> **EXEMPLE**   VOUS ENTENDEZ: Quel est ton restaurant préféré?
> VOUS INDIQUEZ: quel ✔️____ quels _____ quelle _____ quelles _____

1. quel ____ quels ____ quelle ____ quelles ____   3. quel ____ quels ____ quelle ____ quelles ____

2. quel ____ quels ____ quelle ____ quelles ____   4. quel ____ quels ____ quelle ____ quelles ____

*Now play the questions again and answer them. Pause the recording to allow enough time to respond.
Remember to make the proper agreement with the adjective **préféré(e)(s)**.

> **EXEMPLE**   VOUS ENTENDEZ: Quel est ton restaurant préféré?
> VOUS ÉCRIVEZ: **Mon restaurant préféré, c'est Pizza Nizza.**

1. _____

2. _____

3. _____

4. _____

🔊 **E. Dictée.** You will hear a conversation between **l'hôtelier** *(the hotel manager)* and a newly-arrived guest.
4-22   The first time, just listen to what they say at normal speed. Then fill in the missing words as the conversation
is repeated more slowly. Pause the recording as needed to allow enough time to fill in the words.

L'HÔTELIER: Alors, vous _____ **(1)** une chambre pour

_____ **(2)**. Nous avons une chambre

_____ **(3)** à _____ **(4)** dollars.

LE CLIENT: _____ **(5)** est calme?

L'HÔTELIER: Oui, monsieur. Elle est _____ **(6)**, loin

_____ **(7)**.

LE CLIENT: Et elle est _____ **(8)**?

L'HÔTELIER: Au premier. Il y a _____ **(9)** derrière vous,

_____ **(10)**.

LE CLIENT: Il y a _____ **(11)** dans l'hôtel?

L'HÔTELIER: Non, mais il y a un restaurant tout près, juste _____ **(12)**.

LE CLIENT: _____ **(13)** ferme _____ **(14)**?

L'HÔTELIER: À _____ **(15)**.

LE CLIENT: Bon, je vais prendre la chambre. _____ **(16)** de la chambre?

L'HÔTELIER: C'est la chambre _____ **(17)**.

En famille

Chapitre **4**

**COMPÉTENCE 1**

Describing your family

By the time you finish this ***Compétence,*** you should be able to name family members and describe them in French.

Partie écrite

A. La famille de Gabriel. Gabriel is identifying some of his family members. Finish his statements to clarify what family member he is talking about.

> **EXEMPLE** C'est le père de mon père. C'est **mon grand-père.**

1. C'est la mère de mon père. C'est _____.
2. Ce sont les parents de ma mère. Ce sont _____.
3. C'est la sœur de mon père. C'est _____.
4. C'est le mari de ma tante. C'est _____.
5. Ce sont les enfants de ma tante. Ce sont _____.
6. C'est le fils de mon frère. C'est _____.
7. C'est la fille de mon frère. C'est _____.

B. La parenté. A friend is showing you pictures of family members. Complete each question asking your friend to clarify her relationship to each one.

> **EXEMPLE** Voilà ma grand-mère.
> C'est **la mère** de ton père ou de ta mère?

1. Voilà ma tante Marie.

   C'est _____ de ton père ou de ta mère?

2. Voilà mon oncle Antoine.

   C'est _____ de la sœur de ton père ou de la sœur de ta mère?

3. Voilà mon grand-père.

   C'est _____ de ton père ou de ta mère?

4. Voilà mon neveu.

   C'est _____ de ton frère ou de ta sœur?

5. Voilà ma nièce.

   C'est _____ de ton frère ou de ta sœur?

C. Une conversation. Gabriel is telling Robert about his family. Complete their conversation.

ROBERT: Vous _____ **(1)** dans ta famille?
_____*(are how many)*

GABRIEL: Nous _____ **(2):** mon père, mon frère, ma sœur et moi.
_____*(are four)*

Mon frère a l'intention de _____ **(3)** ici avec moi.
_____*(spend the weekend)*

ROBERT: Il est plus jeune ou _____ **(4)** toi?
_____*(older than)*

_____ **(5)**?
_____*(How old is he)*

GABRIEL: _____ **(6).**
_____*(He's fourteen years old)*

ROBERT: _____ **(7)**?
_____*(What's his name)*

GABRIEL: _____ **(8)** Marc.
_____*(His name is)*

D. Comment sont-ils? Indicate whether the following descriptions describe Charles or Vincent by writing **C** for Charles and **V** for Vincent next to each one. The first one has been done as an example.

Charles

_C_ Il est de taille moyenne et il est mince.

____ Il est grand et un peu gros parce qu'il aime manger.

____ Il a environ quarante-cinq ans.

____ Il a environ soixante-cinq ans.

____ Il a les cheveux gris.

____ Il a les cheveux noirs.

____ Il n'a pas de moustache.

____ Il a une moustache mais il n'a pas de barbe.

Vincent

*Now, write similar sentences describing two male celebrities. Write four sentences for each, then complete the last statement with the name of each one.

_____

_____

_____

_____

Il s'appelle _____.

_____

_____

_____

Il s'appelle _____.

E. Descriptions. Say how these people are feeling using an expression with **avoir.**

avoir peur / avoir chaud / avoir froid / avoir sommeil / avoir soif / avoir faim

EXEMPLE J'...   **1.** Anne...   **2.** Les enfants...   **3.** Mes amis et moi...

EXEMPLE J'ai froid.

1. Anne _____.

2. Les enfants _____.

3. Mes amis et moi _____.

F. Une fête d'anniversaire (A birthday party). Complete the following statements between parents at Robert's niece's birthday party using the logical expressions with **avoir** in parentheses.

EXEMPLE (avoir l'intention de, avoir faim, avoir soif)
Si *(If)* vous **avez soif,** il y a de l'eau minérale, du coca et de la limonade et si vous **avez faim,** il y a de la pizza et des sandwichs. Nous **avons l'intention de** manger le gâteau *(cake)* plus tard.

1. (avoir faim, avoir envie de, avoir besoin de)

J' _____ servir le gâteau. Les enfants

_____ et ils _____ manger le

gâteau maintenant.

2. (avoir l'air, avoir... ans, avoir raison)

— Votre fille _____ cinq _____? Elle _____ plus âgée!

— Oui, vous _____. Elle est assez grande pour son âge.

3. (avoir envie de, avoir raison, avoir tort)

— Mon fils de sept ans _____ un téléphone

portable pour son anniversaire mais je pense qu'il est trop jeune. Est-ce que

j'_____ de refuser un portable à mon fils?

— Non, vous _____. Il est trop jeune.

*G. Et vous? Talk about yourself by completing the following sentences. Use a verb in the infinitive.

1. Demain, j'ai l'intention de (d') _____.

2. Cette semaine, j'ai besoin de (d') _____.

3. Ce week-end, j'ai envie de (d') _____.

4. Quelquefois, j'ai peur de (d') _____.

*H. Quelques questions. Answer each question with a complete sentence in French.

1. Vous êtes combien dans votre famille? Combien de frères et de sœurs est-ce que vous avez? Ils/Elles sont plus âgé(e)s que vous?

   _____

   _____

   _____

2. Votre famille habite dans quelle ville? Est-ce que vous passez beaucoup de temps chez vos parents?

   _____

   _____

3. Avec quel membre de votre famille passez-vous le plus de temps *(the most time)*? Comment s'appelle-t-il/elle? Quel âge a-t-il/elle? Il/Elle a les yeux et les cheveux de quelle couleur? Il/Elle porte des lunettes ou des lentilles *(contacts)*? Qu'est-ce que vous aimez faire ensemble?

   _____

   _____

   _____

   _____

   _____

4. Est-ce que vous avez l'intention de passer le week-end prochain avec votre famille? Qu'est-ce que vous avez envie de faire?

   _____

   _____

   _____

Partie auditive

4-23

A. Qui est-ce? Listen as Thomas points out family members and fill in the missing words. Pause the recording as needed to have time to respond.

EXEMPLE VOUS ENTENDEZ: C'est le père de mon père.
  VOUS ÉCRIVEZ: C'est **le père** de **mon père.**

1. C'est _____ de _____.
2. C'est _____ de _____.
3. C'est _____ de _____.
4. C'est _____ de _____.
5. Ce sont _____ de _____.
6. C'est _____ de _____.

Now listen to Thomas's statements again. This time, identify the name of each relationship he describes. After a pause for you to answer, you will hear the correct response.

EXEMPLE VOUS ENTENDEZ: C'est le père de mon père.
  VOUS DITES: **C'est son grand-père.**
  VOUS ENTENDEZ: C'est son grand-père.

4-24

B. Je vous présente... You will hear the first part of some introductions. For each one, repeat what you hear and complete the sentence with the corresponding female family member from the following list. After a pause for you to respond, you will hear the correct answer. Verify your response and indicate the number of the statement next to the person named.

EXEMPLE VOUS ENTENDEZ: Voici mon père et…
  VOUS DITES: **Voici mon père et ma mère.**
  VOUS ENTENDEZ: Voici mon père et ma mère.
  VOUS INDIQUEZ: **Exemple** *next to* **ma mère**

____ ma cousine   ____ ma grand-mère   ____ ma nièce   ____ ma tante

____ ma fille   **EXEMPLE** ma mère   ____ ma sœur

4-25

C. Les parents de Gisèle. Fill in the missing words as you hear Gisèle describe her parents. Then pause the recording and indicate whether each statement is **vrai (V)** or **faux (F)** according to the illustration. The first one has been done as an example.

__F__ **Mon père** s'appelle Christian.

____ Il a _____ ans.

____ Il _____ sportif.

____ Il est _____.

____ Il a les cheveux _____.

____ Il a _____
  et _____.

____ _____ s'appelle Diane.

____ Elle a _____ ans.

____ Elle _____ intellectuelle.

____ Elle est assez _____.

____ Elle a les cheveux _____.

____ Elle porte _____.

Paul, 48 ans et Diane, 42 ans

Line art on this page: © Cengage Learning

Nom _____ Date _____

🔊 **D. Stratégie:** *Asking for clarification.* A new acquaintance is talking about her family. You should
4-26 understand everything she says except one word or name. For each statement you hear, indicate the letter of
the expression that you should use to ask for clarification.

a. Comment? Répétez, s'il vous plaît.   **b.** Qu'est-ce que ça veut dire?   **c.** Ça s'écrit comment?

1. _____   **2.** _____   **3.** _____   **4.** _____   **5.** _____   **6.** _____

🔊 **E. Une sortie.** Thomas and Robert are spending the day with Robert's nephew and niece in New Orleans.
4-27 How would Robert answer each of Thomas's questions that you hear? Indicate the logical response as you say it
aloud. Then listen to the correct answer and repeat again.

EXEMPLE   VOUS VOYEZ: _____ Oui, j'ai chaud.   _____ Oui, j'ai froid.
              VOUS ENTENDEZ: Tu portes un short et un tee-shirt?
              VOUS INDIQUEZ ET VOUS DITES: **X** Oui, j'ai chaud.   _____ Oui, j'ai froid.
              VOUS ENTENDEZ: Oui, j'ai chaud.
              VOUS RÉPÉTEZ: **Oui, j'ai chaud.**

1. ____ Oui, tu as raison. Ils sont gentils, ces chiens.   ____ Oui, les enfants ont peur de ces chiens.

2. ____ Oui, nous avons sommeil.   ____ Oui, nous avons soif.

3. ____ Oui, il a faim.   ____ Oui, il a une barbe.

4. ____ Oui, elle a peur des chiens.   ____ Oui, il a cinq ans et elle a sept ans.

5. ____ Oui, ça a l'air intéressant.   ____ Oui, j'ai besoin de dormir un peu.

6. ____ Oui, ils ont sommeil.   ____ Oui, ils ont envie d'aller au cinéma.

🔊 **F. La famille de Thomas.** You will hear Thomas talk about his family. After you listen, indicate whether
4-28 the following statements are **vrai** or **faux**.

_____ **1.** Thomas a deux frères.

_____ **2.** Yannick est plus âgé que Philippe.

_____ **3.** Philippe est divorcé.

_____ **4.** Thomas a deux tantes et trois oncles.

_____ **5.** Thomas a seulement *(only)* deux cousins.

_____ **6.** Les parents de sa mère habitent chez la famille de Thomas.

🔊 ***G. Et votre meilleur ami?** Answer the questions you hear about your best male friend in French. Pause
4-29 the recording in order to respond.

1. _____

2. _____

3. _____

4. _____

5. _____

6. _____

COMPÉTENCE 2

Saying where you go in your free time

By the time you finish this **Compétence,** you should be able to tell in French where you go in your free time and suggest activities to your friends.

Partie écrite

A. Où va-t-on? Say where one goes to do each of the activities. Complete the sentences using the pronoun **on** and the logical place from the list.

> **au parc / à la plage / au café / au centre commercial / à un concert / à la librairie / au musée**

EXEMPLE   Pour écouter de la musique, **on va à un concert.**

1. Pour prendre un verre, _____.
2. Pour voir une exposition, _____.
3. Pour faire du shopping, _____.
4. Pour acheter des livres, _____.
5. Pour jouer avec son chien, _____.
6. Pour nager ou prendre un bain de soleil, _____.

B. Conversation. Gabriel and Thomas are talking about their plans for the afternoon. Complete their conversation.

GABRIEL: _____ **(1)** des vêtements.
             (I need to buy)

             _____ **(2)** au centre commercial?
             (How about going)

THOMAS: D'accord, mais _____ **(3)** manger
                           (let's go)

             _____ **(4)** d'abord *(first)*.
             (something)

GABRIEL: _____ **(5)**! Moi aussi, _____ **(6).**
             (Good idea)   *(I'm hungry)*

             _____ **(7)** au MacDo?
             (How about going)

THOMAS: _____ **(8)** au restaurant La Guadeloupe. C'est
             (Let's go instead)

un nouveau restaurant où on sert de la cuisine antillaise. C'est comme la cuisine de ma mère.

             _____ **(9)**?
             (How does that sound)

GABRIEL: Oui. J'adore manger _____ **(10).**
                                 (at your mother's house)

C. La préposition à. Complete the following passage with the appropriate form of **à** and the definite article **le, la, l',** or **les.** Remember that **à + le** contracts to **au** and **à + les** contracts to **aux.** The first one has been done as an example.

Yannick est toujours très occupé *(busy).* En semaine, il va tous les jours **(1)** _____ à l' _____ école *(school).* À midi, il va déjeuner **(2)** _____ café avec ses amis. Après les cours, ils vont ensemble **(3)** _____ bibliothèque où ils préparent leurs devoirs. Ensuite, ils vont **(4)** _____ maison de Yannick pour jouer au basket.

Le vendredi soir, Thomas et Yannick aiment aller **(5)** _____ cinéma ou **(6)** _____ parc. Le samedi, Yannick va **(7)** _____ centre commercial avec ses amis pour faire du shopping. Le dimanche matin, toute la famille va **(8)** _____ église et à midi, ils vont **(9)** _____ restaurant parce que sa mère n'aime pas faire la cuisine *(to cook)* le dimanche.

D. Où vont-ils? Gabriel is talking about his family. Complete the following sentences telling how often the indicated people go to the places shown. Use the adverb in parentheses.

EXEMPLE Mes grands-parents…
(rarement)

1. Mes amis et moi, nous...
(souvent)

2. Moi, je...
(rarement)

EXEMPLE Mes grands-parents **vont rarement au théâtre.**

1. Mes amis et moi, nous _____.

2. Moi, je _____.

3. Mon meilleur ami…
(tous les dimanches)

4. Ma famille...
(ne… jamais)

5. Mes amis...
(le samedi d'habitude)

3. Mon meilleur ami _____.

4. Ma famille _____.

5. Mes amis _____.

E. Comment? Robert was not paying attention to what Gabriel said in **D. Où vont-ils?** and asks the following questions. Answer each one with a complete sentence using the pronoun **y.**

> **EXEMPLE**   Tes grands-parents vont souvent au théâtre?
> **Non, ils y vont rarement.**

1. Tes amis et toi, vous allez souvent à la piscine?

_____

2. Tu vas souvent à des concerts?

_____

3. Ton meilleur ami va souvent à l'église?

_____

4. Ta famille et toi, vous allez souvent au centre commercial?

_____

5. Tes amis vont souvent au parc?

_____

*F. Où va-t-on? Where do people go in your city to do the indicated things? Create complete sentences using the pronoun **on** with a specific place as in the example. Remember that the name of a place generally follows the type of place. For example, for *Tinseltown Cinema,* you say **le cinéma Tinseltown.**

> **EXEMPLE**   Pour acheter des livres, **on va à la librairie Barnes & Noble.**

1. Pour assister à *(to attend)* un concert, _____.

2. Pour acheter des vêtements chers, _____.

3. Pour voir des expositions intéressantes, _____.

4. Pour bien manger, _____.

G. En Amérique. A French friend is going to visit both Louisiana and Quebec. Where would you tell her to do the following things? Write a **tu** form command of the verb in parentheses and indicate the logical place.

> **EXEMPLE**   __Écoute__ (écouter) de la musique zydeco.   AU QUÉBEC ____ EN LOUISIANE ✔

1. _____ (manger) des spécialités créoles.   AU QUÉBEC ____ EN LOUISIANE ____

2. _____ (aller) voir le festival de neige *(snow).*   AU QUÉBEC ____ EN LOUISIANE ____

3. _____ (passer) une semaine à Montréal.   AU QUÉBEC ____ EN LOUISIANE ____

4. _____ (acheter) des vêtements chauds *(warm).*   AU QUÉBEC ____ EN LOUISIANE ____

5. _____ (être) sûre de visiter La Nouvelle-Orléans.   AU QUÉBEC ____ EN LOUISIANE ____

H. Suggestions. Would you tell a group of people visiting New Orleans to do or not to do the following things if you want them to experience the culture there? Give logical suggestions by changing the infinitives in parentheses to the command form for **vous.** Negate the verbs as needed to make appropriate suggestions.

EXEMPLE ___Ne soyez pas___ (être) pas timides.

1. _____ (être) à l'heure à l'aéroport.

2. _____ (manger) de la cuisine créole.

3. _____ (aller) toujours manger dans des fast-foods.

4. _____ (écouter) du jazz.

5. _____ (avoir) peur.

6. _____ (laisser) les bons temps rouler *(to let the good times roll)* (regional).

I. Des projets. It is Friday night and you are making plans with a classmate. Answer your friend's questions by making suggestions with the **nous** form of the verb to say *Let's . . .*

EXEMPLE Alors, on va au cinéma ce soir ou on regarde un DVD à la maison?
Allons au cinéma! / Regardons un DVD à la maison!

1. On regarde un film français ou un film américain?

_____

2. On invite d'autres étudiants de la classe de français ou on regarde le film seuls?

_____

3. On mange quelque chose avant ou après?

_____

4. Et demain, on reste à la maison ou on va au parc?

_____

*Journal. Describe your best friend. Tell his/her name. Describe his/her physical appearance, including age, hair and eye color, and personality. Then, using the pronoun **on** to say *we,* tell how often the two of you go different places and what you like to do there.

_____

_____

_____

_____

_____

_____

_____

_____

_____

_____

Partie auditive

4·30

A. Où vont-ils? Robert and his friends are visiting these places this week. For each picture, you will hear two places named. Identify the place that corresponds to the picture. After a pause for you to respond, you will hear the correct answer. Verify your response and your pronunciation and write the name of the place under the illustration. Be sure to include the prepositions and articles that are used to say *to the* or *to a*. Pause the recording as needed to have time to respond.

EXEMPLE
    VOUS ENTENDEZ: Où vont-ils? Ils vont dans les petits magasins ou au café?
    VOUS RÉPONDEZ: **Ils vont au café.**
    VOUS ENTENDEZ: Ils vont au café.
    VOUS ÉCRIVEZ:

EXEMPLE   <u>au café</u>

1. _____

2. _____

3. _____

4. _____

5. _____

6. _____

7. _____

8. _____

9. _____

10. _____

Line art on this page: © Cengage Learning

CHAPITRE 4 *Compétence 2* • *Partie auditive*   **107**

Nom _____ Date _____

🔊 **B. Invitations.** Your friend would like to do a variety of activities. For each activity, suggest you go to a
4-31   logical place from the list below. First, use **on** to say *Shall we . . .* , then use **nous** to say *Let's . . .* After a pause
for you to respond, you will hear the correct answers. Verify your response and indicate the number of that
question in the blank next to the name of the place.

> **EXEMPLE**   VOUS ENTENDEZ: Je voudrais aller voir une pièce de théâtre.
> VOUS DITES: **On va au théâtre? Allons au théâtre!**
> VOUS ENTENDEZ: On va au théâtre? Allons au théâtre!
> VOUS ÉCRIVEZ:

____ au parc   **Exemple** au théâtre   ____ à la piscine   ____ au musée

____ au café   ____ au centre commercial   ____ à la librairie

🔊 **C. Qu'est-ce qu'on fait?** Robert and Thomas are making plans for this evening. The first time, just
4-32   listen to what they say at normal speed. Then fill in the missing words as it is repeated more slowly. Pause the
recording as needed to allow enough time to write.

THOMAS: Alors, _____ **(1)** ce soir ou on sort?

ROBERT: _____ **(2)**. Il y a un festival de jazz.

_____ **(3)** c'est toujours excellent.

THOMAS: _____ **(4)** quelque chose avant

d' _____ **(5)**?

ROBERT: Oui, il y a un restaurant où on sert de la _____ **(6)** créole

tout _____ **(7)**. C'est un de mes restaurants préférés.

_____ **(8)**?

THOMAS: _____ **(9)**! _____ **(10)**

vraiment bien ici en Louisiane.

Now pause the recording and find all of the places where the pronoun **on** is used. For each one, indicate
whether it means *we* and is used to make a suggestion *(Shall we . . . ?)*, or whether it is used to talk about
people in general and is translated as *one, they,* or *you*. List each verb with **on** according to its use. The first one
has been done as an example.

Making a suggestion *(we):* **on reste,** _____

Talking about people in general *(one, they, you):* _____

🔊 **D. Prononciation: Les lettres *a, au* et *ai*.** Pause the recording and review the *Prononciation* section
4-33   on page 152 of the textbook. Then turn on the recording and repeat the following sentences, making sure to
distinguish between the vowel sounds **a, au,** and **ai.** As you listen, determine whether **a, au,** or **ai** is missing
from each place's name and fill in the blank.

1. On va au cinéma G_____ *mont* samedi après-midi.

2. J'aime faire du shopping au magasin G_____ *leries* L_____ *fayette.*

3. J'achète souvent des livres à la librairie _____ *vicenne.*

4. Aujourd'hui, je vais manger au restaurant _____ *x Lyonn* _____ *s.*

108   *Horizons,* Sixth Edition • **Student Activities Manual**

 **COMPÉTENCE 3**

Saying what you are going to do

By the time you finish this *Compétence,* you should be able to talk about your plans for tomorrow, this weekend, and the near future in French.

Partie écrite

*A. Le week-end. Answer the following questions about your typical Saturday with complete sentences in French. *Use the present tense.*

> **EXEMPLE** Jusqu'à quelle heure est-ce que vous restez au lit généralement le samedi?
> **Généralement le samedi, je reste au lit jusqu'à… heures.**

1. À quelle heure est-ce que vous quittez la maison le samedi?

   _____

2. Est-ce que vous allez souvent boire un café avec des amis?

   _____

3. Avec qui est-ce que vous passez la soirée?

   _____

4. Est-ce que vous rentrez souvent tard le samedi soir?

   _____

5. Est-ce que vous aimez partir pour le week-end? Où est-ce que vous aimez aller?

   _____

6. Est-ce que vous allez souvent voir des amis ou des cousins dans une autre ville?

   _____

B. Une conversation. Robert and Thomas are making plans for the weekend. Complete their conversation.

THOMAS: Qu'est-ce qu'on fait ce week-end?

ROBERT: _____ **(1)** pour
                            (I don't have plans)

         vendredi. Je vais _____ **(2)** à
                               (spend the evening)

         la maison et regarder des DVD. Samedi, on va _____ **(3)** mon père.
                                          (go see)

         _____ **(4),** on va déjeuner ensemble.
              (First)

         _____ **(5),** on va _____ **(6)**
             (Next)   *(go see)*

         une exposition au musée de Lafayette.

THOMAS: Et samedi soir?

ROBERT: Après l'exposition, on va rentrer _____ (7).
                                                              (to my father's house)

_____ (8), on va aller à un festival de _____ (9).
          (And then)   *(Cajun music)*

THOMAS: _____ (10)!
              (Great)

C. Projets. Robert, Gabriel, and Thomas are back in Quebec and Robert is talking about what they are going to do this weekend. Fill in each blank with the correct form of **aller** followed by the logical infinitive from the list. The first one has been done as an example.

réviser / quitter / rester

Samedi matin, je _____ **vais quitter** _____ la maison tôt mais Thomas _____ (1) au lit.

Gabriel _____ (2) ses cours à la maison.

louer / aller / nager

Samedi après-midi, Thomas _____ (3) à la bibliothèque

et après, nous _____ (4) à la piscine. Ensuite, je

_____ (5) un DVD.

boire / aller / rentrer

Dimanche après-midi, je _____ (6) au parc avec Gabriel pour

jouer au frisbee. Plus tard, on _____ (7) quelque chose au café

avec une amie. On _____ (8) tard.

Line art on this page: © Cengage Learning

D. Qu'est-ce qu'ils vont faire? Robert is talking to Thomas about what they and others are going to do today and tomorrow. Complete each sentence with the correct form of the verb **aller** and a logical activity from the list.

aller à un concert	voir l'exposition	faire du shopping	aller danser
jouer au basket	acheter des livres	dîner	voir une pièce

EXEMPLE   Ce matin, je **vais acheter des livres** à la librairie.

1. Je _____ avec des amis au parc vers une heure.

2. Ce soir, on _____ au festival de musique.

3. Tu _____ au centre commercial avec ta copine cet après-midi?

4. Ta copine et toi, vous _____ au restaurant ce soir?

5. Après, est-ce qu'elle _____ en boîte avec toi?

6. Demain, Gabriel et moi _____ au musée.

7. Demain soir, Gabriel et ses amis _____ au théâtre.

*E. Des projets d'avenir. Create sentences in French telling what the indicated people are going to do at each of the following times. If you don't know, guess! Use the immediate future (**aller** + infinitive).

EXEMPLE   Demain matin, je **vais quitter la maison tôt pour aller en cours.**

1. Ce soir, je _____.

2. Demain soir, mon (ma) meilleur(e) ami(e) _____.

3. Le week-end prochain, mes amis et moi _____.

4. Le dernier jour du semestre, les étudiants _____.

5. L'année prochaine, je _____.

F. C'est quand? If today is March 15 **(le quinze mars),** when are the following dates? Create sentences with the date and the logical expression in parentheses, as in the example.

EXEMPLE   16/3 (la semaine prochaine, demain)
   Le seize mars, c'est **demain.**

1. 18/3 (dans trois semaines, dans trois jours)

   _____ c'est _____.

2. 23/3 (la semaine prochaine, le mois prochain)

   _____ c'est _____.

3. 1/4 (la semaine prochaine, le mois prochain)

   _____ c'est _____.

4. 15/9 (dans six mois, l'année prochaine)

   _____ c'est _____.

G. Quelle est la date? Which of the two indicated activities would Robert most likely say people are going to do on these dates? Complete the date with the name of the month, then finish the statement with the correct form of **aller** and the logical choice in parentheses.

> **EXEMPLE**   25/12 (sortir avec des amis, passer la journée avec ma famille)
> Le vingt-cinq **décembre,** je **vais passer la journée avec ma famille.**

1. 1/1 (rester à la maison, être en cours)

   Le premier _____, mes frères _____.

2. 14/2 (aller à un match de basket avec ses amis, sortir avec sa femme)

   Le quatorze _____, mon père _____.

3. 4/7 (aller voir des feux d'artifice *[fireworks]*, voir des matchs de football américain à la télé)

   Le quatre _____, on _____.

4. 31/10 (faire une fête, aller à l'église)

   Le trente et un _____, mes amis et moi _____.

5. 12/5 (terminer mon deuxième semestre à Laval, commencer mon deuxième semestre à Laval)

   Le douze _____, je _____.

*H. Quelques questions. Answer each question with a complete sentence in French.

1. Quelle est la date aujourd'hui? Qu'est-ce que vous allez faire ce soir? Avec qui allez-vous passer la soirée?

   _____

   _____

   _____

2. Quelle est la date samedi prochain? Qu'est-ce que vous allez faire samedi matin? samedi après-midi? samedi soir?

   _____

   _____

   _____

3. Quelle est la date de votre anniversaire? Qu'est-ce que vous allez faire pour fêter *(to celebrate)* votre anniversaire?

   _____

   _____

   _____

4. (Regardez la liste des fêtes dans le vocabulaire supplémentaire à la page 160 du livre.) Quelle est votre fête préférée? Cette fête est en quel mois? Qu'est-ce que vous allez faire cette année?

   _____

   _____

   _____

Partie auditive

 A. Ce week-end. Look at the pictures illustrating what various friends are or are not going to do this weekend. After you hear each cue, ask if the friend is going to do the activity mentioned. Then after you hear the response, indicate whether or not the friend is going to do the activity.

> **EXEMPLE** VOUS ENTENDEZ: quitter l'appartement tôt samedi
> VOUS DEMANDEZ: **Tu vas quitter l'appartement tôt samedi?**
> VOUS ENTENDEZ: Non, je ne vais pas quitter l'appartement tôt samedi.
> VOUS INDIQUEZ: **non**

EXEMPLE oui ____ non ✓   **1.** oui ____ non ____   **2.** oui ____ non ____   **3.** oui ____ non ____

4. oui ____ non ____   **5.** oui ____ non ____   **6.** oui ____ non ____   **7.** oui ____ non ____

 B. Les expressions qui indiquent le futur. You will hear several pairs of expressions of time. Write the one that is the most distant in the future. Pause the recording as needed to have time to respond.

> **EXEMPLE** VOUS ENTENDEZ: demain matin / demain soir
> VOUS ÉCRIVEZ: **demain soir**

1. _____   **4.** _____   **7.** _____

2. _____   **5.** _____   **8.** _____

3. _____   **6.** _____   **9.** _____

 C. Présent ou futur? For each statement Robert's friend Christine makes, decide if she is talking about what she generally does on Saturdays (**le présent**) or what she is going to do this Saturday (**le futur**). Fill in the blank with a **P** for **le présent** and an **F** for **le futur**.

1. ____   **2.** ____   **3.** ____   **4.** ____   **5.** ____   **6.** ____   **7.** ____   **8.** ____   **9.** ____

🔊 **D. Les années et les mois de l'année.** Listen to the following years and months and repeat after the
4-37 speaker, paying careful attention to your pronunciation. As you repeat, fill in the missing years and months
from the list.

1789	1978	janvier	avril	_____	octobre
1864	1999	février	mai	_____	novembre
_____	_____	_____	juin	septembre	décembre

🔊 **E. Dates.** Write the dates that you hear using numerals as in the example. Remember that the number for
4-38 the day is written before the month in French. Pause the recording as needed to have time to respond.

> **EXEMPLE** VOUS ENTENDEZ: le quinze mars mille neuf cent cinquante et un
> VOUS ÉCRIVEZ: **15 / 3 / 1951**

1. _____ / _____ / _____
2. _____ / _____ / _____
3. _____ / _____ / _____
4. _____ / _____ / _____
5. _____ / _____ / _____
6. _____ / _____ / _____

🔊 **F. Qu'est-ce qu'on fait?** Listen as Robert and Thomas discuss their plans for this evening. Then stop the
4-39 recording and select the correct answer based on what you heard. Play this section again as needed.

_____ 1. Ce soir, ils vont…	**a.** regarder la télé	**b.** regarder un DVD	**c.** aller au cinéma
_____ 2. Ils vont voir…	**a.** un film français	**b.** un film italien	**c.** un film américain
_____ 3. C'est un…	**a.** très bon film	**b.** film amusant	**c.** film triste
_____ 4. C'est l'histoire (story)…	**a.** d'un couple	**b.** d'une petite fille	**c.** d'un jeune garçon

🔊 **G. Qu'est-ce que tu vas faire?** Two friends are talking about their plans for today. The first time, just
4-40 listen to what they say at normal speed. Then fill in the missing words as it is repeated more slowly. Pause the
recording as needed to allow enough time to complete the conversation.

— Alors, _____ **(1)** aujourd'hui?

— _____, _____ **(2)** travailler un peu sur

l'ordinateur. _____ **(3)**, cet après-midi, _____

_____ **(4)** la nouvelle exposition au musée. _____ **(5)**

d'aller au musée?

— Combien de temps _____ **(6)** au musée?

— _____ **(7)** vers quatre heures.

— Alors oui, _____ **(8)** avec toi. _____ **(9)** après ça,

_____ **(10)** ce soir?

— Je n'ai pas de _____ **(11)** pour ce soir.

COMPÉTENCE 4

Planning how to get there

By the time you finish this **Compétence,** you should be able to talk about where you are going to go and how you are going to get there in French.

Partie écrite

A. Moyens de transport. This family is visiting France. The mother is talking about how they are going to get around. Complete each sentence with the means of transportation.

EXEMPLE On…

1. On…

2. Nos amis…

3. Mon fils…

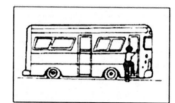

4. Moi, je…

5. Mon chéri, tu… ?

EXEMPLE On va prendre la **voiture** pour aller à Deauville.

1. On va prendre l' _____ pour aller à Paris.

2. Nos amis vont prendre un _____ pour aller d'une plage à l'autre.

3. Mon fils va prendre son _____ pour aller au parc.

4. Moi, je vais prendre le _____ pour aller en ville.

5. Mon chéri, tu vas prendre le _____ pour aller à Strasbourg?

B. Comment? A friend of the woman in **A. Moyens de transport** did not hear what she said and asks the following questions. Answer using the pronoun **y** and the verb **aller.**

EXEMPLE Comment est-ce que vous allez à Deauville?
On y va en voiture.

1. Comment est-ce que vous allez à Paris?

_____

2. Comment est-ce que vos amis vont à l'autre plage?

_____

3. Comment est-ce que ton fils va au parc?

_____

4. Comment est-ce que tu vas en ville?

_____

5. Comment est-ce que ton mari va à Strasbourg?

_____

C. Une conversation. Robert and Thomas are meeting some friends at the park. Complete their conversation.

ROBERT: _____ (1), on va partir bientôt. Tu es _____ (2)?
         (Listen)   *(ready)*

THOMAS: Oui. _____ (3)?
             (Shall we go there by car)

ROBERT: Non, _____ (4). Ce n'est pas
              (let's go to the park on foot)

_____ (5).
        (far)

THOMAS: Ça _____ (6) pour
           (takes how much time)

_____ (7)?
        (to go there)

ROBERT: Ça prend _____ (8), pas plus.
                 (around twenty minutes)

THOMAS: _____ (9) va-t-on rester au parc?
        (How long)

ROBERT: _____ (10) vers cinq heures?
        (Shall we come back)

D. Des touristes. Two tourists are returning from a trip. Answer each question with a complete sentence according to the illustrations.

© Cengage Learning

1. À quelle heure prennent-ils le petit déjeuner?

_____

2. Prennent-ils un café ou un jus d'orange?

_____

3. Comment vont-ils de l'hôtel à l'aéroport: en taxi, en métro ou en bus?

_____

4. Prennent-ils le train ou l'avion?

_____

5. À quelle heure prennent-ils l'avion?

_____

6. À quelle heure est-ce qu'ils prennent quelque chose à manger dans l'avion?

_____

E. Au café. A mother is asking what everyone wants to order in a café. Complete their conversation with the verb **prendre.** The first one has been done an example.

— Les enfants, vous _____ **prenez** _____ **(1)** une limonade ou un coca?

— Nous _____ **(2)** une limonade.

— Et toi, chéri, tu _____ **(3)** une eau minérale ou un demi?

— Je _____ **(4)** un demi. Et toi, qu'est-ce que tu vas

_____ **(5)**?

— Je vais _____**(6)** un café.

Now the mother is ordering for her family. Based on the previous dialogue, complete what she says with the verb **prendre** in the present tense.

1. Les enfants _____ une limonade.

2. Mon mari _____ un demi.

3. Et moi, je _____ un café.

F. Le verbe *venir*. A friend is talking to you on campus. Complete what she says with the correct form of the verb **venir** in the present tense.

Ce semestre, je _____ **(1)** à la fac tous les jours. D'habitude,

je _____ **(2)** à pied et ma colocataire _____ **(3)**

en bus, mais quelquefois nous _____ **(4)** à vélo. Beaucoup

d'étudiants _____ **(5)** à la fac à vélo parce qu'il n'y a pas assez de parkings.

Et toi? Comment est-ce que tu _____ **(6)** à la fac? Tes amis et toi, vous

_____ **(7)** à l'université le week-end pour étudier ou pour assister

(to attend) aux matchs de football américain ou de basket?

*Now answer the questions asked in **6** and **7** with complete sentences in French.

6. _____

7. _____

*G. En cours de français. A friend is asking you these questions. Complete his questions with the correct form of the verb indicated in parentheses. Then answer them with complete sentences.

1. Est-ce que tu _____ (venir) en cours à pied? Combien de temps

    est-ce que ça _____ (prendre) pour venir de chez toi en cours de français:

    quinze minutes? une heure?

    _____

    _____

2. Comment est-ce que les étudiants _____ (venir) en cours en général?

    Est-ce que beaucoup d'étudiants _____ (prendre) le bus pour venir à la fac?

    _____

    _____

3. Dans quels cours est-ce que tu _____ (apprendre) beaucoup? peu?

    _____

    _____

4. Généralement, est-ce que les étudiants _____ (comprendre) bien le

    prof de français?

    _____

5. Est-ce que le cours de français _____ (devenir) difficile?

    _____

---

*Journal. Write about your plans for tomorrow. Use the immediate future and include the following information.

- where you are going to have breakfast and at what time
- what time you are going to leave your house, apartment, or dormitory
- where you are going to go, why you are going to each place, and how you are going to go there
- what time you are going to return home

_____

_____

_____

_____

_____

_____

_____

_____

_____

_____

Partie auditive

4-41

A. Comment est-ce qu'on y va? The following illustrations show how Robert and his acquaintances are traveling. Answer each question affirmatively or negatively with the pronoun **y** and the correct means of transportation. Indicate whether you answered affirmatively or negatively by selecting **oui** or **non.**

EXEMPLE   VOUS ENTENDEZ: Thomas et Gabriel vont à Montréal en train?
            VOUS DITES: **Non, ils y vont en avion.**
            VOUS ENTENDEZ: Non, ils y vont en avion.
            VOUS INDIQUEZ:

EXEMPLE oui ____ non ✓   **1.** oui ____ non ____   **2.** oui ____ non ____   **3.** oui ____ non ____

4. oui ____ non ____   **5.** oui ____ non ____   **6.** oui ____ non ____   **7.** oui ____ non ____

4-42

B. Prononciation: Les verbes *prendre* et *venir*. Pause the recording and review the ***Prononciation*** section on page 164 of the textbook. Then turn on the recording and fill in the verb forms as you hear them pronounced.

prendre

Je _____ souvent le bus.

Tu _____ souvent le train?

On _____ le métro?

Nous _____ le bus.

Vous _____ souvent le bus?

Les Parisiens _____ souvent le train.

venir

Je _____ à l'université à pied.

Comment _____-tu en cours?

Il _____ en cours en bus.

Nous _____ en cours en voiture.

Vous _____ toujours en cours?

Ils _____ en cours à l'heure.

Now listen as Thomas, who is at school, talks about how some of his friends get around. Indicate whether he is talking about just one friend or about a group of friends.

1. ____ un ami   ____ un groupe   **4.** ____ un ami   ____ un groupe

2. ____ un ami   ____ un groupe   **5.** ____ un ami   ____ un groupe

3. ____ un ami   ____ un groupe   **6.** ____ un ami   ____ un groupe

Line art on this page: © Cengage Learning

C. Comment est-ce que vous y allez? Restate each sentence you hear using the verb **prendre.** You will then hear the correct answer. Verify your response and fill in the missing means of transportation.

EXEMPLE VOUS VOYEZ: Thomas prend _____ pour aller en ville.
            VOUS ENTENDEZ: Thomas va en ville en bus.
            VOUS DITES: **Thomas prend le bus pour aller en ville.**
            VOUS ENTENDEZ: Thomas prend le bus pour aller en ville.
            VOUS COMPLÉTEZ: Thomas prend **le bus** pour aller en ville.

1. Je prends _____ pour aller à l'université.

2. Nous prenons _____ pour aller à Québec.

3. Tu prends _____ pour aller au parc?

4. On prend _____ pour aller au musée?

5. Vous prenez _____ pour aller au centre commercial?

6. Gabriel et Thomas prennent _____ pour aller en Louisiane.

D. Comment est-ce qu'on y va? You will hear two means of transportation proposed. Suggest taking the one that is usually faster. You will then hear the correct answer. Verify your response, repeat again, and fill in the blank with the selected means of transportation.

EXEMPLE VOUS ENTENDEZ: On prend la voiture ou on y va à pied?
            VOUS DITES: **Prenons la voiture!**
            VOUS ENTENDEZ: Prenons la voiture!
            VOUS RÉPÉTEZ: **Prenons la voiture!**
            VOUS INDIQUEZ: **la voiture**

1. _____   3. _____   5. _____

2. _____   4. _____   6. _____

E. Un départ. Two of Thomas's friends are flying down to meet him in New Orleans, and they are about to leave for the airport **(l'aéroport).** Listen to their conversation, then pause the recording and complete the following sentences.

1. Leur avion va partir à _____ heures _____.

2. Ils vont aller à l'aéroport en _____.

3. Ils ne prennent pas la voiture pour aller à l'aéroport parce qu'il n'aime pas _____ _____ au parking de l'aéroport.

4. Pour aller à leur hôtel à La Nouvelle-Orléans, ils vont _____.

*F. Et vous? Imagine that a classmate asks you these questions in class. Answer the questions with complete sentences, pausing the recording in order to respond.

1. _____

2. _____

3. _____

4. _____

5. _____

Nom _____ Date _____

Les projets
Chapitre 5

Saying what you did

By the time you finish this **Compétence,** you should be able talk about what you did yesterday.

Partie écrite

A. La journée d'Alice. Alice is talking about what she did last Saturday. Complete her statements according to the illustrations. In the blank, write the verb in the past tense (**passé composé**). Then indicate the correct italicized completion. The first part of number 1 has been done as an example.

  1   2   3   4   5

1. Samedi matin, j'**ai dormi** (dormir) *sur le divan / (dans mon lit) / sous une tente.*

J' _____ (dormir) jusqu'à *dix heures / sept heures / huit heures* du matin.

2. J' _____ (prendre) mon petit déjeuner *au café / chez moi / au restaurant.*

J' _____ (manger) *avec mon mari / avec mes enfants / seule.*

3. J' _____ (déjeuner) *chez moi / au parc / en ville.*

J' _____ (déjeuner) *avec un ami / avec une amie / seule.*

4. Le soir, j' _____ (retrouver) une amie *au cinéma / au centre commercial / à la bibliothèque.*

J' _____ (voir) *une pièce de théâtre / un film / un DVD.*

5. Plus tard *(later)* à la maison, j' _____ (lire) *le journal / un livre / une lettre.*

B. Conversation. Reread the conversation between Cathy and Jérémy on page 183 of your textbook. Then, complete this conversation between two other students with the indicated words.

INÈS: Tu _____ **(1)** un bon week-end?
                    (had [use **passer**])

HUGO: Bof, pas trop. Samedi matin, _____ **(2)**
                                              (I played)

à des jeux vidéo et _____ **(3)**, j'ai travaillé.
                        (Saturday afternoon)

CHAPITRE 5 *Compétence 1 • Partie écrite*   **121**

© 2015 Cengage Learning. All Rights Reserved. May not be scanned, copied or duplicated, or posted to a publicly accessible website, in whole or in part.

INÈS: _____ (4) dimanche?
                   (What did you do)

HUGO: Dimanche matin, _____ (5) et dimanche
                              (I slept)

       après-midi, _____ (6).
                       (I watched TV)

INÈS: Et _____ (7)?
                   (last night)

HUGO: _____ (8).
               (Last night, I did nothing)

C. La journée d'Alice.
Alice is talking about her day last Sunday. Complete the following paragraph by putting the verbs in parentheses in the **passé composé.** The first item has been done as an example.

Dimanche dernier, j' _____ *ai dormi* _____ (1) (dormir) jusqu'à huit heures et demie.

Le matin, je _____ (2) (ne rien faire) de spécial. Vincent et

moi _____ (3) (prendre) le petit déjeuner avec les enfants et

après, Vincent et les enfants _____ (4) (faire) une promenade.

Vers onze heures, j' _____ (5) (téléphoner) à mon amie Sophie

pour l'inviter à déjeuner avec Vincent et moi. Nous _____ (6) (retrouver) Sophie

et son mari en ville où nous _____ (7) (manger) dans

un excellent restaurant. Après le déjeuner, Vincent et moi _____ (8) (faire)

du shopping et nous _____ (9) (prendre) le bus pour

rentrer à la maison. Nous _____ (10) (passer) la soirée à la maison. Nous

_____ (11) (voir) un bon film à la télé et après, Vincent et les enfants

_____ (12) (surfer) sur Internet.

D. Un peu d'histoire.
Tell a little about francophone history in North America by putting the verbs in the following sentences in the **passé composé.**

    EXEMPLE   En 1534, l'explorateur français, Jacques Cartier **a pris** (prendre) possession
                      du Canada (la Nouvelle-France) pour la France.

1. En 1604, les Français _____ (commencer) à coloniser la Cadie (plus

    tard l'Acadie), aujourd'hui la Nouvelle-Écosse *(Nova Scotia),* le Nouveau-Brunswick et l'Île-du-Prince-

    Édouard. En 1608, Samuel de Champlain _____ (fonder) la ville de Québec.

2. En 1682, les Français _____ (prendre) possession de la Louisiane.

3. Les Anglais _____ (gagner) le contrôle de l'Acadie en 1713 et en 1755,

    ils _____ (commencer) à expulser *(to remove)* les Français de la région.

4. Entre 1756 et 1763, les Anglais et les Français _____ (faire) la guerre

(war). Les Anglais _____ (gagner) la guerre et en 1763, la France

_____ (céder) ses territoires canadiens aux Anglais. Entre 1764 et 1785,

des vagues d'Acadiens _____ (trouver) un nouveau pays en Louisiane.

5. En 1803, les Américains _____ (acheter) la Louisiane à la France pour

$15.000.000. Mais les Acadiens _____ (être) isolés pendant plus de

cent ans dans le sud de la Louisiane. Entre 1880 et 1905, ils _____

(commencer) à avoir plus de contact avec les anglophones après l'arrivée du chemin de fer *(railroad),* de

l'électricité et de l'industrie pétrolière.

E. Pour mieux lire: *Using the sequence of events to make logical guesses.* In a logical
sequence of events, what might the italicized verbs mean in these sentences describing what Cathy did last
Saturday? Give the *English* equivalent of each italicized verb in the blank in parentheses. The first part of
number 1 has been done as an example.

1. À onze heures, une amie a téléphoné. Cathy *a répondu* (**answered**) au téléphone et elle a parlé à son amie

pendant une demi-heure. Elles ont décidé d'aller faire du shopping et elles ont terminé la conversation.

Après la conversation, Cathy *a raccroché* (_____) le téléphone.

2. L'après-midi, Cathy a retrouvé son amie au centre commercial où elle a acheté beaucoup de choses. À un

certain moment, elle *a perdu* (_____) sa carte bancaire *(bank/debit card).* Elle l'a

cherchée partout et finalement elle a trouvé sa carte bancaire et ses lunettes par terre.

3. Son amie et elle ont pris quelque chose au café. Quand Cathy a payé, elle *a reçu* (_____)

trop de monnaie, alors elle *a rendu* (_____) cinq euros au serveur.

4. Le soir, Cathy *a mis* (_____) ses nouveaux vêtements, elle a quitté la

maison, elle a retrouvé ses amis en ville et ils ont dansé toute la soirée.

5. Vers deux heures du matin, elle a pris un taxi pour rentrer à la maison. Elle est allée dans sa chambre, elle *a*

enlevé (_____) ses vêtements, elle *a mis* (_____) son

pyjama et elle a dormi jusqu'au lendemain.

F. Qu'est-ce qu'elle a fait? Reread the story *Qu'est-ce qu'elle a fait?* on
page 187 of the textbook. Then, for each location, say one thing Cathy did and
one thing she didn't do.

EXEMPLE   (boire, commander) Au café, Cathy **a commandé** un coca mais
elle **n'a pas bu** le coca.

1. (acheter, prendre) À la station de métro, Cathy _____ un billet mais

elle _____ le métro.

2. (acheter, demander) Au magasin de vélos, Cathy _____ le prix d'un vélo

mais elle _____ de vélo.

*Now explain in *a few words in English* why Cathy did what she did.

_____

_____

*G. Toujours des questions. Imagine that a friend wants to ask you about your activities last Saturday. Use **est-ce que** with the elements given to create his questions. Then, answer each question.

    EXEMPLE   faire samedi dernier *(what)*
          — **Qu'est-ce que tu as fait samedi dernier?**
          — **J'ai bricolé. / Je n'ai rien fait.**

  1. dormir *(until what time)*

    — _____

    — _____

  2. passer la matinée *(where)*

    — _____

    — _____

  3. quitter la maison *(at what time)*

    — _____

    — _____

  4. déjeuner *(with whom)*

    — _____

    — _____

  5. manger *(where)*

    — _____

    — _____

  6. faire samedi après-midi *(what)*

    — _____

    — _____

  7. passer la soirée *(where)*

    — _____

    — _____

Partie auditive

5-2

A. Une journée chargée. You will hear Alice say some of the things she did yesterday. Indicate the number of each sentence you hear under the corresponding picture. The first one has been done as an example.

a. _____

b. _____

c. _____

d. __1__

e. _____

f. _____

5-3

B. Et vous? Now you will hear several sentences in which Cathy says what she did the last day she went to class. After each one, pause the recording and fill in the blank to say whether you did the same thing the last day you went to French class.

EXEMPLE	VOUS ENTENDEZ:	J'ai téléphoné à un ami.
	VOUS ÉCRIVEZ:	Moi, **j'ai téléphoné** à un ami.
		Moi, **je n'ai pas téléphoné** à un ami.

1. Moi, _____ jusqu'à midi.

2. Moi, _____ la matinée chez moi.

3. Moi, _____ mon petit déjeuner au lit.

4. Moi, _____ le journal.

5. Moi, _____ le bus.

6. Moi, _____ les mots de vocabulaire.

7. Moi, _____ mes devoirs avant les cours.

8. Moi, _____ la leçon *(the lesson)*.

9. Moi, _____ un film / de film au cinéma.

10. Moi, _____ la télé.

C. Tu as passé un bon week-end? Listen to a conversation between two students about last weekend and indicate if the following sentences are true (**vrai**) or false (**faux**).

1. Un des étudiants n'a pas fait grand-chose *(not much).* _____ VRAI _____ FAUX

2. Cet étudiant a travaillé sur l'ordinateur. _____ VRAI _____ FAUX

3. Il a beaucoup dormi. _____ VRAI _____ FAUX

4. L'autre étudiant a retrouvé des amis en ville samedi. _____ VRAI _____ FAUX

5. Dimanche, il a dormi toute la journée. _____ VRAI _____ FAUX

D. Dictée. You will hear two friends, Olivia and Arthur, discuss their weekend. The first time, just listen to what they say at normal speed. Then fill in the missing words as the conversation is repeated more slowly.

OLIVIA: _____ **(1)** un bon week-end?

ARTHUR: Oui, _____ **(2)**. Et toi? Qu'est-ce que

_____ **(3)**?

OLIVIA: Samedi à midi, _____ **(4)** des

amis au café et _____ **(5)** ensemble. Après,

_____ **(6)** un tour de la ville et le soir,

_____ **(7)** un film.

ARTHUR: Et dimanche?

OLIVIA: Dimanche matin, _____ **(8)** le journal et après,

_____ **(9)** le petit déjeuner avec un ami.

ARTHUR: Qu'est-ce que _____ **(10)** après?

OLIVIA: _____ **(11)** une promenade.

*E. Et vous? Answer these questions about your own activities yesterday with complete sentences in French. Remember to use the **passé composé.**

1. _____

2. _____

3. _____

4. _____

5. _____

6. _____

7. _____

 **COMPÉTENCE 2**

Telling where you went

By the time you finish this **Compétence,** you should be able to tell in French where you went and when you did something.

Partie écrite

*A. Mon voyage. Talk about the last time you left town. Fill in the blanks with the verbs in the **passé composé** and complete the sentences as indicated.

> **EXEMPLE**   Je **suis allé(e)** (aller) à **Madrid** *[quelle ville].*

1. Je _____ (aller) à _____ *[quelle ville].*

2. Je _____ (partir) _____ *[quand].*

3. J'y _____ (aller) en _____ *[comment].*

4. Je _____ (arriver) _____ *[quand].*

5. Je _____ (rester) _____ *[où].*

6. Je _____ (rentrer) _____ *[quand].*

B. Conversation. Reread the conversation between Claire and Alice on page 188 of your textbook. Then, complete this conversation between two other friends with the indicated words.

SARAH: Qu'est-ce que tu as fait _____ **(1)**?
                                                              (last weekend)

THÉO: _____ **(2)** à Tours.
                        (I went)

SARAH: _____ **(3)**! J'adore Tours! Tu as pris le train?
                  (What luck)

THÉO: Oui, _____ **(4)** samedi matin vers 11h et _____ **(5)**
                     (I left)   *(I arrived)*

vers midi et demi. _____ **(6)** hier soir.
                                  (I returned)

SARAH: Où est-ce que tu es descendu?

THÉO: _____ **(7)** dans un petit hôtel en centre-ville.
                  (I stayed)

SARAH: Moi, j'ai visité Tours en juin. Je suis restée _____ **(8)**.
                                                                            (at some relatives' house)

C. Le dernier cours. Say whether or not the following people did the things indicated in parentheses the last day you went to French class. Use the **passé composé,** and don't forget the agreement of the past participle when needed.

> **EXEMPLE**   Je **suis parti(e) / ne suis pas parti(e)** (partir) tôt de la maison.

1. Tous les étudiants _____ (aller) en cours de français.

2. Je _____ (arriver) en cours en retard *(late).*

3. Nous _____ (aller) à la salle d'informatique.

4. Le professeur _____ (sortir) de la salle de cours pendant *(during)* le cours.

5. Je _____ (rentrer) chez moi après le cours.

6. Les autres étudiants _____ (rester) dans la salle de cours après le cours.

7. Je _____ (revenir) le soir pour travailler avec d'autres étudiants à la bibliothèque.

D. La journée d'Éric.
Complete the following passage about what Éric and his family did yesterday by supplying the correct form of the appropriate auxiliary verb **avoir** or **être**. The first one has been done as an example.

Éric ____*a*____ **(1)** commencé sa journée à 7h30. D'abord, il _____ **(2)** fait du jogging dans le quartier et après, il _____ **(3)** rentré à la maison où il _____ **(4)** pris son petit déjeuner. Ensuite, il _____ **(5)** allé en ville. L'après-midi, il _____ **(6)** joué au football avec des amis. Éric _____ **(7)** parti à 5h30 pour rentrer à la maison. Hier soir, une amie _____ **(8)** invité Éric à dîner chez elle. Alors Vincent, Alice et les autres enfants _____ **(9)** dîné en ville et ils _____ **(10)** allés au cinéma. Toute la famille _____ **(11)** rentrée très fatiguée à 11h du soir.

E. Qui?
Based on the illustrations, write a sentence to say who did each of the indicated things: **Vincent, Alice,** or **Vincent et Alice.** Make sure you choose the correct auxiliary, **avoir** or **être.**

Alice   **Vincent**   **Vincent et Alice**   **Vincent et Alice**

EXEMPLE **Vincent est resté** (rester) à la maison pendant la journée.

1. _____ (travailler) sur l'ordinateur.

2. _____ (sortir) vers 7h30.

3. _____ (faire) une promenade.

4. _____ (passer) la soirée chez des amis.

5. _____ (prendre) un verre avec leurs amis.

6. _____ (beaucoup parler) avec leurs amis.

7. _____ (rentrer) assez tard.

8. _____ (monter) à leur appartement vers minuit.

F. Quand? Translate these expressions into French. The first one has been done as an example.

1. *a few minutes ago*   il y a quelques minutes
2. *last month* _____
3. *yesterday morning* _____
4. *last year* _____
5. *yesterday afternoon* _____
6. *two hours ago* _____
7. *last week* _____
8. *last night* _____

G. Déjà? Say whether you have *already* done these things or whether you have *not yet* done them. Use **déjà** or **ne… pas encore.**

    EXEMPLE   prendre le petit déjeuner aujourd'hui:
        J'ai déjà pris le petit déjeuner aujourd'hui.
        Je n'ai pas encore pris le petit déjeuner aujourd'hui.

1. déjeuner aujourd'hui: _____ aujourd'hui.

2. faire tous les devoirs pour mon prochain cours: _____

   tous les devoirs pour mon prochain cours.

3. sortir de chez moi aujourd'hui: _____ de chez moi

   aujourd'hui.

4. être en cours cette semaine: _____ en cours cette semaine.

H. Tu as passé un bon week-end? Two men are talking about the weekend. Complete their conversation by putting the verbs in parentheses into the **passé composé** and supplying the missing expressions of past time. Be careful to distinguish which verbs take **avoir** as their auxiliary verb and which ones require **être.**

— Je _____ **(1)** de Deauville _____ **(2).**
        (rentrer)   *[last night]*

  Et toi, tu _____ **(3)** _____ **(4)?**
              (voyager)   *[recently]*

— Je (J') _____ **(5)** à la plage avec ma copine et ses
          (aller)

  parents _____ **(6).**
        [two months ago]

— Quand est-ce que vous _____ **(7)?**
                 (partir)

— Nous _____ **(8)** Paris vendredi, le 6.
       (quitter)

— Vous _____ **(9)** à Deauville
       (rester)

_____ **(10)?**
     [for how long]

— Nous y _____ **(11)** _____ **(12)**.
            (rester)   *[for five days]*

— Vous _____ **(13)** à l'hôtel?
            (descendre)

— Non, nous _____ **(14)** chez des amis.
                     (rester)

---

*Journal. Write a paragraph about a trip you took to another city. Tell the following:

- where you went, when you left, how you went there
- who you traveled with, how long you stayed, and where you stayed
- a few things you did
- when you came back

_____

_____

_____

_____

_____

_____

_____

_____

_____

_____

_____

_____

_____

_____

_____

_____

_____

Partie auditive

5-7 **A. Alice et Vincent ont fait un voyage.** Listen as Alice talks about a weekend trip she and Vincent took. Then pause the recording and choose the best completion for each of these statements based on what she says.

1. Ils sont allés _____ *à Deauville* / _____ *à Nice.*

2. Ils y sont allés _____ *en train* / _____ *en voiture.*

3. Ils sont partis _____ *l'après-midi* / _____ *le matin* et ils sont

   arrivés _____ *vers une heure* / _____ *une heure plus tard.*

4. Ils sont restés _____ *dans un hôtel* / _____ *chez des parents.*

5. Dimanche, ils sont allés _____ *à la plage* / _____ *en ville.*

6. Ils sont rentrés tard _____ *dimanche* / _____ *lundi.*

5-8 **B. Prononciation: Les verbes auxiliaires *avoir* et *être*.** Pause the recording and review the ***Prononciation*** section on page 190 of the textbook. Then start the recording and repeat the following forms of the verbs **avoir** and **être** after the speaker, being careful to pronounce them distinctly.

1. tu as _____   tu es _____   3. il a _____   il est _____

2. tu as _____   tu es _____   4. ils ont _____   ils sont _____

Now you will hear a friend's questions about the last time you went away for the weekend (**la dernière fois que tu es parti[e] en week-end**), with either **avoir** or **être** as the auxiliary verb. Indicate the auxiliary verb that you hear in items 1–4 *above.*

*Now play the questions again. This time, *answer* the questions with complete sentences.

1. _____

2. _____

3. _____

4. _____

5-9 **C. Claire décrit son week-end.** Claire has spent a weekend in Deauville. Listen as she describes her weekend to Alice. The first time, simply listen to the conversation at normal speed. It will then be repeated at a slower speed with pauses for you to fill in the missing words in the sentences.

ALICE: Alors, Claire, raconte-moi ton week-end à Deauville!

CLAIRE: D'abord, _____ **(1)** le

   train et _____ **(2)** dans un charmant

   petit hôtel. Le premier soir, _____ **(3)** dans un très

   bon restaurant où nous avons goûté *(tasted)* des spécialités de la région. C'était *(It was)* très bon!

   Dimanche, _____ **(4)** la

   journée à la plage.

ALICE: Est-ce que _____ (5) au casino?

CLAIRE: Oui, dimanche soir, mais _____ (6).

Mon mari n'aime pas jouer pour de l'argent. Après, _____ (7)

à un concert de jazz au centre culturel. _____ (8) la

musique. _____ (9) à l'hôtel à trois heures du matin!

🔊 **D. Les expressions qui désignent le passé.** Pause the recording and match each phrase expressing
5-10 present time on the left with a parallel expression of past time from the lettered list on the right. The first
one has been done as an example. Afterward, turn on the recording and correct your work. Repeat each time
expression after the speaker to practice pronunciation.

_**g**_ 1. aujourd'hui   **a.** la semaine dernière

____ 2. ce matin   **b.** hier soir

____ 3. cet après-midi   **c.** le mois dernier

____ 4. ce soir   **d.** hier après-midi

____ 5. ce week-end   **e.** le week-end dernier

____ 6. cette semaine   **f.** l'année dernière

____ 7. ce mois-ci   **g.** hier

____ 8. cette année   **h.** hier matin

🔊 **E. Cathy est occupée *(busy)*.** Listen as Cathy talks about her recent activities. Then replay the passage
5-11 and indicate which of the things listed for each time are true. Pause the recording as needed.

1. Le mois dernier:

____ elle a beaucoup travaillé   ____ elle a passé beaucoup de temps en famille

2. La semaine dernière:

____ elle a fait du shopping   ____ elle a travaillé

3. Le week-end dernier:

____ elle est restée chez elle   ____ elle est allée à la campagne

4. Hier matin:

____ elle a pris son petit déjeuner à la maison   ____ elle est allée en ville

5. Hier après-midi:

____ elle est restée seule   ____ elle a retrouvé des amis

6. Hier soir:

____ elle a retrouvé un ami au café   ____ elle est allée au cinéma

COMPÉTENCE 3

Discussing the weather and your activities

By the time you finish *this **Compétence,*** you should be able to describe the weather and say what people do in different seasons.

Partie écrite

A. Quel temps fait-il? Say two things about what the weather is like in each of these four scenes. Use the *present* tense.

EXEMPLE **Il fait chaud et il fait du soleil.**

Exemple   1   2   3

1. _____

2. _____

3. _____

*Now say two things about what the weather is like in your region in these seasons.

EXEMPLE été: **En été ici, il fait beau et il fait du soleil.**

1. hiver: _____

2. automne: _____

3. printemps: _____

4. été: _____

B. Conversation. Reread the vocabulary and the conversation between Alice and Cathy on pages 194–195 of your textbook. Then, complete this conversation between two friends.

CHLOÉ: En _____ **(1)** préfères-tu voyager?
                      (what season)

OLIVIA: J'aime voyager _____ **(2)** parce que j'aime
                                     (in summer)

_____ **(3)** et
                      (to go boating)

_____ **(4).**
                      (to waterski)

CHLOÉ: Moi, je préfère voyager _____ **(5)** parce

_____ *(in spring)*

qu' _____ **(6)**. J'aime aller

_____ *(it's cool)*

_____ **(7)**

_____ *(to the mountains)*

pour _____ **(8)** et pour

_____ *(to go camping)*

_____ **(9)**. _____ **(10)**

(to go hiking). _____ *(If it's sunny)*

ce week-end, j' _____ **(11)** faire du camping à la campagne.

(intend to)

C. Un après-midi. Complete the following conversation between Alice and Vincent by filling in each blank with the correct form of **faire** in the *present* tense or in the *infinitive*. The first one has been done as an example.

— Où sont les enfants? Qu'est-ce qu'ils ____**font**____ **(1)** cet après-midi?

— Cathy _____ **(2)** du shopping avec son amie et les garçons

_____ **(3)** du vélo.

— Et toi, qu'est-ce que tu _____ **(4)**?

— Je ne _____ **(5)** rien de spécial. Et ton ami et toi, vous

_____ **(6)** du shopping comme d'habitude?

— Non, je n'ai pas l'intention de _____ **(7)** du shopping aujourd'hui.

— Alors, on _____ **(8)** quelque chose ensemble?

— Nous ne _____ **(9)** pas assez d'exercice en ce moment. Allons au

parc pour _____ **(10)** une promenade.

D. Des photos. Alice is looking at various photos and saying what the weather was like and what everyone did the day each photo was taken. Complete her sentences with the illustrated weather condition and a verb in the **passé composé**.

Exemple   **1**   **2**   **3**

EXEMPLE Ce jour-là *(That day)*, il **a fait froid** et Vincent **a fait une promenade.**

1. Ce jour-là, il _____ et Éric _____.

2. Ce jour-là, il _____ et moi, j'_____.

3. Ce jour-là, il _____ et les enfants _____.

E. Suggestions. Review how to form commands on page 154 in *Chapitre 4* of the textbook. Imagine that you are trying to get a friend to have some fun with you, rather than doing what he should around the house. Tell him not to do what he is supposed to and suggest doing the other activity with you.

    EXEMPLE   faire les courses / faire du jogging
               Ne fais pas les courses! Faisons du jogging!

1. faire du bateau / faire la lessive

_____

2. faire la vaisselle / faire une promenade

_____

3. faire du vélo / faire le ménage

_____

4. faire la cuisine / faire du ski

_____

F. Hier. Alice is talking about what happened yesterday. The first statement she makes is true, but only one of the follow-up statements is logical. Compose sentences in the **passé composé,** putting the appropriate verb in the negative form.

    EXEMPLE   Hier matin, Alice **est sortie** (sortir).
                Elle **n'est pas restée** (rester) à la maison.
                Elle **a fait** (faire) les courses.

1. Vincent _____ (passer) la matinée à la maison.

    Il _____ (faire) le ménage.

    Il _____ (jouer) au golf avec ses amis.

2. Cathy et Michel _____ (aller) au centre commercial.

    Ils _____ (faire) du shopping.

    Ils _____ (aider *[to help]*) avec le ménage.

3. Hier après-midi, il _____ (faire) beau.

    Il _____ (pleuvoir).

    Il _____ (faire) du soleil.

4. Alice et Vincent _____ (aller) au cinéma.

    Ils _____ (voir) un film.

    Ils _____ (rester) chez eux.

5. Hier soir, Alice et Vincent _____ (manger) à la maison.

    Ils _____ (dîner) au restaurant.

    Ils _____ (faire) la cuisine.

6. Après le dîner, Cathy _____ (rester) dans la cuisine.

    Elle _____ (faire) la vaisselle.

    Elle _____ (sortir) avec ses amis.

*G. Et toi? A friend is asking you questions. Answer his questions in complete sentences in French.

1. Quelle saison préfères-tu? Qu'est-ce que tu aimes faire pendant cette saison?

_____

_____

2. Quel temps fait-il aujourd'hui?

_____

3. Qu'est-ce que tu aimes faire quand il fait très froid? Et quand il fait très chaud?

_____

_____

4. Quel temps va-t-il probablement faire le week-end prochain? Qu'est-ce que tu as l'intention de faire s'il fait beau samedi? Et s'il fait mauvais?

_____

_____

_____

5. Quel temps a-t-il fait samedi dernier? Qu'est-ce que tu as fait?

_____

_____

6. Est-ce que tu aimes mieux faire la lessive ou faire le ménage? faire la cuisine ou faire la vaisselle? faire les courses ou faire du jardinage?

_____

_____

7. Qu'est-ce que tu fais d'habitude le week-end? Qu'est-ce que tu as besoin de faire ce week-end? Qu'est-ce que tu as envie de faire?

_____

_____

_____

Partie auditive

🔊 **A. Quel temps fait-il?** You will hear several short exchanges about the weather. Match each one to the
5-12 appropriate illustration.

EXEMPLE   VOUS ENTENDEZ: — Quel temps fait-il?
— Il fait chaud.

VOUS INDIQUEZ:

a. _____   b. _____   c. _____

d. _____   e. _____   f. _____   g. EXEMPLE

🔊 **B. La météo.** You will hear a weather report for France. The first time, just listen as it is read at normal speed.
5-13 Then, complete the sentences as you hear it again more slowly with pauses for you to fill in the missing words.

Voici le bulletin météorologique pour demain: _____ **(1)**

sur l'ensemble du pays, sauf en Normandie où _____ **(2)**

le matin et _____ **(3)** dans le courant de l'après-midi. Les

températures vont varier entre _____ **(4)** et _____ **(5)**

degrés dans le nord du pays et à Paris. Mais _____ **(6)**

dans le sud, où les températures vont atteindre _____ **(7)** degrés. En montagne,

sortez vos skis – _____ **(8)**!

🔊 **C. Le verbe *faire*.** Pause the recording and fill in the blanks with the correct form of the verb **faire** in the
5-14 *present* tense. The first one has been done as an example.

— Qu'est-ce que tu ___*fais*___ **(1)** samedi?

— Je ne _____ **(2)** rien.

— Alors, on _____ **(3)** quelque chose ensemble?

— Mes amis et moi, nous _____ **(4)** souvent du sport le samedi.

  Tes amis et toi, vous _____ **(5)** souvent de l'exercice?

— Mes amis _____ **(6)** souvent du jogging et moi, je _____ **(7)** du yoga.

Now listen to the recording and repeat each sentence of the preceding conversation after the speakers, paying
attention to the pronunciation of the forms of the verb **faire.** Listen carefully. In only one of the forms, the
letter combination **ai** is pronounced irregularly like the **e** of **je.** Which form is it?

The **ai** is pronounced like the **e** of **je** in the form:

____ fais/fait   ____ faisons   ____ faites

D. Préférences. You will hear Éric say which of each pair of activities he prefers. For each pair, indicate the illustration of the activity he prefers. The first one has been done as an example.

5-15

1

a. _____ b. ___✓___

2

a. _____ b. _____

3

a. _____ b. _____

4

a. _____ b. _____

5

a. _____ b. _____

*Now you will hear a friend ask which activities you prefer. Fill in the blank with your preference.

1. Pendant mon temps libre, je préfère _____.

2. Comme exercice, je préfère _____.

3. J'aime mieux _____.

4. J'aime mieux _____.

5. Je préfère _____.

6. Quand je fais un voyage, je préfère _____.

7. J'aime mieux _____.

*E. Et vous? Answer the questions you hear in complete sentences in French.

5-16

1. _____

2. _____

3. _____

4. _____

5. _____

6. _____

COMPÉTENCE 4

Deciding what to wear and buying clothes

By the time you finish this **Compétence,** you should be able to talk about your clothing and buy clothes in a store.

Partie écrite

A. Les vêtements. Identify these items using words from the box.

un parapluie	un pull	un costume	un short	une chemise
un chemisier	un pantalon	une jupe	un survêtement	un maillot de bain
une robe	un anorak	un imperméable	un jean	

EXEMPLE   _un jean_   _____   _____   _____   _____

_____   _____   _____   _____   _____

_____   _____   _____   _____

*B. C'est logique. Fill in the blanks with the name of a logical clothing item or an accessory.

1. Quand on va à la plage, on met _____ et _____.

2. Quand il fait froid, on met _____ et _____.

3. Quand il pleut, il est bon d'avoir _____ ou _____.

4. Pour savoir l'heure qu'il est, on porte _____.

5. On met son argent dans _____ ou dans _____.

*C. Conversation. Reread the conversation at the clothing store on page 201 of the textbook. Now imagine that you want to buy a new bathing suit. Complete the following conversation with the salesperson in a logical way.

La vendeuse: Bonjour, monsieur / madame. Je peux vous aider?

Vous: _____.

La vendeuse: Vous faites quelle taille?

Vous: _____.

La vendeuse: Quelle couleur est-ce que vous préférez?

Vous: Je préfère quelque chose en _____.

La vendeuse: Nous avons ces maillots-ci et ils sont tous en solde.

Vous: J'aime bien ce maillot-ci. Est-ce que je peux _____?

La vendeuse: Mais bien sûr! Voilà la cabine d'essayage.

La vendeuse: Alors, qu'en pensez-vous?

Vous: _____.

D. Cathy fait du shopping. Cathy is shopping and is taking everything she likes. According to the indications for each item pictured, complete the first sentence to say whether or not she likes it. Then write a second sentence to say whether or not she is taking it. Use a direct object pronoun.

EXEMPLE 1 Elle n'aime pas **ce jean.**
Elle **ne le prend pas.**

EXEMPLE 2 Elle aime bien **cette jupe.**
Elle **la prend.**

Exemple 1

Exemple 2

1

2

3

4

5

6

1. Elle n'aime pas _____. Elle _____.

2. Elle aime bien _____. Elle _____.

3. Elle aime bien _____. Elle _____.

4. Elle n'aime pas _____. Elle _____.

5. Elle n'aime pas _____. Elle _____.

6. Elle aime bien _____. Elle _____.

Line art on this page: © Cengage Learning

E. Que faites-vous? Use the appropriate direct object pronoun (**le, la, l', les**) to say whether you often do these things on Saturdays.

     EXEMPLE   faire *les devoirs* le samedi matin
                         Je **les fais** souvent le samedi matin. / Je **ne les fais pas** souvent le samedi matin.

1. passer *la matinée* chez vous le samedi

    Je _____ souvent chez moi le samedi.

2. prendre *votre petit déjeuner* au café

    Je _____ souvent au café.

3. faire *les courses* le samedi matin

    Je _____ souvent le samedi matin.

4. écouter *la radio* le samedi soir

    Je _____ souvent le samedi soir.

Review the placement of the direct object pronouns with infinitives on page 202 of the textbook. Then, use a direct object pronoun and the immediate future to say whether you are going to do these things on Saturday.

     EXEMPLE   faire *les devoirs* samedi matin
                         Je **vais les faire** samedi matin. / Je **ne vais pas les faire** samedi matin.

1. prendre *votre petit déjeuner* au café

    Je _____ au café.

2. passer *la journée* chez vous

    Je _____ chez moi.

3. faire *mes exercices de français* samedi soir

    Je _____ samedi soir.

4. inviter *votre meilleur(e) ami(e)* au restaurant

    Je _____ au restaurant.

Review the placement of object pronouns in the **passé composé** and the agreement of the past participle on page 202 of the textbook. Then, say whether or not you did these things last Saturday. Use a direct object pronoun and the **passé composé** in your answers.

     EXEMPLE   faire *les devoirs* samedi matin.
                         Je **les ai faits** samedi matin. / Je **ne les ai pas faits** samedi matin.

1. faire *votre lit* avant de prendre le petit déjeuner

    Je _____ avant de prendre le petit déjeuner.

2. passer *la matinée* chez vous

    Je _____ chez moi.

3. mettre *vos lunettes de soleil* avant de sortir

    Je _____ avant de sortir.

4. faire *les courses* samedi matin

    Je _____ samedi matin.

*F. Encore des pronoms! Answer the following questions, replacing the italicized direct objects with the appropriate pronoun (**le, la, l', les**).

> **EXEMPLE**   Où est-ce que vous retrouvez *vos amis* pour prendre un verre?
>
> **Je les retrouve au café Mozart's pour prendre un verre.**

1. Est-ce que vous invitez souvent *vos amis* chez vous? Est-ce que vous allez inviter *vos amis* chez vous ce soir? Est-ce que vous avez invité *vos amis* chez vous récemment?

    _____

    _____

    _____

2. Vous aimez regarder *la télé*? Vous allez regarder *la télé* ce soir? Vous avez regardé *la télé* pendant le dîner hier?

    _____

    _____

    _____

3. Est-ce que vous faites souvent *la cuisine*? Qui prépare *le dîner* chez vous normalement? Vous avez préparé *le dîner* hier soir?

    _____

    _____

    _____

---

*Journal. Write a paragraph describing your day yesterday. Include the following information.

- until what time you slept
- what clothes you put on (use **mettre**)
- what time you left your house
- where you went
- what you did yesterday morning, afternoon, and evening
- what time you returned home

© Cengage Learning

_____

_____

_____

_____

_____

_____

_____

_____

_____

_____

Partie auditive

5-17
A. Quels vêtements? You will hear several short conversations. Indicate the illustrations of all the clothing and accessories you hear mentioned.

5-18
B. Je les prends. Alice is buying clothes only for herself today, and none for her husband. After the salesclerk names an item, pause the recording and complete Alice's statement saying whether she is or is not taking it, using the appropriate direct object pronoun. Then, turn on the recording and check your work as you hear the correct response.

EXEMPLES	VOUS ENTENDEZ:	Cette jupe?		VOUS ENTENDEZ:	Ce costume?
	VOUS ÉCRIVEZ:	**Je la prends.**		VOUS ÉCRIVEZ:	**Je ne le prends pas.**
	VOUS ENTENDEZ:	Je la prends.		VOUS ENTENDEZ:	Je ne le prends pas.

1. Je _____.

2. Je _____.

3. Je _____.

4. Je _____.

5. Je _____.

6. Je _____.

C. Qu'est-ce qu'elle va mettre? Look at the illustrations of Alice's weekend activities and indicate whether or not she is going to wear each piece of clothing named. Complete each sentence using a direct object pronoun. Then, turn on the recording and check your work as you hear the correct answers.

EXEMPLES   VOUS VOYEZ: Son nouveau chemisier?
VOUS ÉCRIVEZ: Elle **va le mettre.**
VOUS ENTENDEZ: Son nouveau chemisier? Elle va le mettre.

VOUS VOYEZ: Sa robe noire?
VOUS ÉCRIVEZ: Elle **ne va pas la mettre.**
VOUS ENTENDEZ: Sa robe noire? Elle ne va pas la mettre.

1. Son short? Elle _____.

2. Sa jupe? Elle _____.

3. Son maillot de bain? Elle _____.

4. Son anorak? Elle _____.

5. Ses lunettes de soleil? Elle _____.

6. Son chemisier blanc? Elle _____.

D. Une cliente exigeante. You will hear a scene in which a young woman is shopping. Listen to the conversation and select the correct ending for each sentence.

1. La jeune femme cherche ____ *un bikini* / ____ *un maillot de bain.*

2. Comme taille, elle fait du ____ *36* / ____ *38.*

3. Elle ne prend pas le premier article suggéré par la vendeuse parce qu'elle n'aime pas ____ *la taille* / ____ *le modèle (style).* Elle n'aime pas le deuxième non plus parce qu'elle cherche quelque chose en ____ *bleu* / ____ *vert.*

4. Elle aime le troisième mais elle ne le prend pas parce qu'il est trop ____ *grand* / ____ *petit* / ____ *cher.*

5. Le quatrième est bleu et il est aussi ____ *en solde* / ____ *très chic.*

*E. Et vous? Answer the questions you hear in complete sentences in French.

1. _____

2. _____

3. _____

4. _____

5. _____

Nom _____ Date _____

Les sorties

Chapitre **6**

Inviting someone to go out

By the time you finish this *Compétence,* you should be able to make plans with friends and accept or refuse invitations.

Partie écrite

A. Invitons des amis! Use **Tu veux…** or **Vous voulez…** and one of the following expressions to invite the indicated people to do the pictured activity. The first one has been done as an example.

étudier   aller prendre un verre   aller danser   faire du shopping

1   2   3   4

1. à votre copain (copine): _____ *Tu veux aller danser* _____ samedi soir?

2. à votre mère: _____ cet après-midi?

3. à des camarades de classe: _____ avec moi ce soir?

4. à des amis: _____ plus tard?

Indicate which of the following expressions could be used instead of **tu veux** or **vous voulez** in the preceding invitations. The first one has been done as an example.

1. ____ Je vous invite à…   **X** Je t'invite à….

2. ____ Vous voudriez…   ____ Tu voudrais…

3. ____ Vous voudriez…   ____ Je t'invite à…

4. ____ Je vous invite à…   ____ Tu voudrais…

*B. On vous invite à… Imagine that a close friend invites you to do the following things. Accept or refuse each invitation. Use a variety of expressions from the choices given.

Oui, je veux bien. Quelle bonne idée! Avec plaisir!	Je regrette mais… je ne suis pas libre. je ne peux vraiment pas. je dois travailler.	Je préfère… J'aime mieux… Allons plutôt à…

EXEMPLE   Tu veux aller au centre commercial avec moi cet après-midi?
             Oui, je veux bien. / Non, je regrette, mais je ne peux vraiment pas. Je dois travailler aujourd'hui. / Allons plutôt au cinéma.

1. Tu as envie d'aller prendre un verre au café?

_____

2. Est-ce que tu voudrais faire la cuisine ce soir?

_____

3. On va voir le nouveau film avec Johnny Depp?

_____

4. Tu veux aller à l'église avec ma famille ce week-end?

_____

5. Tu es libre jeudi matin? Tu voudrais aller au musée?

_____

C. Les séances. The university film club is having a classic film festival. Give the show times using official time. Write out all numbers.

À bout de souffle	lun. / mer. / vend.	12h15	14h45	17h15
Les Quatre Cents Coups	mar. / jeu.	11h20	13h30	15h45
La Belle et la Bête	sam. / dim.	18h05	20h15	22h25

EXEMPLE   *À bout de souffle:* 12h15 = à **douze heures quinze**
14h45 = à **quatorze heures quarante-cinq**
17h15 = à **dix-sept heures quinze**

1. *Les Quatre Cents Coups:*

11h20 = à _____

13h30 = à _____

15h45 = à _____

2. *La Belle et la Bête:*

18h05 = à _____

20h15 = à _____

22h25 = à _____

Now convert the show times to conversational time as in the example. Write out all numbers.

EXEMPLE   *À bout de souffle:* 12h15 = à **midi et quart**
14h45 = à **trois heures moins le quart de l'après-midi**
17h15 = à **cinq heures et quart de l'après-midi**

1. *Les Quatre Cents Coups:*

11h20 = à _____

13h30 = à _____

15h45 = à _____

2. *La Belle et la Bête:*

18h05 = à _____

20h15 = à _____

22h25 = à _____

D. Conversation. Reread the conversation between Michèle and Éric on page 225 of your textbook. Then, complete this phone conversation between Aurélie and her friend Didier with the indicated words.

AURÉLIE: _____ **(1)**?
          (Hello)

DIDIER: Salut, Aurélie. _____ **(2)**, Didier. Ça va?
                        (It's me)

AURÉLIE: Oui, très bien. Et toi?

DIDIER: Moi, ça va. Écoute, tu es _____ **(3)** ce soir? Tu voudrais sortir?
                                    (free)

AURÉLIE: _____ **(4)**, mais ce soir _____ **(5)**.
          (I'm sorry)   *(I can't)*

Je suis libre demain soir.

DIDIER: Alors, qu'est-ce que tu _____ **(6)**?
                                  (feel like doing)

Tu veux aller voir ce film avec Bérénice Bejo?

AURÉLIE: Oui, je veux bien. À quelle heure?

DIDIER: Il y a _____ **(7)** à dix-neuf heures.
                  (a showing)

AURÉLIE: Veux-tu _____ **(8)** six heures et quart?
                  (come by my house around)

DIDIER: _____ **(9)**. À demain, Aurélie.
          (Okay)

AURÉLIE: Au revoir, Didier.

E. Encore une invitation. Éric is inviting Michèle to go out again. Complete the following invitation with the *present tense* of the verbs in parentheses. The first one has been done as an example.

ÉRIC: Tu es libre samedi après-midi? Tu _____**veux**_____ **(1)** (vouloir) faire quelque chose avec moi?

MICHÈLE: Je ne _____ **(2)** (pouvoir) vraiment pas, parce que je _____ **(3)**
(devoir) rester à la maison avec mes deux petits frères.

ÉRIC: Ils _____ **(4)** (pouvoir) venir avec nous si tu _____ **(5)** (vouloir). Nous
_____ **(6)** (pouvoir) aller au parc.

MICHÈLE: Bon, d'accord, mais nous _____ **(7)** (devoir) rentrer avant cinq heures.

Now complete these statements logically about Éric and Michèle's conversation with the correct forms of
vouloir, pouvoir, or **devoir** in the *present tense.* Use each verb only once in each sentence. The first blank
has been completed as an example.

1. Éric _____**veut**_____ faire quelque chose avec Michèle samedi après-midi, mais elle ne _____

   pas sortir parce qu'elle _____ rester à la maison avec ses deux petits frères.

2. Ils _____ aller tous *(all)* ensemble au parc s'ils _____, mais ils _____

   rentrer avant cinq heures.

*F. Pourquoi pas? Alice is explaining that the following people want to do the activity in the first illustration, but they cannot because they have to do the second. Complete her sentences using the verbs **vouloir, pouvoir,** and **devoir** in the *present tense.*

EXEMPLE Vincent et moi **voulons aller à la plage mais nous ne pouvons pas parce que nous devons aller au centre commercial.**

1. Éric _____

_____

_____

_____ .

2. Vincent et moi _____

_____

_____

_____ .

3. Les enfants _____

_____

_____

_____ .

*G. Et vous? Complete the following questions about yourself and your friends with the *present tense* of the verb in parentheses. Then answer each question with a complete sentence.

1. Qu'est-ce que vos amis _____ (vouloir) faire le week-end, en général?

_____

2. Qu'est-ce que vous _____ (vouloir) faire ce soir?

_____

3. Quels soirs est-ce que vous _____ (pouvoir) sortir avec vos amis?

_____

4. Généralement, est-ce que vous _____ (devoir) travailler le week-end?

_____

5. Où est-ce qu'on _____ (pouvoir) aller près du campus pour prendre

un verre avec des amis?

_____

Partie auditive

A. Tu veux bien... ? Éric's friend Dominique always goes out with friends, *except* when they want to exercise or play sports. You will hear friends invite her to do various things. In each case, indicate her probable response.

1. Avec plaisir! _____   Je regrette, mais je dois partir maintenant! _____

2. Oui, je veux bien! _____   Je regrette, mais je ne suis pas libre. _____

3. Mais oui! Avec plaisir! _____   Je regrette, mais je suis occupée *(busy).* _____

4. D'accord! _____   Je regrette, mais je dois travailler. _____

5. Quelle bonne idée! _____   Je regrette, mais je ne peux vraiment pas! _____

B. Succès du box-office. A film festival is showing the six French movies that were the biggest box office hits of all times in France. As you hear the show times given in official time, write the number of the statement under the corresponding clock.

      EXEMPLE   VOUS ENTENDEZ: Aujourd'hui, on passe *Bienvenue chez les Ch'tis* à quatorze heures cinquante.

                    VOUS INDIQUEZ:

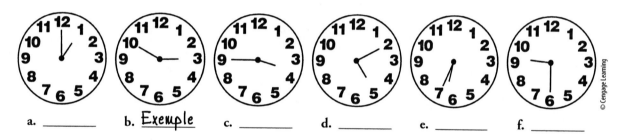

a. _____   b. *Exemple*   c. _____   d. _____   e. _____   f. _____

C. Prononciation: Les verbes *vouloir, pouvoir* et *devoir*. Repeat the phrases after the speaker, paying attention to the pronunciation of the forms of **vouloir**, **pouvoir**, and **devoir**.

Je veux aller au cinéma, mais je ne peux pas. Je dois travailler.
Tu veux sortir ce soir, mais tu ne peux pas. Tu dois réviser tes cours.
Éric veut aller au musée, mais il ne peut pas. Il doit rester avec son petit frère.
Nous voulons partir en week-end, mais nous ne pouvons pas. Nous devons travailler.
Vous voulez aller à la plage, mais vous ne pouvez pas. Vous devez faire le ménage.
Ils veulent aller au café, mais ils ne peuvent pas. Ils doivent aller en classe.

Notice the difference between the pronunciation of the third-person singular and plural forms of these verbs. Listen and repeat.

Elle veut aller au cinéma. Elles veulent aller au cinéma.
Elle ne peut pas. Elles ne peuvent pas.
Elle doit rester à la maison. Elles doivent rester à la maison.

Nom _____ Date _____

Now, listen to Alice talk about Vincent and Éric. For each statement, indicate whether she is just talking about **Vincent** or whether she is talking about both **Vincent and Éric.**

1. Vincent ____   Vincent et Éric ____   **4.** Vincent ____   Vincent et Éric ____

2. Vincent ____   Vincent et Éric ____   **5.** Vincent ____   Vincent et Éric ____

3. Vincent ____   Vincent et Éric ____   **6.** Vincent ____   Vincent et Éric ____

Now you will hear these sentences again. Complete each sentence with the missing words.

1. _____ cet après-midi.

2. _____ avec moi ce soir.

3. _____

parce qu' _____.

4. _____ à Deauville ce week-end.

5. _____ ce week-end.

6. _____ à la maison aujourd'hui.

🔊
5-25
D. Pour mieux comprendre: *Noting the important information.* It's Monday afternoon and Alice is listening to messages on her answering machine. After each message, pause the recording and fill in the requested information in the chart. The first one has been done as an example.

	Qui parle?	Quelle est l'activité proposée?	Quel jour?	À quelle heure?
Message 1	Vincent	aller voir un film	cet après-midi	à 16h30
Message 2				
Message 3				
Message 4				

🔊
5-26
E. Au cinéma. Alice and Vincent have just arrived at the movie theater. Listen to their conversation. Then pause the recording and indicate if these statements are true or false by selecting **vrai** or **faux.**

1. Alice n'a jamais vu *Les Quatre Cents Coups.*   vrai ____   faux ____

2. Vincent a envie de voir un autre film.   vrai ____   faux ____

3. Les séances des deux films sont à des heures différentes.   vrai ____   faux ____

4. Alice va voir un film de Steven Spielberg avec Vincent.   vrai ____   faux ____

Now play this section again and complete the following statements.

1. Vincent a déjà vu le film *Les Quatre Cents Coups* _____ fois.

2. Alice a aimé le film parce que _____ est touchante, les acteurs sont excellents

et elle adore les films en _____.

3. Après le film, Alice voudrait aller au _____ avant de rentrer.

COMPÉTENCE 2

Talking about how you spend and used to spend your time

By the time you finish this **Compétence,** you should be able to compare how things are now with how they used to be in the past.

Partie écrite

*A. Ici ou en France? A high school student has just moved from France to the United States, and is comparing his new school here with his former school in France. Write sentences in the *present tense* that he would probably say about how things are at his high school compared to how things used to be at his **lycée** in France.

EXEMPLES En France, j'avais cours du lundi au samedi.
Ici, j'ai cours du lundi au vendredi.

En France, j'avais une spécialisation en maths.
Ici, je n'ai pas de spécialisation.

1. En France, on étudiait deux ou trois langues étrangères généralement.

   Ici, on _____ généralement.

2. En France, la langue étrangère la plus populaire était l'anglais.

   Ici, la langue étrangère la plus populaire _____.

3. En France, les élèves *(pupils, students)* avaient de neuf à douze cours.

   Ici, les étudiants _____ cours.

4. En France, j'étais avec le même groupe d'élèves dans presque tous mes cours.

   Ici, je _____ dans tous mes cours.

5. En France, je ne pouvais pas participer à beaucoup d'activités extrascolaires *(extracurricular)*.

   Ici, je _____.

6. En France, le sport n'était pas très important.

   Ici, le sport _____.

7. En France, l'école n'avait pas de fanfare *(f) (marching band)*.

   Ici, l'école _____.

8. En France, nous avions deux semaines de vacances d'hiver en février entre les vacances de Noël et les vacances de printemps.

   Ici, nous _____ en février.

9. En France, les vacances d'été commençaient en juillet.

   Ici, les vacances d'été _____.

10. En France, on avait deux mois de vacances en été.

    Ici, on _____.

B. Conversation. Reread the conversation between Michèle and Éric on page 231 of your textbook. Then, complete this conversation in which they talk about when Éric was a little boy. Put the verbs in the **imparfait.**

MICHÈLE: _____ **(1)** le
(What did you used to like to do)

week-end quand tu étais petit?

ÉRIC: Le samedi matin, _____ **(2)** ou midi.
(I liked to sleep until eleven o'clock)

MICHÈLE: Et le samedi après-midi, qu'est-ce que tu faisais généralement?

ÉRIC: J'aimais jouer avec _____ **(3)** du quartier.
(my pals)

On _____ **(4)** ou on jouait à des jeux vidéo.
(skateboarded)

MICHÈLE: Et qu'est-ce que tu faisais le dimanche?

ÉRIC: Le dimanche matin, on _____ **(5)** à l'église et
(went)

l'après-midi _____ **(6).**
(I didn't do anything special)

C. M. Monotone. One of Michèle's professors, poor **M. Monotone,** has done the same thing for years. Here is a description of his day yesterday. It is exactly the same as what he did years ago. Complete the second paragraph in the **imparfait** describing his daily routine when he first began teaching.

Avant de quitter la maison hier matin, M. Monotone **a pris** un café avec sa femme et ils **ont mangé** un croissant. Il **a quitté** la maison à 7h45 et il **a pris** le bus à 7h52 à l'arrêt de bus devant son immeuble. Quand il **est arrivé** sur le campus, il **est entré** dans son bureau et il **a commencé** à travailler. Il **est resté** à la fac toute la journée jusqu'à 16h55, quand il **a quitté** son bureau pour rentrer à la maison. Quand il **est arrivé** à la maison, sa femme **a préparé** le dîner et ils **ont mangé.** Après le dîner, sa femme **a pris** un bain et M. Monotone **a fait** la vaisselle. Ensuite, ils **ont regardé** la télé pendant une heure avant de se coucher *(going to bed).*

Avant de quitter la maison tous les matins, M. Monotone **prenait** un café avec sa femme et ils

_____ **(1)** un croissant. Il _____ **(2)** la maison à 7h45 et il

_____ **(3)** le bus à 7h52 à l'arrêt de bus devant son immeuble. Quand il

_____ **(4)** sur le campus, il _____ **(5)** dans son bureau et il

_____ **(6)** à travailler. Il _____ **(7)** à la fac toute la journée

jusqu'à 16h55, quand il _____ **(8)** son bureau pour rentrer à la maison. Quand il

_____ **(9)** à la maison, sa femme _____ **(10)** le dîner et ils

_____ **(11).** Après le dîner, sa femme _____ **(12)** un bain et

M. Monotone _____ **(13)** la vaisselle. Ensuite, ils _____ **(14)**

la télé pendant une heure avant de se coucher.

Nom _____ Date _____

D. La routine de Michèle. Talk about Michèle's habits by filling in the blanks with the correct *present tense* form of the verb in parentheses. The first one has been done as an example.

Michèle ___**a**___ (avoir) cours tous les jours. Pendant la semaine, elle _____ **(1)** (dormir) jusqu'à sept heures et elle _____ **(2)** (partir) pour l'université vers huit heures. À midi, elle _____ **(3)** (déjeuner) au resto-u. Elle _____ **(4)** (sortir) de ses cours à quatre heures et elle _____ **(5)** (rentrer) à la maison. Elle _____ **(6)** (être) souvent fatiguée et elle _____ **(7)** (dormir) un peu. Le week-end, elle _____ **(8)** (sortir) souvent avec ses copains. Ils _____ **(9)** (faire) du roller ou ils _____ **(10)** (jouer) au tennis. Le samedi soir, ils _____ **(11)** (sortir) ensemble. Ils _____ **(12)** (rentrer) tard et ils _____ **(13)** (dormir) tard le dimanche. Ils _____ **(14)** (aimer) aussi voyager et ils _____ **(15)** (partir) souvent en voyage ensemble en été.

*Now imagine that a friend is asking about your routine. Complete his questions with the correct *present tense* form of the verb given. Then, answer his questions with complete sentences.

EXEMPLE   Quels jours de la semaine est-ce que tu **as** (avoir) cours?
J'ai cours le mardi et le jeudi.

1. Le premier jour de la semaine où tu as cours, tu _____ (dormir) jusqu'à quelle heure?
_____

2. À quelle heure est-ce que tu _____ (partir) de chez toi pour aller en cours?
_____

3. Est-ce que des étudiants _____ (dormir) quelquefois dans tes cours ou à la bibliothèque?
_____

4. À quelle heure est-ce que tu _____ (sortir) de ton dernier cours?
_____

5. D'habitude, qu'est-ce que tu _____ (vouloir) faire après les cours?
_____

6. Est-ce que tu _____ (pouvoir) faire une sieste *(take a nap)* après les cours si tu _____ (vouloir)?
_____

7. Tes copains (copines) et toi, est-ce que vous _____ (sortir) souvent le week-end?
_____

8. Quand tu _____ (sortir) avec tes copains (copines), est-ce que tu _____ (pouvoir) rentrer quand tu _____ (vouloir) ou est-ce que tu _____ (devoir) rentrer avant une certaine heure?
_____

*E. Et au lycée? Using the answers to the questions in the second part of *D. La routine de Michèle* as a guide, write a paragraph describing your life when you were in high school. Use the **imparfait**.

> **EXEMPLE** **Quand j'étais au lycée, j'avais cours tous les jours sauf le week-end.**

_____

_____

_____

_____

_____

_____

_____

_____

---

*Journal. Write three paragraphs describing your Saturdays. In the first paragraph, use the *present tense* to say four things you generally do on Saturdays now. In the second paragraph, use the **passé composé** to state four things you did last Saturday. Finally, in the third paragraph, use the **imparfait** to talk about four things you used to do on Saturdays in high school. Mention several different things in each paragraph.

Le samedi, _____

_____

_____

_____

_____

Samedi dernier, _____

_____

_____

_____

_____

Quand j'étais au lycée, le samedi, _____

_____

_____

_____

_____

_____

Partie auditive

5-27 **A. À l'université ou au lycée?** Michèle is comparing her life now with how things were in high school. Listen to what she says. Pause the recording after each sentence and fill in the missing word or words.

1. Maintenant, _____ .

   À l'âge de quinze ans, _____ .

2. Maintenant, _____ du lundi au vendredi.

   Au lycée, _____ le samedi matin aussi.

3. _____ à l'université,

   mais quand j'étais jeune, _____ .

4. Le week-end, _____ et _____

   beaucoup. Quand _____ ,

   _____ aussi.

5. Le week-end, _____ avec _____ et le samedi

   on joue au tennis. Quand _____ , je sortais avec des copains

   et le samedi _____ .

5-28 **B. Prononciation: Les terminaisons de l'imparfait.** Pause the recording and review the *Prononciation* section on page 232 of the textbook. Then turn on the recording and repeat the sentences to practice the pronunciation of the endings of the imperfect tense. Complete each sentence with the missing verb.

Quand j'étais jeune, j' _____ avec ma famille.

Quand tu étais jeune, où _____ -tu?

Nous habitions à la campagne. Nous _____ souvent en ville.

Vous habitiez en ville? Vous _____ une jolie maison?

Il y avait beaucoup de jeunes dans le village. On _____ le car pour aller en ville.

Mes amis aimaient sortir. Ils _____ souvent au cinéma.

5-29 **C. La jeunesse de Michèle.** Michèle's life has changed very little from when she was young. Listen to statements about her present situation and say that they also used to be true when she was young. Use the **imparfait.** Verify your response and fill in the missing words as you hear the correct answer.

EXEMPLE   VOUS ENTENDEZ: Ses parents travaillent beaucoup.
             VOUS DITES: **Ses parents travaillaient beaucoup quand elle était jeune.**
             VOUS ENTENDEZ: Ses parents travaillaient beaucoup quand elle était jeune.
             VOUS COMPLÉTEZ: Ses parents **travaillaient beaucoup** quand elle était jeune.

1. Elle _____ quand elle était jeune.

2. Ils _____ quand elle était jeune.

3. Leur appartement _____ quand elle était jeune.

4. Elle _____ quand elle était jeune.

5. Ses parents _____ quand elle était jeune.

6. Son père _____ quand elle était jeune.

7. Sa mère _____ quand elle était jeune.

D. Prononciation: Les verbes *sortir*, *partir* et *dormir*. Pause the recording and review the
Prononciation section on page 234 of the textbook. Then turn on the recording and repeat these verb forms
after the speaker. As you repeat the forms of **partir** and **sortir**, fill in the missing ending, using **dormir** as a
model.

DORMIR *(TO SLEEP)*	PARTIR *(TO LEAVE)*	SORTIR *(TO GO OUT, TO LEAVE)*
je dors	je par ____	je sor ____
tu dors	tu par ____	tu sor ____
il dort	il par ____	il sor ____
elle dort	elle par ____	elle sor ____
on dort	on par ____	on sor ____
nous dormons	nous par ____	nous sor ____
vous dormez	vous par ____	vous sor ____
ils dorment	ils par ____	ils sor ____
elles dorment	elles par ____	elles sor ____

Now, listen to Alice talk about Éric and Cathy. For each statement, indicate whether she is just talking about
Éric or whether she is talking about both **Éric and Cathy.**

1. Éric ____   Éric et Cathy ____

2. Éric ____   Éric et Cathy ____

3. Éric ____   Éric et Cathy ____

4. Éric ____   Éric et Cathy ____

5. Éric ____   Éric et Cathy ____

6. Éric ____   Éric et Cathy ____

*E. Chez vous? A friend is asking you about your habits. Answer her questions with complete sentences.

1. _____

2. _____

3. _____

4. _____

5. _____

6. _____

Nom _____ Date _____

Talking about the past

By the time you finish this *Compétence,* you should be able to tell what happened in the past and describe the circumstances.

Partie écrite

*A. Une sortie. Answer the following questions about the last time you got together with friends at a restaurant for dinner. Use the same tenses as in the questions in each clause of your answer.

1. Est-ce que vos amis étaient déjà au restaurant quand vous êtes arrivé(e)?

_____

_____

2. Quelle heure était-il quand vous êtes arrivé(e) au restaurant?

_____

_____

3. Est-ce que vous aviez faim quand vous êtes arrivé(e) au restaurant?

_____

_____

4. Après le repas, êtes-vous parti(e) tout de suite parce que vous étiez fatigué(e) ou est-ce que vous êtes resté(e) au restaurant parce que vous vouliez parler avec vos amis?

_____

_____

5. Quelle heure était-il quand vous avez quitté le restaurant?

_____

_____

B. Conversation. Reread the conversation between Manon and Cathy on page 237 of your textbook. Then, complete this conversation between Cathy and another friend about a date she had.

CATHY: Tu _____ **(1)** avec Didier le week-end dernier?
                                    (went out)

AURÉLIE: Oui, nous _____ **(2)** un film avec Bérénice Bejo.
                                    (went to see)

CATHY: _____ **(3)**?
                      (Did you like it)

AURÉLIE: Beaucoup. _____ **(4).**
                                    (It was really good)

CATHY: _____ **(5)** avec Didier après?
                      (What did you do)

AURÉLIE: _____ **(6).** J'étais _____ **(7)** et je suis rentrée.
                (Nothing at all)   *(tired)*

C. Leur journée. Complete the following sentences in the past. Put the verb stating what happened in the **passé composé** and the verb describing the circumstances in the **imparfait**. Be careful, the first clause is not always in the **passé composé**.

> **EXEMPLE**   Alice **est allée** (aller) au bureau parce qu'elle **avait** (avoir) beaucoup de choses à faire.

1. Il _____ (pleuvoir) quand Vincent _____ (aller) au parc.

2. Éric _____ (beaucoup manger) au petit déjeuner parce qu'il

   _____ (avoir) très faim.

3. Vincent _____ (vouloir) aller voir un film, alors il

   _____ (chercher) un film sur Internet.

4. Vincent et les enfants _____ (aller) au cinéma Rex parce qu'il y

   _____ (avoir) un bon film d'aventure.

5. Alice _____ (rester) à la maison parce qu'elle

   _____ (être) fatiguée après sa longue journée au bureau.

D. Situations. Vincent is describing the people in each picture when these snapshots were taken. Complete each sentence, using the logical verb in parentheses.

> **EXEMPLE**   (porter, être, faire)
> Alice **était** en ville. Elle **faisait** des courses.
> Elle **portait** une robe.

1. (être, faire, porter)

   Éric et moi _____ du jogging.

   Nous _____ au parc.

   Nous _____ des survêtements.

2. (être, faire, porter)

   Moi, je _____ un tee-shirt et un jean.

   J' _____ à la maison.

   Je _____ la lessive.

3. (aller, vouloir, porter)

   Éric et son ami _____ à la piscine.

   Ils _____ des maillots de bain.

   Ils _____ nager.

E. Une panne d'électricité. Using one of the verbs from the list, say what the following people were doing at the Li household yesterday when the electricity went out. Use the **imparfait**.

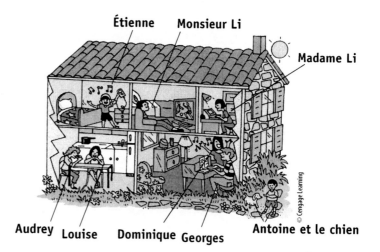

Étienne   Monsieur Li   Madame Li
Audrey   Louise   Dominique   Georges   Antoine et le chien

chanter	écouter	jouer
manger	regarder	surfer

EXEMPLE   Louise et son amie Audrey **mangeaient** quelque chose.

1. Madame Li _____ sur Internet.

2. Monsieur Li _____ la télé.

3. Étienne _____ de la musique.

4. Dominique _____ et son copain Georges _____ du piano.

Now say who was doing these things when the electricity went off. Use the **imparfait**.

EXEMPLE   **Monsieur Li voulait** (vouloir) voir un match de football.

5. _____ (être) dans la cuisine.

6. _____ (avoir) l'iPod de sa sœur Dominique.

7. _____ (faire) des recherches (*searches*) sur Internet.

8. _____ (dormir) devant la télé.

9. _____ (vouloir) danser avec son copain dans le salon.

F. Beaucoup de problèmes. Use the **imparfait** of the verb **aller** followed by the logical activity in parentheses to say what Éric and his classmates were going to do today. Then use the **imparfait** of the other verb in parentheses to explain the circumstances that didn't allow them to do so.

EXEMPLE   **J'allais faire mes devoirs,** mais je ne **ne comprenais pas les exercices.**
(ne pas comprendre les exercices, faire mes devoirs)

1. J' _____, mais je _____
_____. (apprendre le vocabulaire, ne pas pouvoir trouver mon livre)

2. Nous _____, mais le lecteur DVD
_____. (voir un film en cours, ne pas marcher [*to work*]).

3. Des étudiants _____, mais ils
_____. (ne pas être prêts, faire une présentation)

4. J' _____, mais il
_____. (pleuvoir, rentrer chez moi à pied)

G. Une soirée. Éric is talking about an outing with his girlfriend last night. Combine the sentences from the two columns, changing the verbs from the present to the past. Put the italicized verbs saying how people felt or describing the circumstances in the **imparfait.** Put the italicized verbs stating the sequence of actions in the **passé composé.** The first one has been done as an example.

HOW PEOPLE FELT / CIRCUMSTANCES

Ma copine Michèle *veut* sortir, alors…
Il *est* six heures et demie quand…
Le film *est* un peu bête et il y *a*
    beaucoup de violence, alors…
Je *veux* partir aussi, mais…
Après le film nous *avons* faim, alors…
Le dîner *est* excellent et…
Nous ne *voulons* pas rentrer, alors…
Il *est* minuit quand…

SEQUENCE OF ACTIONS

nous *allons* au cinéma.
je *retrouve* Michèle au cinéma.
beaucoup de gens *partent* avant
    la fin *(the end)*.
nous *restons*.
nous *dînons* dans un petit restaurant.
je *mange* bien.
nous *prenons* un dessert.
nous *rentrons*.

Hier soir, ma copine Michèle voulait sortir, alors nous sommes allés au cinéma.

_____

_____

_____

_____

_____

_____

_____

_____

*H. Et vous? Answer the following questions about the last time you went to the movies with someone.

1. Avec qui êtes-vous allé(e) au cinéma? C'était le week-end ou pendant la semaine?

_____

_____

2. Comment s'appelait le film? Quels acteurs étaient dans le film? Comment était le film?

_____

_____

3. Est-ce qu'il y avait beaucoup de monde *(a big crowd)* au cinéma? Est-ce que vous aviez une bonne place *(seat)*? Pouviez-vous voir le film sans problème?

_____

_____

4. Quelle heure était-il et quel temps faisait-il quand vous êtes sorti(e) du cinéma?

_____

_____

Nom _____   Date _____

Partie auditive

🔊 **A. Des vacances.** Two of Alice's friends, Catherine and David, came to visit her in Paris. Repeat each
5-32 question about the day they went to the airport (**l'aéroport**) to leave for their trip and match the number of the
question with its correct answer.

EXEMPLE   VOUS ENTENDEZ: Où était Catherine quand David est sorti pour
faire du jogging?

VOUS RÉPÉTEZ: **Où était Catherine quand David est sorti
pour faire du jogging?**

VOUS INDIQUEZ:

_____   Non, il ne pleuvait pas.

_____   Elle était déjà dans le taxi.

_____   Il était six heures et demie.

_____   Il était onze heures moins le quart.

_____   Il était midi.

_____   Non, ils n'avaient pas beaucoup de temps.

_____   Oui, il était encore à l'aéroport.

_____*Exemple*_____   Elle était encore au lit.

_____   Non, elle ne dormait pas.

🔊 **B. Prononciation: Le passé composé et l'imparfait.** Pause the recording and review the
5-33 *Prononciation* section on page 238 of the textbook. Then turn on the recording. Listen and repeat to practice
distinguishing the present, the imperfect, and the **passé composé.**

____ je parle   ____ tu regardes   ____ il est   ____ nous arrivons   ____ vous mangez   ____ ils dansent

____ je parlais ____ tu regardais ____ il était ____ nous arrivions ____ vous mangiez ____ ils dansaient

____ j'ai parlé ____ tu as regardé ____ il a été ____ nous sommes arrivés ____ vous avez mangé ____ ils ont dansé

Now you will hear one of the verb forms from each column above. Identify the form that you hear.

🔊 ***C. Passé composé ou imparfait?** Listen to a series of questions about your high school years. Select
5-34 **PC** for **passé composé** if you are being asked about a single event that happened or **IMP** for **imparfait** if being
asked about how things used to be in general. Then, listen again and answer each question with a complete
sentence.

1. PC____   IMP____   _____

2. PC____   IMP____   _____

3. PC____   IMP____   _____

4. PC____   IMP____   _____

5. PC____   IMP____   _____

6. PC____   IMP____   _____

Line art on this page: © Cengage Learning

Nom _____ Date _____

5-35

D. La journée d'Alice. Listen as Alice describes her day. Each sentence has one verb in the **imparfait** to describe what was already in progress or the circumstances and one in the **passé composé** to tell what happened. Pause the recording after each sentence and put the two verbs and their subjects in the appropriate column.

> **EXEMPLE**   VOUS ENTENDEZ: Il faisait beau quand je suis
> sortie de l'appartement.
>
> VOUS ÉCRIVEZ:

WHAT WAS IN PROGRESS / CIRCUMSTANCES	WHAT HAPPENED
EXEMPLE **il faisait**	**je suis sortie**

1. _____   _____

2. _____   _____

3. _____   _____

4. _____   _____

5. _____   _____

6. _____   _____

5-36

E. Une sortie. Listen as Alice talks about the last time she and Vincent went to a restaurant. First, listen to the conversation at normal speed. Then, listen again and fill in the missing words as it is repeated at a slower speed. Pause the recording as needed to have sufficient time to respond. Play this section again to correct your work.

On _____ **(1)** ensemble au restaurant samedi soir. On _____ **(2)** la maison vers sept heures. Comme *(Since)* il _____ **(3)** beau, on _____ **(4)** au restaurant à pied. Il _____ **(5)** environ sept heures et demie quand on _____ **(6)**. Je _____ **(7)** très faim et on _____ **(8)** tout de suite. On _____ **(9)** un verre de vin avant. Le repas _____ **(10)** délicieux et j'_____ **(11)**. Après, nous _____ **(12)** trop fatigués; alors nous _____ **(13)** une promenade. Il _____ **(14)** environ dix heures quand nous _____ **(15)** et nous _____ **(16)** directement au lit. Le lendemain, c'_____ **(17)** dimanche et j'_____ **(18)** jusqu'à onze heures.

COMPÉTENCE 4

Narrating in the past

By the time you finish this **Compétence,** you should be able to recount a story in the past.

Partie écrite

A. Le Magicien d'Oz. Éric is telling Michèle about his favorite childhood movie when he was growing up in America, *The Wizard of Oz.* Complete the following sentences by putting the verb describing what was already in progress in the **imparfait** and the verb saying what happened while it was in progress in the **passé composé.** The first one has been done as an example.

1. Une jeune fille appelée Dorothy _____**habitait**_____ (habiter) chez son oncle et sa tante au Kansas quand une violente tornade _____**est arrivée**_____ (arriver).

2. La tornade _____ (transporter) la maison où Dorothy _____ (dormir) dans un pays imaginaire.

3. Quand elle _____ (sortir) de la maison après la tornade, elle n' _____ (être) plus *(no longer)* au Kansas.

4. Après quelques minutes dans ce pays fabuleux, elle _____ (rencontrer) les Microsiens *(Munchkins)*, les petites personnes qui y _____ (habiter).

5. Les Microsiens _____ (poser) des questions à Dorothy quand Glinda, la bonne sorcière du Nord *(witch of the North)* _____ (arriver).

6. Dorothy _____ (parler) à Glinda quand elle _____ (voir) une mauvaise sorcière morte sous sa maison.

7. Glinda _____ (donner) à Dorothy les chaussures de rubis que la sorcière morte _____ (porter).

8. Ensuite, une autre mauvaise sorcière, la sœur de la sorcière morte, _____ (venir) chercher les chaussures de rubis parce qu'elles _____ (être) magiques.

9. Avant de partir, elle _____ (avertir *[to warn]*) Dorothy qu'elle _____ (aller) l'avoir *(to get her)*.

10. La bonne sorcière _____ (recommander) à Dorothy de suivre un chemin *(road)* de briques jaunes pour aller voir le Magicien d'Oz à la cité d'Émeraude si elle _____ (vouloir) rentrer au Kansas.

11. Sur le chemin de briques jaunes, Dorothy _____ (rencontrer) un épouvantail *(scarecrow)* sans cervelle *(brain)*, un homme en fer blanc *(tin)* sans cœur *(heart)* et un lion qui _____ (avoir) peur de tout.

12. Ils _____ (décider) d'accompagner Dorothy à la cité d'Émeraude pour voir si le magicien _____ (pouvoir) les aider aussi.

B. Conversation. Reread the conversation where Cathy asks Éric about his weekend on page 242 of your textbook. Then, complete this conversation in which Éric asks Cathy about her weekend.

ÉRIC: Tu _____ **(1)** samedi soir?
              (stayed home)

CATHY: Oui, _____ **(2)**, alors _____ **(3)**
                    (I was tired)   *(I rented)*

          le film *Le Cinquième Élément* en DVD.

ÉRIC: J'adore ce film! C'est un bon film d'action avec un peu d'humour. _____ **(4)**?
                                                                                        (Did you like it)

CATHY: Oui, _____ **(5)**. C'était excellent.
                    (I liked it a lot)

          Les acteurs, les dialogues et _____ **(6)** vraiment
                                                    (the special effects were)

          extra, mais _____ **(7)**.
                              (there was a little too much violence)

C. Un entretien (interview). Alice is telling about an interview with an applicant for a position with her company. First, read a version in English and identify the six verbs indicating something that happened in the sequence of events of the interview. The first one has been done as an example.

1. _____arrived_____   4. _____

2. _____   5. _____

3. _____   6. _____

When I *arrived* at the office, she *was* already there. She *was* a pleasant young woman, but she *looked* very nervous. She *was wearing* a very nice dress and it *was* evident that she really *wanted* to have this position. We *went* into my office and we *began* to talk. She *was* Belgian and she *was going* to finish her studies in Brussels soon, where she *wanted* to work in our new office. She *spoke* not only French, but also English, Dutch, and a little German. We *did* part of the interview in English and her accent *was* excellent. We *spoke* for more than an hour. When she *left*, I *was* almost sure that I *was going* to hire her, but I *could* not say anything because there *were* still two other candidates.

Now, complete the same paragraph in French. Use the **passé composé** for the six verbs indicating something that happened in the sequence of events and the **imparfait** for the remaining verbs. Remember, these indicate something that was already true or in progress when those events happened. The first one has been done as an example.

Quand je (j') ___*je suis arrivée*___ **(1)** (arriver) au bureau, elle _____ **(2)** (être) déjà là.

C'_____ **(3)** (être) une jeune femme agréable, mais elle _____ **(4)** (avoir)

l'air très nerveuse. Elle _____ **(5)** (porter) une très belle robe et c'_____ **(6)**

(être) évident qu'elle _____ **(7)** (vouloir) vraiment avoir ce poste. Nous

_____ **(8)** (aller) dans mon bureau et nous _____ **(9)**

(commencer) à parler. Elle _____ **(10)** (être) belge et elle _____ **(11)**

(aller) bientôt terminer ses études à Bruxelles où elle _____ **(12)** (vouloir) travailler dans

notre nouveau bureau. Elle _____ **(13)** (parler) non seulement français, mais aussi anglais,

néerlandais et un peu allemand. Nous _____ **(14)** (faire) une partie de l'entretien en anglais et son accent _____ **(15)** (être) excellent. Nous _____ **(16)** (parler) plus

d'une heure. Quand elle _____ **(17)** (partir), j'_____ **(18)** (être) presque

certaine que je (j') _____ **(19)** (aller) l'embaucher, mais je ne (n') _____ **(20)**

(pouvoir) rien dire parce qu'il y _____ **(21)** (avoir) encore deux autres candidats.

D. Le Petit Chaperon rouge. Retell the story of *Little Red Riding Hood* by
putting the verbs in parentheses in the **passé composé** or the **imparfait.** The first
one has been done as an example.

Une petite fille _____*habitait*_____ **(1)** (habiter) avec sa mère dans une grande

forêt. Elle _____ **(2)** (ne pas avoir) de père mais sa grand-mère

_____ **(3)** (habiter) dans une petite maison de l'autre côté de la

forêt. On appelait cette petite fille le Petit Chaperon rouge parce qu'elle _____ **(4)** (porter)

toujours un chaperon rouge. Un jour, sa mère _____ **(5)** (demander) au Petit Chaperon rouge

d'apporter un panier *(to take a basket)* de bonnes choses à manger à sa grand-mère et la petite fille

_____ **(6)** (partir) tout de suite. Elle _____ **(7)** (traverser *[to*

cross]) la forêt quand un grand loup *(wolf)* _____ **(8)** (sortir) de derrière un arbre. Il

_____ **(9)** (avoir) très faim et il _____ **(10)** (vouloir) savoir *(to know)* où le

Petit Chaperon rouge _____ **(11)** (aller) avec toutes ces choses à manger. Le Petit Chaperon

rouge _____ **(12)** (expliquer *[to explain]*) qu'elle les _____ **(13)**

(apporter) chez sa grand-mère. Le loup _____ **(14)** (partir) dans la forêt et la petite fille

_____ **(15)** (continuer) son chemin *(way)*. Mais le loup _____ **(16)**

(prendre) un chemin plus court pour aller chez la grand-mère et il _____ **(17)** (arriver) le

premier. Comme la porte _____ **(18)** (ne pas être) fermée, il _____ **(19)**

(entrer) dans la maison. Il _____ **(20)** (manger) la grand-mère toute entière

(whole) et _____ **(21)** (prendre) sa place. Quelques minutes plus tard, sa petite-fille

_____ **(22)** (entrer) dans la chambre. Il y _____ **(23)** (avoir) très peu de

lumière *(light)* et le Petit Chaperon rouge _____ **(24)** (ne pas pouvoir)

très bien voir. La petite fille _____ **(25)** (commencer) à parler à sa grand-mère.

À ce moment-là, le loup _____ **(26)** (sauter *[to jump]*) du lit,

il _____ **(27)** (manger) le Petit Chaperon rouge tout entier et il _____ **(28)**

(sortir) de la maison. Par hasard *(By chance),* un chasseur *(hunter)* _____ **(29)**

(passer) devant la maison à ce moment-là. Il _____ **(30)** (voir) le loup

et il le (l') _____ **(31)** (tuer *[to kill]*). Quand il a ouvert le ventre *(belly)* du loup,

la petite fille et sa grand-mère _____ **(32)** (sortir) vivantes *(alive)*

parce que le loup les avait mangées tout entières.

E. Leur départ. David and Catherine, two of Alice's American friends, went to visit her in Paris. Say what happened the day they left by putting the verbs in the **passé composé** or the **imparfait.**

© Cengage Learning

Le jour de leur départ, David et Catherine __*pouvaient*__ (pouvoir) prendre leur temps parce que leur

avion _____ **(1)** (aller) partir à onze heures et demie, alors David _____ **(2)**

(sortir) faire du jogging à six heures et demie parce qu'il _____ **(3)** (vouloir) faire un peu

d'exercice. Catherine _____ **(4)** (vouloir) rester au lit et elle _____ **(5)** (dormir)

encore un peu. Quand David _____ **(6)** (rentrer) du parc, ils _____ **(7)**

(prendre) un bain et ils _____ **(8)** (faire) leurs bagages. Ils _____ **(9)** (prendre)

tranquillement leur petit déjeuner quand soudainement, David _____ **(10)** (remarquer) qu'il

_____ **(11)** (être) déjà dix heures. Ils _____ **(12)** (devoir) être à l'aéroport

au moins une heure avant leur vol, alors ils _____ **(13)** (ne pas avoir) beaucoup de temps. Ils

_____ **(14)** (sortir) rapidement de la cuisine pour aller chercher leurs bagages et Catherine

_____ **(15)** (aller) dans le salon pour appeler un taxi. Le taxi _____ **(16)**

(arriver) vingt minutes plus tard et ils _____ **(17)** (partir) pour l'aéroport à onze heures moins le

quart. Heureusement, ils _____ **(18)** (arriver) à temps parce que l'avion _____ **(19)**

(partir) à midi, avec trente minutes de retard. Catherine _____ **(20)** (être) très fatiguée et elle

_____ **(21)** (dormir) pendant le vol.

---

*Journal. Write a paragraph in French recounting a recent outing or a trip with friends. Set the scene and give the background information using the **imparfait** and name as many things as you can that happened using the **passé composé.** Include such details as what day it was, what the weather was like, and who was with you. Then tell when you got there, what it was like, and what happened or what you did.

_____

_____

_____

_____

_____

_____

_____

_____

_____

_____

Partie auditive

5-37

A. La Belle et la Bête. Listen as the narrator recounts the summary of the story of *Beauty and the Beast* from page 242 of the textbook. Afterward, you will hear a series of questions. Indicate the answer to each one.

1. deux _____   trois _____

2. plus jeune _____   plus âgée _____

3. horrible et féroce _____   jolie et douce _____

4. horrible et féroce _____   jolie et douce _____

5. il a pris sa place _____   il l'a emprisonné _____

6. de prendre sa place _____   de l'emprisonner _____

7. tout de suite _____   petit à petit _____

8. Belle _____   la Bête _____

9. à apprécier la Bête _____   à aimer _____

5-38

B. Leur arrivée à Paris. Alice's friends David and Catherine came to visit her in Paris. Listen to the description of their arrival and complete it with the missing verbs.

Quand David et Catherine _____ **(1)** à Paris, ils _____ **(2)** très fatigués et le premier soir ils _____ **(3)** se reposer *(to rest)* un peu avant de téléphoner à Alice. Ils _____ **(4)** un taxi pour aller à leur hôtel, qui _____ **(5)** loin de la tour Eiffel. À l'hôtel, il y _____ **(6)** un petit problème parce que leur réservation _____ **(7)** pour la semaine suivante. Comme *(Since)* il n'y _____ **(8)** pas d'autres chambres disponibles *(available)*, ils _____ **(9)** chercher un autre hôtel. Le réceptionniste de l'hôtel _____ **(10)** à d'autres hôtels pour trouver une autre chambre quand tout d'un coup il y _____ **(11)** une annulation *(cancellation)* à l'hôtel. David et Catherine _____ **(12)** rester là où ils _____ **(13)**. Ils _____ **(14)** tout de suite dans leur chambre. C'_____ **(15)** une très belle chambre avec une vue magnifique de la tour Eiffel. Comme ils _____ **(16)** fatigués, ils _____ **(17)** quelques heures avant de sortir.

Line art on this page: © Cengage Learning

Now complete the following sentences with the indicated verbs in the **passé composé** or **imparfait** and the appropriate ending in the last blank.

EXEMPLE   David et Catherine **n'ont pas téléphoné** (ne pas téléphoner) à Alice tout de suite parce qu'ils *étaient* (être) trop **fatigués.**

1. Pour aller à leur hôtel, ils _____ (prendre) un _____.

2. Ils _____ (avoir) un problème à l'hôtel parce que leur réservation _____ (être) pour la semaine _____.

3. Le réceptionniste _____ (téléphoner) à d'autres hôtels quand il y _____ (avoir) une _____.

4. Leur chambre _____ (être) très belle et ils _____ (avoir) une très belle vue de la _____.

C. Pourquoi? Indicate the logical circumstances explaining why David and Catherine did each thing you hear mentioned. Then as you hear the correct response, check your work.

EXEMPLE   VOUS VOYEZ: Ils cherchaient du travail. / Ils voulaient voir Alice.
              VOUS ENTENDEZ: Pourquoi est-ce que David et Catherine ont fait un voyage à Paris?
              VOUS INDIQUEZ: **Ils voulaient voir Alice.**
              VOUS ENTENDEZ: Ils ont fait un voyage à Paris parce qu'ils voulaient voir Alice.

1. Ils voulaient dormir un peu. ____   Ils ne voulaient pas voir Alice. ____

2. Ils trouvaient Paris ennuyeux. ____   Ils étaient fatigués. ____

3. Ils avaient une réservation pour la semaine suivante. ____   Ils avaient une jolie chambre. ____

4. Ils avaient une vue magnifique de la tour Eiffel. ____   Ils n'avaient pas de fenêtres. ____

5. Ils aimaient beaucoup leur chambre d'hôtel. ____   Ils voulaient voir Paris. ____

6. Ils n'avaient pas faim. ____   Ils aimaient la cuisine française. ____

7. Ils parlaient français. ____   Ils ne parlaient pas français. ____

*D. Et vous? Answer the following questions about the last time you went out with someone.

1. _____

2. _____

3. _____

4. _____

5. _____

6. _____

La vie quotidienne Chapitre

 COMPÉTENCE 1

Describing your daily routine

By the time you finish this **Compétence,** you should be able to describe your daily routine.

Partie écrite

A. D'abord. Number the activities in each pair in the order they would logically occur.

EXEMPLE __2__ Je me lève.
  __1__ Je me réveille.

1. ___ Je me déshabille.
  ___ Je prends un bain.

2. ___ Je quitte la maison.
  ___ Je m'habille.

3. ___ Je rentre de mes cours.
  ___ Je me repose.

4. ___ Je m'endors.
  ___ Je me couche.

5. ___ Je me lève.
  ___ Je me brosse les dents.

6. ___ Je m'habille.
  ___ Je me lève.

B. Ma routine. Complete the sentences by choosing the logical verb in parentheses for each blank.

EXEMPLE **Je m'endors** facilement tous les soirs, mais le matin, **je me réveille** avec difficulté. (je me réveille, je m'endors)

1. _____ vers sept heures et demie d'habitude et _____ tout de suite, mais quelquefois je reste au lit une demi-heure si je suis fatiguée. (je me réveille, je me lève)

2. _____ presque toujours avant de prendre le petit déjeuner. Généralement, _____ une jupe et un pull pour aller en cours. (je m'habille, je mets)

3. Après le petit déjeuner, _____ les dents et _____ la figure. (je me lave, je me brosse)

4. Après ça, _____ et _____ les cheveux. (je me maquille, je me brosse)

5. Le soir, je révise mes cours et après, _____ un peu. Vers dix heures, _____ et je mets mon pyjama. (je me déshabille, je me repose)

6. _____ vers onze heures et _____ rapidement. (je m'endors, je me couche)

C. Conversation. Reread the conversation between Rosalie and Rose on page 263 of your textbook. Then, complete this paragraph in which Rose's cousin Patricia describes her routine.

D'habitude, _____ **(1)** vers 7 heures et je fais _____ **(2)**
        (I get up)   *(quickly)*

ma toilette. Je passe _____ **(3)** dans la salle de bains.
                        (a half hour)

_____ **(4)** et _____ **(5)**.
        (I put on make-up)   *(I get dressed)*

Je suis _____ **(6)** en moins d' _____ **(7)**.
        (ready)   *(one hour)*

Je dois _____ **(8)** mon mari parce qu'on quitte la maison ensemble.
        (to wait for)

D. Que font-ils? Complete the following sentences in French saying what these people are doing. Choose from the verbs listed and be sure to conjugate the verb.

se réveiller	s'habiller	prendre un bain
se brosser les dents	prendre une douche	se laver la figure
se coucher	se brosser les cheveux	

Exemple
EXEMPLE Abdul **s'habille.**

1. Francine _____.

2. Lucie _____.

3. Lin _____.

4. Clara _____.

5. Manon _____.

6. Sarah _____.

7. Arthur _____.

Line art on this page: © Cengage Learning

E. Chez Rose. Rose is talking about her family's routine back at home in Atlanta. Complete what she says by conjugating the verbs in parentheses in the *present tense*. The first one has been done as an example.

Le matin, je **me réveille (1)** (se réveiller) vers 6h30 et ma mère et moi, nous

_____ **(2)** (se lever) vers 6h45. Mes deux frères _____ **(3)** (se lever)

bien après, vers 8h30. Quelquefois, mon frère Alain _____ **(4)** (se recoucher)

parce qu'il _____ **(5)** (se coucher) très tard le soir et il est fatigué. Je

_____ **(6)** (prendre) mon bain le soir, alors, le matin je _____

(7) (se laver) la figure et les mains, je _____ **(8)** (se maquiller) et je

_____ **(9)** (s'habiller). Ma mère _____ **(10)** (ne pas

se maquiller). Mes deux frères font leur toilette et ils _____ **(11)** (s'habiller).

Et vous? À quelle heure est-ce que vous _____ **(12)** (se lever)?

F. Pour mieux lire: *Using word families.* Skim the paragraph on the right and find the verb from the same word family as each of the following nouns.

> **EXEMPLE**   un habitant   **habite**

1. un passage   _____
2. une plante   _____
3. un arrêt de bus   _____
4. un regard   _____
5. l'admiration   _____
6. la ressemblance   _____
7. la vie   _____

> André Dupont habite depuis toujours à Rouen. Il passe des heures dans son jardin où il plante des rosiers ravissants. Tous les gens du quartier s'arrêtent pour regarder son beau jardin. Un jour, une jeune fille admire son jardin. Elle ressemble à quelqu'un qu'André aimait quand il était jeune, une fille qui est partie vivre aux États-Unis.

G. André et Rosalie. Reread the story **Il n'est jamais trop tard!** on pages 268–269 of the textbook and select the correct completion for each sentence below.

© Cengage Learning

1. André est *célibataire / marié / divorcé / veuf.*
2. Rosalie est *célibataire / mariée / divorcée / veuve.*
3. André est tombé amoureux de Rosalie *il y a longtemps / récemment.*
4. Rosalie s'est mariée avec *un Anglais / un Américain / un Français.*
5. Rosalie a quitté *Rouen / Paris* pour aller vivre *à Houston / à Atlanta.*
6. Rosalie est revenue en France pour voir *son frère / son ami André / ses parents.*
7. Rosalie est venue en France avec *sa fille / son mari / sa petite-fille.*

*H. Et votre journée? Answer the following questions with complete sentences.

1. Est-ce que vous vous réveillez facilement le matin?

   _____

2. Est-ce que vous vous levez tout de suite?

   _____

3. Quel jour est-ce que vous vous levez le plus tôt *(the earliest)*?

   _____

4. Préférez-vous prendre un bain ou une douche?

   _____

5. Est-ce que vous vous lavez les cheveux tous les jours?

   _____

6. Combien de fois par jour est-ce que vous vous brossez les dents?

   _____

7. Est-ce que vous vous habillez avant le petit déjeuner ou après?

   _____

8. Avec qui est-ce que vous vous amusez le plus *(the most)*?

   _____

9. Est-ce que vous vous ennuyez quand vous êtes seul(e)?

   _____

10. Est-ce que vous vous reposez ou est-ce que vous travaillez le week-end?

    _____

11. À quelle heure est-ce que vous vous couchez le samedi soir?

    _____

12. Est-ce que vous vous endormez facilement ou avec difficulté en général?

    _____

Partie auditive

A. Chez Henri et Patricia. You will hear several statements about the daily lives of Patricia and Henri. Label each drawing with the number of the statement describing it. The first one has been done as an example.

6-2

a. ___1___

b. _____

c. _____

d. _____

e. _____

f. _____

B. Ma routine quotidienne. Indicate the most logical ending to each sentence you hear. Then listen to the completed sentence to check your work, repeating after the speaker.

6-3

EXEMPLE VOUS ENTENDEZ: Je me réveille…
VOUS INDIQUEZ: ___ la figure et les mains. / _✓_ et je me lève tout de suite.
VOUS ENTENDEZ: Je me réveille et je me lève tout de suite.
VOUS RÉPÉTEZ: **Je me réveille et je me lève tout de suite.**

1. ___ une douche. / ___ avant le petit déjeuner.

2. ___ les cheveux. / ___ un bain.

3. ___ dans la salle de bains. / ___ un bain.

4. ___ je n'ai rien à faire. / ___ je m'amuse avec mes amis.

5. ___ les cheveux. / ___ les mains.

6. ___ la figure et les mains. / ___ sur le canapé.

7. ___ je prends ma douche. / ___ je sors.

8. ___ je n'ai rien à faire. / ___ je me réveille.

9. ___ je dois beaucoup travailler. / ___ je sors avec des amis.

10. ___ je m'endors. / ___ je quitte la maison.

Line art on this page: © Cengage Learning

🔊 **C. La routine chez Patricia.** You will hear Patricia talk about her daily routine. First, listen to what she
6-4 says at normal speed. Then, fill in the missing words as it is repeated more slowly.

Le matin, _____ **(1)** en premier. Henri

_____ **(2)** facilement et _____ **(3)**

un peu après moi. Ensuite, les enfants _____ **(4)** et

nous mangeons. Après, Henri et moi, _____ **(5)**

et _____ **(6)**. Henri _____ **(7)**

et _____ **(8)**. Les enfants

_____ **(9)** et _____ **(10)**.

Le soir, Henri et les enfants _____ **(11)** ensemble mais

_____ **(12)**. _____ **(13)**

et _____ **(14)** vers 10 heures. Et toi, à quelle heure est-ce

que _____ **(15)**? _____ **(16)**

facilement?

🔊 **D. Les enfants de Patricia et Henri.** Rose is going to babysit her cousin's
6-5 children for the weekend. Listen to their conversation, then indicate the appropriate
completion for each of these sentences.

© Cengage Learning

1. Le samedi, les enfants se lèvent vers _____ *8h* _____ *9h* _____ *10h.*

2. Ils s'habillent _____ *avant* _____ *après* leur petit déjeuner.

3. Pour s'amuser quand il pleut, ils aiment _____ *aller dans le jardin* _____
   jouer à des jeux vidéo _____ *regarder un DVD.*

4. En semaine, ils se couchent à 9h mais _____ *le samedi* _____ *le dimanche*, ils se couchent un
   peu plus tard.

5. Avant de se coucher, ils _____ *mangent quelque chose* _____ *jouent à des jeux vidéo* _____
   prennent un bain.

🔊 ***E. Et vous?** Answer the questions you hear in complete sentences in French.
6-6

1. _____

2. _____

3. _____

4. _____

5. _____

6. _____

COMPÉTENCE 2

Talking about relationships

By the time you finish this **Compétence,** you should be able to talk about personal relationships.

Partie écrite

A. André et Rosalie se retrouvent. Tell what happens between André and Rosalie, using the indicated verbs in the *present tense.*

se disputer   s'embrasser   se parler   se quitter   se regarder   se retrouver

| Exemple | 1 | 2 | 3 | 4 | 5 |

EXEMPLE   André et Rosalie **se regardent.**

1. Ils _____.

2. Ils _____ pendant des heures.

3. Ils _____ vers 7 heures.

4. Ils _____ au café presque tous les jours.

5. Ils _____ rarement.

B. Conversation. Reread the conversation between Rose and Rosalie on page 270 of your textbook. Then, complete this conversation between Rose and Isabelle.

ISABELLE: Ton copain et toi, vous _____ **(1)** en général?
(get along well)

ROSE: Non, nous _____ **(2)** très bien. Nous
(don't get along)

_____ **(3)** souvent. Nous passons beaucoup de temps
(argue)

ensemble mais nous ne nous parlons pas de choses importantes.

ISABELLE: _____ **(4)**! Et comment est
(That's too bad)

_____ **(5)** entre Rosalie et André?
(the relationship)

ROSE: Moi, je _____ **(6)** d'une telle relation. Ils _____ **(7)**
(dream)   *(meet each other)*

tous les jours et ils _____ **(8)** bien
(get along)

_____ **(9)**. Tu sais, ils vont _____ **(10)**
(most of the time)   *(to marry)*

et ils vont _____ **(11)** à Rouen. Je suis certaine qu'ils vont être très

       (to settle)

_____ **(12)** ensemble.

    (happy)

*C. Entre amis. A classmate is asking about you and your best friend. Complete his questions with the correct form of the indicated verb, then answer them with complete sentences.

    EXEMPLE   Vous **vous disputez** (se disputer) quelquefois?
                      Oui, on se dispute quelquefois. / Non, on ne se dispute jamais.

1. Où est-ce que vous _____ (se retrouver) le plus souvent *(the most often)*

    quand vous sortez ensemble?

    _____

2. Est-ce que vous _____ (se parler) de tout?

    _____

3. Vous _____ (s'entendre) toujours bien?

    _____

4. Quand vous _____ (se disputer), est-ce que vous

    _____ (se réconcilier) facilement?

    _____

    _____

D. Préférences. Say whether or not these people like to do the indicated things. Then say whether they are or are not going to do them tomorrow.

    EXEMPLE   se lever tôt
                      Moi, j'aime me lever tôt. / Moi, je n'aime pas me lever tôt.
                      Demain, je vais me lever tôt. / Demain, je ne vais pas me lever tôt.

1. se lever tout de suite

    Moi, je/j' _____.

    Demain matin, je _____.

2. s'amuser ensemble

    Mes amis et moi, nous _____.

    Demain soir, nous _____.

3. se coucher très tôt

    Mon meilleur ami (Ma meilleure amie) _____.

    Demain, il/elle _____.

4. se retrouver chez moi

    Mes amis _____.

    Demain soir, ils _____.

E. Et vous? First, review the **-re** verbs on page 276 of the textbook. Then, complete these sentences with the *present tense* of the verb given in either the affirmative or the negative to make them true for you.

EXEMPLE Je **perds / ne perds pas** (perdre) facilement patience.

1. En cours de français, les étudiants _____ (entendre) le professeur sans problème.

2. La plupart du temps, je _____ (répondre) correctement aux questions du prof.

3. Le prof _____ (s'entendre) bien avec les étudiants.

4. En cours, nous _____ (perdre) notre temps.

5. Je/J' _____ (attendre) le week-end avec impatience!

F. Les verbes en -re. Complete the following description of Rosalie's date with André with the indicated **-re** verbs. Remember, you also use the *simple present tense* to say someone *is doing* something in French (*I am waiting* = **j'attends**). The first one has been done as an example.

Rosalie fait le lit quand elle **entend** (1) *(hears)* le téléphone sonner.

Elle _____ (2) *(answers)* et c'est André qui veut

_____ (3) *(to visit)* Rosalie chez son

frère. Rosalie préfère aller au café en ville. À l'arrêt de bus, elle rencontre deux

vieilles amies de son enfance *(childhood)* qui _____ (4) *(are waiting for)*

le bus. En ville, ses amies _____ (5) *(get off)* du bus au même

arrêt que Rosalie et elles parlent pendant presque une heure. Quand Rosalie arrive au café, elle est très en

retard *(late)*, mais André _____ (6) *(is waiting)* parce qu'il ne

_____ (7) *(loses)* presque jamais patience.

Now tell the preceding story in the past. Use the **passé composé** for verbs narrating the sequence of events and the **imparfait** for those that set the scene or describe an action already in progress when something else happened. The first sentence has been done as an example.

Rosalie faisait le lit quand elle **a entendu** (1) (entendre) le téléphone sonner. Elle

_____ (2) (répondre) et c' _____ (3)

(être) André qui _____ (4) (vouloir) rendre visite à Rosalie

chez son frère. Rosalie _____ (5) (préférer) aller au café en ville.

Quand elle _____ (6) (arriver) à l'arrêt de bus pour aller

retrouver André en ville, elle _____ (7) (rencontrer) deux

vieilles amies de son enfance qui _____ (8) (attendre)

le bus. En ville, ses amies _____ (9) (descendre) du bus au même arrêt

que Rosalie et elles _____ (10) (parler) pendant presque une heure.

Quand Rosalie _____ (11) (arriver)

au café, elle _____ (12) (être) très en retard, mais André

_____ (13) (attendre) parce qu'il ne perd presque jamais patience.

*G. Et toi? Your friend is asking you about your travel habits. Complete his questions with the correct form of the given verb in the *present tense*. Then, answer his questions with complete sentences.

1. Avec qui préfères-tu voyager? Est-ce que tu _____ (s'entendre) toujours bien

    avec cette personne?

    _____

    _____

2. Tu _____ (rendre souvent visite) à des amis ou à des parents

    qui habitent dans une autre ville?

    _____

    _____

3. Si tu voyages en avion et que la compagnie aérienne _____ (perdre) tes bagages,

    est-ce que tu _____ (perdre) patience ou est-ce que tu _____

    (attendre) patiemment?

    _____

    _____

4. Tu _____ (descendre) souvent dans un hôtel de luxe?

    _____

5. Tu _____ (se perdre) facilement dans une nouvelle ville?

    _____

*Journal. Describe an ideal relationship between a happy couple. How often do they talk to each other? phone each other? get together? What do they do for each other? Do they talk to each other about everything? How do they get along? Do they argue? Write at least six sentences.

Dans un couple heureux, on…

_____

_____

_____

_____

_____

_____

_____

_____

_____

Partie auditive

A. Rosalie et André. You will hear a series of statements about Rosalie and André's interactions. After each one, stop the recording and write a statement to restate what they do to or for each other. Turn on the recording and check your response.

EXEMPLE VOUS ENTENDEZ: André rencontre Rosalie et Rosalie rencontre André.
VOUS ÉCRIVEZ: Ils **se rencontrent.**
VOUS ENTENDEZ: Ils se rencontrent.

1. Ils _____.

2. Ils _____.

3. Ils _____.

4. Ils _____.

5. Ils _____.

B. Mon ami(e) et moi. You will hear a series of statements about what you and your best friend do to and for each other. Complete each statement that follows with what you hear, then circle **vrai** or **faux** to indicate whether it is true of your relationship.

EXEMPLE VOUS ENTENDEZ: Mon ami(e) et moi, nous nous téléphonons tous les jours.
VOUS COMPLÉTEZ: Mon ami(e) et moi, **nous nous téléphonons** tous les jours.
VOUS INDIQUEZ **VRAI** *or* **FAUX**

1. Mon ami(e) et moi, _____ tous les jours.   VRAI   FAUX

2. Mon ami(e) et moi, _____ très souvent des textos.   VRAI   FAUX

3. Cet(te) ami(e) et moi, _____ souvent au café.   VRAI   FAUX

4. Cet(te) ami(e) et moi, _____ presque jamais.   VRAI   FAUX

5. Mon ami(e) et moi, _____ presque toujours bien.   VRAI   FAUX

C. Qui? Patricia is talking about what she and Henri and André and Rosalie are going to do tomorrow. Repeat what Patricia says as you write the number of each statement under the corresponding illustration.

EXEMPLE VOUS ENTENDEZ: Henri et moi, nous allons nous lever à six heures.
VOUS RÉPÉTEZ: **Henri et moi, nous allons nous lever à six heures.**
VOUS ÉCRIVEZ:

a. _____   **b. Exemple**   **c.** _____   **d.** _____   **e.** _____   **f.** _____

D. Prononciation: Les verbes en -re. Some students are talking about their French class. Pause the recording and complete each sentence or question with the correct form of the **-re** verb given in the *present tense*. Then turn on the recording and repeat the sentences after the speaker.

1. Nous _____ (répondre) bien.

2. Les étudiants _____ (s'entendre) bien.

3. Le professeur _____ (attendre) ta réponse.

4. Je _____ (rendre) mes devoirs.

5. Tu _____ (entendre) toujours bien le prof en cours?

E. La routine de Rose. Rose is describing her daily routine at home in Atlanta. The first time, just listen to what she says. Then, fill in the missing words as it is repeated more slowly with pauses.

Le matin, j' _____ **(1)** le bus devant mon appartement. Quelquefois,

le bus est en retard *(late)* et je _____ **(2)** patience. Je n'aime pas

_____ **(3)**! Quand le bus arrive, je monte et je

_____ **(4)** à l'université. En cours, les étudiants ne _____ **(5)**

pas toujours correctement, mais le prof ne _____ **(6)** jamais patience avec

nous. Nous ne _____ **(7)** pas notre temps en cours – nous travaillons

bien! Après les cours, je vais souvent à mon magasin préféré où on _____ **(8)**

des livres et des DVD. Quelquefois, je _____ **(9)** à mon ami Trentin. Nous

_____ **(10)** très bien.

*F. Et toi? Answer each question a friend asks about your French class with a complete sentence.

1. _____

2. _____

3. _____

4. _____

5. _____

Talking about what you did and used to do

By the time you finish this *Compétence,* you should be able to talk about your daily routine or a relationship in the past.

Partie écrite

A. Le matin chez Rose. Use a **passé composé** form of the verbs below to complete Rose's sentences.

se lever   s'habiller   se peigner   se réveiller   prendre un bain   se brosser les dents

EXEMPLE   Le réveil a sonné et je **me suis réveillée.**

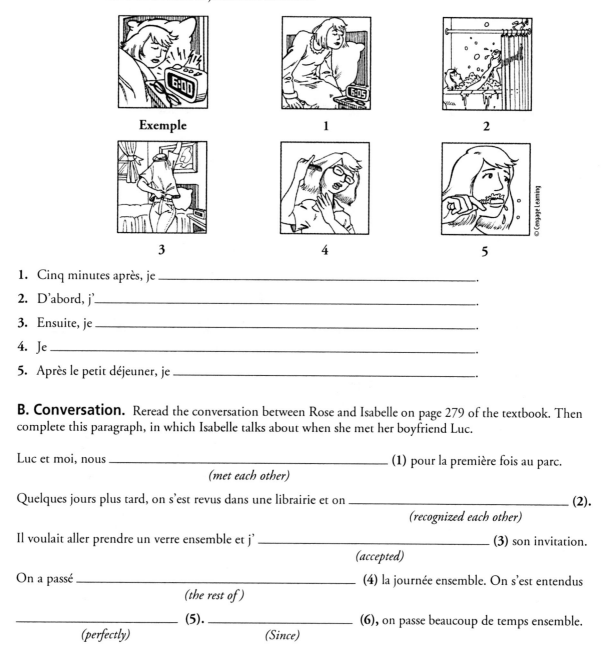

1. Cinq minutes après, je _____.

2. D'abord, j'_____.

3. Ensuite, je _____.

4. Je _____.

5. Après le petit déjeuner, je _____.

B. Conversation. Reread the conversation between Rose and Isabelle on page 279 of the textbook. Then complete this paragraph, in which Isabelle talks about when she met her boyfriend Luc.

Luc et moi, nous _____ **(1)** pour la première fois au parc.
                        (met each other)

Quelques jours plus tard, on s'est revus dans une librairie et on _____ **(2)**.
                                                                    (recognized each other)

Il voulait aller prendre un verre ensemble et j' _____ **(3)** son invitation.
                                                  (accepted)

On a passé _____ **(4)** la journée ensemble. On s'est entendus
              (the rest of)

_____ **(5).** _____ **(6),** on passe beaucoup de temps ensemble.
    (perfectly)   *(Since)*

C. La rencontre. Tell the story of how Rosalie and André met again after all of these years, using the words given. Remember that **se parler** does not require agreement of the past participle.

se quitter   se regarder   se rencontrer   se promener   s'embrasser   se parler

EXEMPLE   Rosalie et André **se sont rencontrés** chez le frère de Rosalie pour la première fois depuis des années. Ils **se sont regardés.**

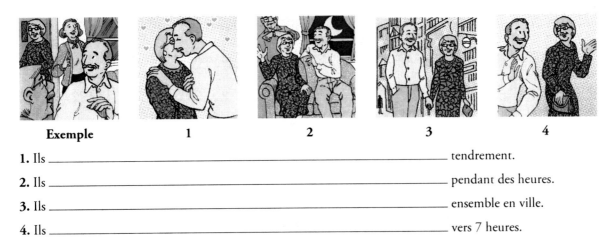

| Exemple | 1 | 2 | 3 | 4 |

1. Ils _____ tendrement.

2. Ils _____ pendant des heures.

3. Ils _____ ensemble en ville.

4. Ils _____ vers 7 heures.

D. Qui a fait ça? Patricia is talking about what happened yesterday. Using the **passé composé,** tell who she says did each of the following things. Note that the verbs with an asterisk do not require agreement of the past participle.

EXEMPLE   s'amuser ensemble: **Mes amis se sont amusés** ensemble.

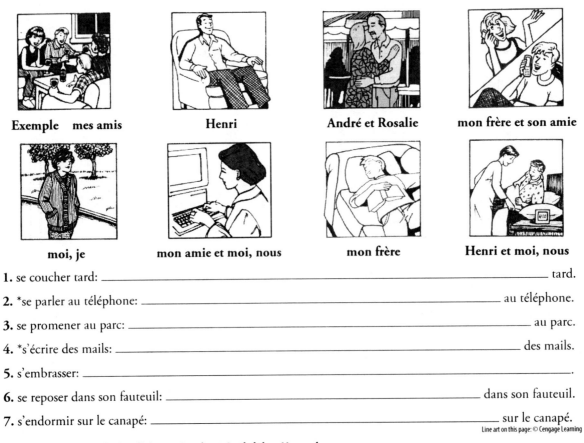

Exemple   mes amis   Henri   André et Rosalie   mon frère et son amie

moi, je   mon amie et moi, nous   mon frère   Henri et moi, nous

1. se coucher tard: _____ tard.

2. *se parler au téléphone: _____ au téléphone.

3. se promener au parc: _____ au parc.

4. *s'écrire des mails: _____ des mails.

5. s'embrasser: _____.

6. se reposer dans son fauteuil: _____ dans son fauteuil.

7. s'endormir sur le canapé: _____ sur le canapé.

E. Ce matin. Complete Rosalie's description of her day by putting the verbs in the **passé composé.** The first one has been done as an example.

Je **me suis réveillée (1)** (se réveiller) vers sept heures ce matin et Rose _____

(2) (se lever) un peu plus tard. J'_____ **(3)** (faire) ma

toilette et Rose _____ **(4)** (se laver) les

cheveux et _____ **(5)** (se maquiller) avant

de sortir. Nous _____ **(6)** (aller) en ville

et nous _____ **(7)** (bien s'amuser). Nous

_____ **(8)** (faire) du shopping, puis nous

_____ **(9)** (aller) dans un café où nous

_____ **(10)** (prendre) un verre et nous

_____ **(11)** (se reposer) un peu. Après le café,

nous _____ **(12)** (se quitter). Rose et ses amis

_____ **(13)** (se retrouver) pour aller au cinéma. Moi,

je _____ **(14)** (se promener) un peu en ville, puis je

_____ **(15)** (rentrer) à la maison.

F. Chez vous. Say whether or not you did each of these things yesterday. Then, say whether you used to do each of them when you were fifteen. Use the **passé composé** and the **imparfait** as appropriate.

> **EXEMPLE** (se réveiller facilement)
> Hier, je **(ne) me suis (pas)** réveillé(e) facilement.
> À l'âge de 15 ans, je **(ne) me réveillais (pas)** facilement.

1. (se lever tout de suite)

Hier, je _____ tout de suite.

À l'âge de 15 ans, je _____ tout de suite.

2. (s'habiller avant le petit déjeuner)

Hier, je _____ avant le petit déjeuner.

À l'âge de 15 ans, je _____ avant le petit déjeuner.

3. (se brosser les dents après le petit déjeuner)

Hier, je _____ après le petit déjeuner.

À l'âge de 15 ans, je _____ après le petit déjeuner.

4. (s'amuser avec des copains [copines])

Hier soir, je _____ avec des copains (copines).

À l'âge de 15 ans, le soir, je _____ avec des copains (copines).

G. Un souvenir du passé. Complete what André says about the past by putting the verbs in the **passé composé** or the **imparfait.** The first one has been done as an example.

Quand j'**avais (1)** (avoir) dix-huit ans, je (j') _____ **(2)** (vouloir) dire à Rosalie

combien je l'_____ **(3)** (aimer), mais j'_____ **(4)** (être) très timide.

Un beau jour, je (j') _____ **(5)** (décider) de déclarer mon amour à Rosalie. Je (J')

_____ **(6)** (prendre) mon vélo et je (j') _____ **(7)** (aller) chez Rosalie.

Mais quand je (j') _____ **(8)** (arriver) chez elle, je (j') _____ **(9)**

(trouver) Rosalie en compagnie d'un jeune Américain et ils _____ **(10)**

(se regarder) d'un regard de couple amoureux. Alors, je _____ **(11)** (rentrer) chez moi.

Peu après ça, Rosalie et son Américain _____ **(12)** (se marier)

et ils _____ **(13)** (s'installer) aux États-Unis.

*H. Ce matin. Answer these questions about your routine this morning.

1. À quelle heure est-ce que vous vous êtes réveillé(e)?

   _____

2. Étiez-vous fatigué(e) quand vous vous êtes levé(e)?

   _____

3. Vous avez pris un bain ou une douche ce matin?

   _____

4. Vous vous êtes brossé les cheveux ou vous vous êtes peigné(e)?

   _____

5. Vous vous êtes habillé(e) avant ou après le petit déjeuner?

   _____

6. À quelle heure avez-vous quitté la maison?

   _____

7. Votre meilleur(e) ami(e) et vous, vous vous êtes vu(e)s ce matin? Vous vous êtes parlé au téléphone?

   _____

   _____

8. La dernière fois que vous étiez ensemble, vous vous êtes bien amusé(e)s? Vous vous êtes disputé(e)s?

   _____

   _____

Partie auditive

A. Hier matin. You will hear pairs of sentences in which people state two things that happened yesterday. Indicate which activity most logically came *first,* **a** or **b.** Then repeat the correct answer after the speaker.

EXEMPLE	VOUS ENTENDEZ:	**a.** Le réveil a sonné. / **b.** Je me suis réveillé.
	VOUS INDIQUEZ:	**a**
	VOUS ENTENDEZ:	**a.** Le réveil a sonné.
	VOUS RÉPÉTEZ:	**a. Le réveil a sonné.**

1. _____ 2. _____ 3. _____ 4. _____ 5. _____ 6. _____

B. Une rencontre. Listen as Rosalie describes how she accidentally ran into André at the café yesterday and how they ended up spending the day together. Label each illustration with the number of the sentence describing it.

a. _____   b. _____   c. _____   d. _____   e. _____

Now play this section again, and indicate if the following statements are **vrai** or **faux.**

1. André et Rosalie se sont vus tout de suite quand ils sont arrivés au café.   VRAI   FAUX

2. Quand ils se sont vus, ils se sont embrassés.   VRAI   FAUX

3. Ils n'ont pas eu le temps de déjeuner ensemble.   VRAI   FAUX

4. André et Rosalie se sont quittés vers 7 heures.   VRAI   FAUX

🔊 6-15 ***C. Au passé composé.** The best way to learn the word order of reflexive and reciprocal verbs in the **passé composé** is to practice saying them until they sound right. As you practice saying each pair of sentences, indicate the sentence that is true for you.

1. ____ Je me suis levé(e) tôt ce matin.

   ____ Je ne me suis pas levé(e) tôt ce matin.

2. ____ Je me suis perdu(e) en ville récemment.

   ____ Je ne me suis pas perdu(e) en ville récemment.

3. ____ Je me suis endormi(e) en cours récemment.

   ____ Je ne me suis pas endormi(e) en cours récemment.

4. ____ Je me suis ennuyé(e) le week-end dernier.

   ____ Je ne me suis pas ennuyé(e) le week-end dernier.

5. ____ Mes parents et moi, nous nous sommes disputés récemment.

   ____ Nous ne nous sommes pas disputés récemment.

6. ____ Mes parents se sont mariés très jeunes.

   ____ Mes parents ne se sont pas mariés très jeunes.

🔊 6-16 **D. Hier chez Henri.** Henri is talking about what he did yesterday. The first time, just listen to what he says. Then, fill in the missing words as it is repeated more slowly with pauses.

Hier matin, _____ **(1)** vers 7 heures

mais _____ **(2)** tout de suite parce que

_____ **(3)** sommeil. _____ **(4)**

mon bain, _____ **(5)** et _____ **(6).**

Après le petit déjeuner, _____ **(7)** les dents et les cheveux et

_____ **(8)** la maison.

   Hier soir, _____ **(9)** vers 7 heures. Les

enfants et moi _____ **(10)** à des jeux vidéo et _____

_____ **(11).** Patricia _____ **(12)**

parce qu'elle _____ **(13)** fatiguée. Après le dîner, elle

_____ **(14).** Les enfants _____ **(15)**

vers 9 heures et _____ **(16)** tout de suite.

🔊 6-17 ***E. Et toi?** Answer a friend's questions about your day yesterday with complete sentences in French.

1. _____

2. _____

3. _____

4. _____

5. _____

Describing traits and characteristics

By the time you finish this *Compétence,* you should be able to talk about a relationship.

Partie écrite

A. Synonymes. Choose a synonym from the list for each set of words and write it in the blank. Then, state how you feel about these characteristics in a potential partner by indicating **a, b,** or **c.** The first part of item 1 has been done as an example.

a. C'est une qualité que j'apprécie chez un(e) partenaire.
b. C'est une qualité qui ne m'importe pas beaucoup chez un(e) partenaire.
c. C'est une qualité que je ne supporte pas chez un(e) partenaire.

la passion   la vanité   l'indifférence   la beauté   la violence   l'infidélité   la jalousie   l'indécision

1. **l'indifférence:** l'apathie, la nonchalance   a ___   b ___   c ✔

2. _____: l'envie, la rivalité   a ___   b ___   c ___

3. _____: l'hésitation, l'irrésolution   a ___   b ___   c ___

4. _____: l'amour intense, l'adoration   a ___   b ___   c ___

5. _____: la prétention, l'égotisme   a ___   b ___   c ___

6. _____: l'élégance, le charme   a ___   b ___   c ___

7. _____: la brutalité, l'agression   a ___   b ___   c ___

8. _____: l'adultère, la déloyauté   a ___   b ___   c ___

B. Traits de caractère. Complete each sentence with the logical ending from the list. The first one has been done as an example.

a un bon sens de l'humour   cultive son esprit
cultive sa spiritualité   ne supporte pas l'insensibilité
cultive sa vie professionnelle   s'intéresse à la nature
cultive son corps   s'intéresse aux arts

1. Quelqu'un qui passe beaucoup de temps dans une salle de gym **cultive son corps.**

2. Quelqu'un qui aime faire des randonnées _____.

3. Quelqu'un qui raconte souvent des histoires amusantes _____

   _____

4. Quelqu'un qui travaille beaucoup _____.

5. Quelqu'un qui apprend quelque chose tous les jours _____.

6. Quelqu'un pour qui la religion est très importante _____.

7. Quelqu'un qui aime la musique et le ballet _____.

8. Quelqu'un qui aime exprimer *(to express)* ses sentiments _____

   _____

C. Conversation. Reread the conversation between Rose and Isabelle on page 285 of the textbook. Then complete the following conversation as indicated.

Rose: Alors, tu as trouvé _____ **(1)** avec Luc?
          (happiness)

Isabelle: Oui et non. Il est un peu _____ **(2)** et ça,
          (jealous)

          _____ **(3)**. En plus, moi, je suis
          (I don't tolerate)

          _____ **(4)** et lui, il est plutôt _____ **(5)**.
          (liberal)   *(conservative)*

          Et ton copain et toi, _____ **(6)**?
          (you are interested in the same things)

Rose: Pas du tout. _____ **(7)** et
          (I am interested in the arts)

          _____ **(8)** sport. _____ **(9)**
          (he is interested in)   *(He cultivates)*

          son corps et je préfère _____ **(10)**.
          (to cultivate my mind)

D. Pronoms relatifs. Combine each pair of sentences to form one sentence by removing the italicized words from the second sentence and linking the two sentences with the indicated relative pronoun, **qui, que,** or **dont.** The first sentence in each set has been done as an example.

QUE (QU')

1. André est un vieil ami. Rosalie retrouve *ce vieil ami* tous les jours en ville.

    André est un vieil ami **que Rosalie retrouve tous les jours en ville.**

2. Rosalie est une femme. André aime beaucoup *cette femme*.

    Rosalie est une femme _____.

3. Rosalie est une personne. Rose admire *cette personne*.

    Rosalie est une personne _____.

4. Le mari de Rosalie était un Américain. Rosalie a accompagné *cet homme* à Atlanta.

    Le mari de Rosalie était un Américain _____.

QUI

1. Le mari de Rosalie était un homme. *Cet homme* aimait beaucoup Rosalie.

    Le mari de Rosalie était un homme **qui aimait beaucoup Rosalie.**

2. Le mari de Rosalie était un homme. *Cet homme* est mort récemment.

    Le mari de Rosalie était un homme _____.

3. André est un ami d'enfance. *Cet ami d'enfance* a passé toute sa vie à Rouen.

    André est un ami d'enfance _____.

4. Rosalie est une vieille amie d'André. *Cette vieille amie d'André* s'est installée à Atlanta.

    Rosalie est une vieille amie d'André _____.

DONT

1. Rosalie est une femme. André était amoureux *de cette femme* quand il était jeune.

   Rosalie est une femme **dont André était amoureux quand il était jeune.**

2. Le jeune Américain était un homme. Rosalie est tombée amoureuse *de cet homme.*

   Le jeune Américain était un homme _____.

3. Rosalie est la femme. André rêve toujours *de cette femme.*

   Rosalie est la femme _____.

4. André est un ami. Rosalie a fait la connaissance *de cet ami* il y a longtemps.

   André est un ami _____.

E. Et vous? Complete the following sentences with **qui, que (qu'),** or **dont.** Then indicate whether each statement is **vrai** or **faux** for you.

1. Je préfère un(e) partenaire _____ n'est pas jaloux (jalouse). V ____ F ____

2. J'ai beaucoup d'ami(e)s _____ s'intéressent à la politique. V ____ F ____

3. J'ai beaucoup d'ami(e)s _____ je suis jaloux (jalouse). V ____ F ____

4. L'infidélité est une chose _____ je ne supporte pas du tout. V ____ F ____

5. Je préfère un(e) partenaire _____ cultive plus son esprit que son corps. V ____ F ____

6. La beauté est une qualité _____ j'apprécie chez un(e) partenaire. V ____ F ____

7. Je préfère passer mon temps avec des amis _____ j'ai fait la connaissance récemment. V ____ F ____

8. Je préfère passer mon temps avec des amis _____ je connais *(I know)* depuis longtemps. V ____ F ____

9. J'aimerais mieux *(I would prefer)* sortir avec quelqu'un _____ je trouve beau mais un peu difficile qu'avec quelqu'un _____ je trouve sympa mais pas très beau. V ____ F ____

F. Lequel des deux? Complete the following sentences in two ways, using the appropriate relative pronouns. Then select the completion that best describes your feelings or situation.

   EXEMPLE   Je préfère me marier avec quelqu'un…
   _____✓_____ ____dont____ je suis amoureux (amoureuse).
   _____ ____qui____ a beaucoup d'argent.

1. L'amour est quelque chose…

   _____ _____ je cherche dans la vie.

   _____ _____ j'ai peur.

2. La beauté d'un(e) partenaire est une qualité…

   _____ _____ je suis facilement jaloux (jalouse).

   _____ _____ je préfère.

   _____ _____ n'a pas beaucoup d'importance pour moi.

3. Mon/Ma partenaire idéal(e) est quelqu'un…

   _____ _____ je connais *(know)* déjà.

   _____ _____ je n'ai pas encore fait la connaissance.

4. La politique est un sujet de conversation…

    _____ je trouve intéressant.

    _____ je n'aime pas parler.

5. Le grand amour est un sentiment…

    _____ arrive comme un coup de foudre.

    _____ il faut *(it is necessary)* cultiver.

6. Le grand amour est quelque chose…

    _____ on peut avoir avec plusieurs partenaires.

    _____ arrive une fois dans la vie.

7. La relation parfaite est quelque chose…

    _____ je rêve encore.

    _____ j'ai déjà trouvé.

---

*Journal. Write a description of your ideal partner. Discuss what traits you prefer and which ones you do not like. Also discuss your interests, what aspects of a relationship are important to you, and what you will not put up with in a relationship.

_____

_____

_____

_____

_____

_____

_____

_____

_____

_____

_____

_____

_____

_____

_____

_____

_____

_____

Partie auditive

A. Qualités. You will hear a series of personality traits. Decide if each one is a desirable trait or not and list it in the appropriate column.

OUI	NON
_____	_____
_____	_____
_____	_____
_____	_____

B. Citations. As you listen, fill in the missing words in these quotations. At the end, pause the recording, reread each one, and indicate whether you agree.

OUI NON **1.** Les privilèges de _____ sont immenses.
(Jean Cocteau, cinéaste)

OUI NON **2.** La fin *(end)* des _____, c'est
_____. (Yves Navarre, écrivain)

OUI NON **3.** _____ de la femme est dans ses charmes.
(Jean-Jacques Rousseau, écrivain et philosophe)

OUI NON **4.** Il y a dans _____ plus d'amour-propre *(self-love)* que d'_____. (François, duc de la Rochefoucauld, écrivain et moraliste)

OUI NON **5.** _____ ruine plus de femmes que
_____. (Marie de Chichy-Chamrond, femme de lettres)

OUI NON **6.** _____ fait les sages *(wise)* et
_____ les monstres. (Denis Diderot, écrivain et philosophe)

C. Luc. Rose is telling her grandmother about her cousin Isabelle's new boyfriend, Luc. Pause the recording and complete what Rose says with **qui, que (qu')**, or **dont.** When you are done, turn on the recording and repeat the correct answers after the speaker, verifying your responses.

1. Luc est un ami _____ a un bon sens de l'humour.
2. C'est un ami _____ Isabelle retrouve tous les jours.
3. C'est un homme _____ Isabelle parle beaucoup.
4. C'est un ami _____ les autres amis d'Isabelle sont quelquefois jaloux.
5. Luc est un homme _____ comprend bien les femmes.
6. C'est un homme _____ nous trouvons très amusant.
7. C'est l'homme _____ Isabelle aime.
8. C'est l'homme _____ Isabelle est amoureuse.

D. Vrai ou faux? You will hear the beginning of a sentence and you will see two possible endings. Select the ending that fits the sentence grammatically. You will then hear the correct answer. Indicate whether or not the completed sentence is true for you.

EXEMPLE   VOUS VOYEZ: ___ j'aime beaucoup. / ___ je suis très amoureux (amoureuse). VRAI FAUX

VOUS ENTENDEZ: Il y a une personne dont…

VOUS SÉLECTIONNEZ: _✓_ je suis très amoureux (amoureuse).

VOUS ENTENDEZ: Il y a une personne dont je suis très amoureux (amoureuse).

VOUS INDIQUEZ: VRAI (FAUX)

1. _____ a beaucoup d'importance pour moi. / _____ je trouve très importante.   VRAI   FAUX

2. _____ je parle peu avec mes amis. / _____ je n'aime pas.   VRAI   FAUX

3. _____ n'est pas très agréable. / _____ je ne supporte pas.   VRAI   FAUX

4. _____ on veut dans une relation. / _____ on a besoin dans une relation.   VRAI   FAUX

5. _____ n'a pas de sens de l'humour. / _____ je trouve ennuyeux.   VRAI   FAUX

E. Une nouvelle relation. Listen to a conversation in which two friends talk about the new girlfriend of a third friend. Then, fill in the missing words as it is repeated more slowly with pauses.

— Alors, Cyril a trouvé la femme _____ **(1)**? Qui est cette

femme, Sophie, dont _____ **(2)**?

— C'est une femme qu'il a rencontrée à la piscine près de son appartement. Ils habitent dans le même

immeuble. C'était _____ **(3)** pour Cyril.

— Tu as fait sa connaissance? Elle est comment?

— Oui, j'ai parlé avec elle l'autre jour. C'est une femme qui est vraiment

_____ **(4)** et qui a _____ **(5),** mais je pense

qu'_____ **(6)** Cyril parce que sa famille est riche.

— Alors, c'est une relation qui est basée sur _____ **(7)** et

_____ **(8)**? Il va y avoir des problèmes, non?

La bonne cuisine Chapitre 8

Ordering at a restaurant

By the time you finish this **Compétence,** you should be able to describe and order a meal at a restaurant.

Partie écrite

A. Un dîner. Indicate whether the following foods are **entrées, légumes, volailles, viandes, fruits de mer,** or **desserts.**

| crudités   soupe   pommes de terre   huîtres   rosbif   petits pois   canard   poulet |
| tarte   moules   bifteck   côtes   haricots verts   glace   homard   crevettes |

EXEMPLE   Les **crudités** sont une **entrée.**

    EXEMPLE   **1**   **2**   **3**

1. La _____ à l'oignon est une _____.

2. Le _____, le _____ et les

_____ de porc sont des _____.

3. Les _____, les _____

et les _____ sont des _____.

      4   **5**   **6**

4. Le _____ et le _____ sont des _____.

5. La _____ aux pommes et la _____ à la vanille

sont des _____.

6. Le _____, les _____,

les _____ et les _____

sont des _____.

Line art on this page: © Cengage Learning

B. Dans quel ordre? Number the following food items from 1 to 6 to indicate in what order the French would most commonly have them at a meal.

_____ de la salade   _____ du pâté   _____ de la viande avec des légumes

_____ du café   _____ du fromage   _____ de la tarte aux cerises

C. Qu'est-ce que c'est? Ask someone to pass you the following things. Since you are referring to specific items, use the definite article **(le, la, l', les)** with each one.

EXEMPLE   1   2   3

4   5   6   7

EXEMPLE   Pouvez-vous me passer la soupe, s'il vous plaît?

1. Pouvez-vous me passer _____, s'il vous plaît?

2. Pouvez-vous me passer _____, s'il vous plaît?

3. Pouvez-vous me passer _____, s'il vous plaît?

4. Pouvez-vous me passer _____, s'il vous plaît?

5. Pouvez-vous me passer _____, s'il vous plaît?

6. Pouvez-vous me passer _____, s'il vous plaît?

7. Pouvez-vous me passer _____, s'il vous plaît?

D. Conversation. Reread the conversation between André, Rosalie, and the server at a restaurant on page 306 of your textbook. Then, complete this conversation where Patricia and Henri order a meal.

LE SERVEUR: Bonsoir, monsieur. Bonsoir, madame. Aimeriez-vous _____ **(1)**?
                                                                                                    (a pre-dinner drink)

PATRICIA: Non, merci, pas ce soir.

HENRI: Pour _____ **(2).**
                          (me neither)

LE SERVEUR: Et pour dîner? _____ **(3)**?
                                            (Have you decided)

HENRI: Nous allons prendre _____ **(4)**.

                              (the 24 euro menu)

LE SERVEUR: Très bien, monsieur. Et qu'est-ce que vous désirez _____ **(5)**?

                                                        (as a first course)

HENRI: La _____ **(6)** pour nous deux.

                           (onion soup)

LE SERVEUR: Et comme _____ **(7)**?

                              (main dish)

PATRICIA: Pour moi, le _____ **(8)** s'il vous plaît.

                                  (tuna)

HENRI: Et pour moi, le _____ **(9)**.

                                  (lobster)

LE SERVEUR: Bien, monsieur. Et comme _____ **(10)**?

                                      (drink)

HENRI: _____ **(11)** de Chablis.

                       (A bottle)

E. Au restaurant. You are ordering the following things at a restaurant. Answer the waiter's questions. The first item has been done for you.

LE SERVEUR: Que voulez-vous comme entrée?

VOUS: **Le pâté,** s'il vous plaît.

LE SERVEUR: Et comme plat principal?

VOUS: Les _____ **(1)**, s'il vous plaît.

LE SERVEUR: Et avec ça, des carottes ou du riz?

VOUS: Je voudrais du _____ **(2)**, s'il vous plaît.

LE SERVEUR: Et comme boisson?

VOUS: Un verre de _____ **(3)** blanc, s'il vous plaît.
       Plus tard:

LE SERVEUR: Est-ce que vous allez prendre un dessert ce soir?

VOUS: Je vais prendre le _____ **(4)** au chocolat, s'il vous plaît.

F. Choix. Complete each blank with the logical noun in parentheses, including the appropriate article (**du, de la, de l', des, de [d']**). Remember to use **de (d')** after a negative expression or an expression of quantity.

EXEMPLE   Je prends **du fromage** à la fin du repas généralement.
Je ne prends jamais **de gâteau** parce que je suis diabétique. (fromage, gâteau)

1. Mon ami est végétarien. À chaque repas, il mange toujours _____ mais

   il ne mange pas _____. (viande, légumes)

2. Je mange _____ tous les jours. Je la préfère sans trop

   _____. (sel, soupe)

3. Au restaurant, je commande souvent _____. Je ne commande jamais

   _____ parce que je n'aime pas les fruits de mer. (rosbif, crevettes)

4. Ma femme ne mange pas _____ ni *(nor)* d'autres viandes rouges, mais

   elle mange souvent _____. (poisson, bifteck)

5. J'adore la cuisine japonaise. Je mange beaucoup _____ teriyaki avec

   _____. (riz, poulet)

6. Si tu veux être plus mince, prends _____ sans beaucoup

   _____. (sucre, desserts)

*G. Qu'est-ce que vous mangez? Complete the following questions with **du, de la, de l', des,** or **de (d')**. Then answer each question to describe your eating habits.

1. Est-ce que vous mangez _____ viande à chaque repas? Mangez-vous assez _____ légumes?

   _____

2. Faites-vous la cuisine avec beaucoup _____ sel et beaucoup _____ poivre?

   _____

3. Au petit déjeuner, prenez-vous _____ café, _____ jus de fruit, _____ lait ou _____ eau?

   _____

4. Mangez-vous beaucoup _____ poisson ou beaucoup _____ fruits de mer?

   _____

5. Avez-vous déjà mangé _____ escargots ou _____ fromage français tel que *(such as)* le brie?

   _____

6. Pour un repas léger *(light)*, préférez-vous manger _____ soupe ou _____ salade?

   _____

7. Mangez-vous plus souvent _____ gâteau, _____ tarte ou _____ glace comme dessert?

   _____

Partie auditive

A. Bon appétit! Listen to the list of dishes for each category and fill in the missing words.

Une entrée ou un hors-d'œuvre:

_____, de la soupe, de la salade de tomates, du pâté,

_____, _____

Un plat principal:

de la viande: _____, du bifteck, _____

de la volaille: _____, du poulet

du poisson: du saumon, _____

des fruits de mer: des moules, _____, des huîtres, _____

Un légume:

_____, des pommes de terre, _____

Pour finir le repas:

_____, du café, du fromage, _____,

de la glace, _____

B. Prononciation: Le _h_ aspiré. Pause the recording and review the *Prononciation* section on page 305 of the textbook. Then turn on the recording. Listen and repeat the following words and indicate whether the **h** is aspirate.

les huîtres / des huîtres / beaucoup d'huîtres	_____ *H* ASPIRÉ	_____ *H* NON-ASPIRÉ
les hors-d'œuvre / des hors-d'œuvre / beaucoup de hors-d'œuvre	_____ *H* ASPIRÉ	_____ *H* NON-ASPIRÉ
l'huile *(oil)* / de l'huile / pas d'huile	_____ *H* ASPIRÉ	_____ *H* NON-ASPIRÉ
le homard / du homard / pas de homard	_____ *H* ASPIRÉ	_____ *H* NON-ASPIRÉ
les hamburgers / des hamburgers / trop de hamburgers	_____ *H* ASPIRÉ	_____ *H* NON-ASPIRÉ
les hot-dogs / des hot-dogs / pas de hot-dogs	_____ *H* ASPIRÉ	_____ *H* NON-ASPIRÉ

C. Pour mieux comprendre: *Planning and predicting.* Listen to the following statements and questions and indicate whether each one is something the server or the customer would say by selecting **le serveur** or **le client**.

> **EXEMPLE**   VOUS ENTENDEZ: Bonsoir, messieurs. Aimeriez-vous un apéritif ce soir?
> VOUS INDIQUEZ: __✓__ le serveur   _____ le client

1. _____ le serveur _____ le client
2. _____ le serveur _____ le client
3. _____ le serveur _____ le client
4. _____ le serveur _____ le client
5. _____ le serveur _____ le client

6. _____ le serveur _____ le client
7. _____ le serveur _____ le client
8. _____ le serveur _____ le client
9. _____ le serveur _____ le client
10. _____ le serveur _____ le client

D. Le Bistrot. Pause the recording and look over the different dishes you can order as an **entrée, plat principal,** or **dessert** from this menu. Then turn on the recording, listen to a scene at the restaurant, and indicate what the woman and the man order.

La femme:

Entrée: _____

Plat principal: _____

Dessert: _____

L'homme:

Entrée: _____

Plat principal: _____

Dessert: _____

E. Qu'est-ce qu'il y a au menu? You are working at a restaurant. Answer each question, telling what there is on the menu. Use the correct forms of the partitive article. You will then hear the correct response. Check your answer and fill in the blank with the form of the partitive article in the answer: **du, de la, de l', des,** or **de.**

> **Le Bistrot - 14 €**
> Service 15% Compris
> *Adrian vous propose son petit Menu Bistrot*
> *composé uniquement de produits frais de saison.*
>
> **Première Assiette**
> 9 Huîtres "Fines de Claires nos" Sur lit de glace
> Assiette de Coquillages farcis à l'aïl
> Cocotte de moules marinières
> Salade aux lardons, Oeuf poché
> Terrine de canard maison, au poivre vert
> Plateau de fruits de mer "l'écailler" + 8 €
>
> **Deuxième Assiette**
> Brochette de poissons, beurre blanc
> Moules de pays, frites
> Sardines grillées aux herbes
> Langue de boeuf, sauce piquante
> Poêlée de Rognon de boeuf, flambée au cognac
> Bavette Poêlée à la fondue d'oignons
>
> **Troisième Assiette**
> Crème Caramel
> Fraises au vin ou fraises au sucre
> Guillantine aux pommes
> Glace et sorbet artisanaux
> Île flottante
> Coupe normande
>
> **Arrivage Journalier**
> **de Poissons, d'Huîtres et de Fruits de Mer**

EXEMPLE	VOUS ENTENDEZ:	Est-ce qu'il y a du pâté?
	VOUS DITES:	**Non, il n'y a pas de pâté.**
	VOUS ENTENDEZ:	Non, il n'y a pas de pâté.
	VOUS INDIQUEZ:	**de**

Comme entrée:

Comme plat principal:

Comme légume:

Comme dessert:

1. _____   3. _____   5. _____   7. _____

2. _____   4. _____   6. _____   8. _____

*F. Et vous? Answer the questions you hear with complete sentences.

1. _____

2. _____

3. _____

4. _____

COMPÉTENCE 2

Buying food

By the time you finish this **Compétence,** you should be able to talk about buying groceries.

Partie écrite

A. Qu'est-ce qu'on peut y acheter? List each of the items given with the store *(shown below or on the next page)* where you can buy it. The first one has been done as an example.

> des saucisses   des crevettes   des conserves   des petits pois   du canard
> une baguette   du bœuf   du poulet   du saucisson   du raisin   du jambon
> des pommes de terre   du porc   du poisson   du homard   un pain complet
> des huîtres   un pain au chocolat   des plats préparés   une tarte aux cerises

1. _____
   _____
   _____
   _____

2. des saucisses, _____
   _____
   _____
   _____

3. _____
   _____
   _____
   _____

4. _____
   _____
   _____
   _____

Line art on this page: © Cengage Learning

Nom _____ Date _____

5. _____

_____

_____

_____

B. Qu'est-ce qu'il faut? Which ingredients from the list are required to make the following dishes? Remember to use the partitive.

tomates, raisin, oignons, œufs, fromage, petits pois, pommes de terre, pommes, oranges, jambon, fraises, pain, carottes, pâté

EXEMPLE   Pour faire un sandwich au pâté, il faut **du pain** et **du pâté.**

1. Pour faire une omelette au jambon, il faut _____ et

_____ .

2. Pour faire une salade de fruits, il faut _____ ,

_____ , _____ et

_____ .

3. Pour faire un sandwich au fromage, il faut _____ et

_____ .

4. Pour faire une soupe de légumes, il faut _____ ,

_____ , _____ ,

_____ et _____ .

C. Conversation. Reread the conversation in which Rosalie is buying fruits and vegetables at the market on page 316 of the textbook. Then, complete this conversation she has at the **charcuterie** with the indicated words.

ROSALIE: Bonjour, monsieur.

LE MARCHAND: Bonjour, madame. _____ (1)?
              (What do you need today)

ROSALIE: Euh... _____ (2), une livre de jambon et
              (let's see)

_____ (3).
(a kilo of sausages)

LE MARCHAND: Alors, qu'est-ce que je peux vous proposer d'autre?

ROSALIE: Donnez-moi aussi 500 _____ (4).
              (grams of salami)

LE MARCHAND: Et voilà, 500 grammes. Et avec ça?

ROSALIE: _____ (5), merci. Ça fait combien?
              (That's all)

LE MARCHAND: Alors, ça fait _____ (6).
              (fifteen euros seventy-five)

D. Les quantités. You are buying groceries. Complete the following sentences with the logical item in parentheses for each quantity given.

> **EXEMPLE**   Je voudrais un kilo **de pommes de terre,** s'il vous plaît. (pommes de terre, vin)

1. Il me faut une douzaine _____, s'il vous plaît. (œufs, rosbif)

2. Donnez-moi cinq tranches _____, s'il vous plaît. (riz, jambon)

3. J'ai besoin d'une bouteille _____, s'il vous plaît. (oignons, eau minérale)

4. Je voudrais aussi une livre _____, s'il vous plaît. (raisin, baguette)

5. Et donnez-moi un morceau _____ aussi, s'il vous plaît. (fromage, conserves)

6. Et avec ça, un kilo _____, s'il vous plaît. (tartelettes aux fraises, oranges)

E. Dans quel magasin? Complete each sentence with the appropriate article (**du, de la, de l', un, une, des**) and the name of the store (besides the supermarket) where you can buy each item in France.

> **EXEMPLE**   On peut acheter **du** pain **à la boulangerie-pâtisserie.**

1. On peut acheter _____ conserves _____.

2. On peut acheter _____ rosbif _____.

3. On peut acheter _____ plats préparés _____.

4. On peut acheter _____ petits pois surgelés _____.

5. On peut acheter _____ tarte aux fraises _____.

6. On peut acheter _____ saumon _____.

7. On peut acheter _____ poires _____.

8. On peut acheter _____ baguette _____.

F. Un dîner de fiançailles (engagement). Complete the following story by selecting the logical articles in parentheses.

Rose a décidé de faire (**1.** un, le) dîner spécial pour Rosalie et André. Elle est allée au marché où elle a acheté tous (**2.** les, des) ingrédients pour préparer (**3.** le, du) poulet au cidre doux, (**4.** une, de la) spécialité de la région. Rose espérait aussi trouver (**5.** la, une) bonne bouteille (**6.** du, de) champagne parce qu'elle voulait célébrer les fiançailles de sa grand-mère et de son futur grand-père. Elle a cherché dans plusieurs *(several)* magasins, mais elle n'a pas trouvé (**7.** du, de) champagne. Comme c'était curieux! Quand elle est rentrée à (**8.** la, une) maison, elle a commencé à tout préparer dans (**9.** la, une) cuisine. Elle faisait la cuisine tranquillement quand soudain Rosalie est entrée.

— Bonjour, mamie, dit Rose, je prépare (**10.** le, un) bon dîner pour André et toi! C'est pour célébrer vos fiançailles.

— Merci, Rose, c'est très gentil! Mais tu sais, il te manque *(you're missing)* (**11.** une, de la) chose obligatoire pour (**12.** la, une) fête de fiançailles normande...

— Oui, je sais, mais je n'ai pas pu trouver (**13.** du, de) champagne en ville...

— Mais non! Ici, en Normandie, on préfère (**14.** le, un) cidre bouché; c'est (**15.** une, de la) vieille tradition. Mais ne t'inquiète pas... J'ai fait des courses et j'ai acheté deux bouteilles (**16.** du, de) cidre, alors nous en avons pour ce soir!

Now complete the following questions with the appropriate article. Then complete the response with the correct items according to the preceding passage.

1. Est-ce que Rose voulait acheter _____ bouteille _____ vin rouge ou _____ bouteille _____

   champagne?

   Elle voulait acheter _____.

2. Elle a acheté tous _____ ingrédients pour faire _____ spécialité de la région. Est-ce qu'elle a acheté

   _____ poulet ou _____ canard?

   Elle a acheté _____.

3. En Normandie, est-ce qu'on préfère _____ cidre *(m)* ou _____ champagne *(m)* pour _____ fête de

   fiançailles?

   On préfère _____ pour un dîner de fiançailles.

---

*Journal. Write a paragraph describing the last time you bought several things at the supermarket. Name as many things as you can that you bought, including at least three quantity expressions explaining how much you bought of different items.

_____

_____

_____

_____

_____

_____

_____

_____

_____

_____

_____

_____

_____

_____

Partie auditive

🔊 **A. Où sont-ils?** You will hear five conversations in which people are buying food items in small shops.
6-29 Match the number of each conversation with the store where it takes place.

a. _____

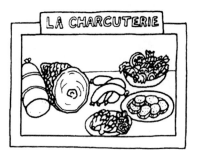

b. _____

c. _____

d. _____   e. _____

Now repeat this section and listen to the conversations again. Pause the recording and, for each conversation, indicate what the customer buys and how much he or she pays. The first one has been done as an example.

1. _du saucisson_____   _5€50_____   4. _____ _____

2. _____ _____   5. _____ _____

3. _____ _____

🔊 **B. Fruits et légumes.** As you hear an item named, identify it as a fruit or a vegetable. After a pause for
6-30 you to respond, you will hear the correct answer. Verify your response and indicate the correct choice.

EXEMPLE	VOUS ENTENDEZ:	Une carotte, c'est un fruit ou un légume?
	VOUS DITES:	**Une carotte, c'est un légume.**
	VOUS ENTENDEZ:	Une carotte, c'est un légume.
	VOUS INDIQUEZ:	___ un fruit ✓ un légume

1. ___ un fruit   ___ un légume   6. ___ un fruit   ___ un légume

2. ___ un fruit   ___ un légume   7. ___ un fruit   ___ un légume

3. ___ un fruit   ___ un légume   8. ___ un fruit   ___ un légume

4. ___ un fruit   ___ un légume   9. ___ un fruit   ___ un légume

5. ___ un fruit   ___ un légume

C. Quantités. Listen to the following items and fill in each expression of quantity that you hear.

1. Je voudrais _____ lait.

2. Je voudrais _____ vin.

3. Je voudrais _____ jambon.

4. Je voudrais _____ pommes de terre.

5. Je voudrais _____ confiture.

6. Je voudrais _____ sucre.

7. Je voudrais _____ œufs.

8. Je voudrais _____ fromage.

D. Quel article? Repeat each question you hear. After each one, pause the recording and identify the article used in the question.

EXEMPLE	VOUS ENTENDEZ:	Est-ce que vous mangez beaucoup de viande?
	VOUS RÉPÉTEZ:	**Est-ce que vous mangez beaucoup de viande?**
	VOUS INDIQUEZ:	

	for likes and preferences				for some or any				for *not any* and after a quantity
EXEMPLE	le ___	la ___	l' ___	les ___	du ___	de la ___	de l' ___	des ___	de ✓
1.	le ___	la ___	l' ___	les ___	du ___	de la ___	de l' ___	des ___	de ___
2.	le ___	la ___	l' ___	les ___	du ___	de la ___	de l' ___	des ___	de ___
3.	le ___	la ___	l' ___	les ___	du ___	de la ___	de l' ___	des ___	de ___
4.	le ___	la ___	l' ___	les ___	du ___	de la ___	de l' ___	des ___	de ___
5.	le ___	la ___	l' ___	les ___	du ___	de la ___	de l' ___	des ___	de ___
6.	le ___	la ___	l' ___	les ___	du ___	de la ___	de l' ___	des ___	de ___
7.	le ___	la ___	l' ___	les ___	du ___	de la ___	de l' ___	des ___	de ___

*Now play this section again and answer each question with a complete sentence. Pause the recording as needed in order to have time to answer.

1. _____

2. _____

3. _____

4. _____

5. _____

6. _____

7. _____

COMPÉTENCE 3

Talking about meals

By the time you finish this **Compétence,** you should be able to describe your typical meals.

Partie écrite

A. Le petit déjeuner. Identify the foods and drinks shown. Use the partitive article with each item: **du, de la, de l',** or **des.**

UN PETIT DÉJEUNER AMÉRICAIN OU CANADIEN

1   2   3   4   5

1. _____   4. _____

2. _____   5. _____

3. _____

UN PETIT DÉJEUNER FRANÇAIS

1   2   3

4   5   6

1. _____   4. _____

2. _____   5. _____

3. _____   6. _____

B. Un repas rapide. Complete these descriptions of things people eat as a quick meal with the appropriate partitive or indefinite article **(du, de la, de l', un, une, des).** Then, in the last blank, give the name of the dish that is described.

> **EXEMPLE**   C'est **une** tranche de pain avec **du** beurre et **de la** confiture. Les Français en mangent souvent le matin. C'est une **tartine.**

1. C'est _____ sandwich avec _____ viande de bœuf, _____ laitue, _____ tomate, des

   cornichons *(pickles)* et de la mayonnaise ou de la moutarde. On en mange beaucoup dans

   les fast-foods avec _____ frites. C'est un _____.

2. C'est _____ spécialité italienne avec de la sauce tomate, _____ fromage et souvent

avec _____ jambon, du pepperoni et des champignons *(mushrooms)*. C'est une _____.

3. C'est _____ plat avec _____ œufs, _____ sel et _____ poivre. On le prépare aussi avec _____

fromage, _____ jambon ou des champignons. C'est une _____.

C. Conversation.

Reread the conversation between Rose and her cousin on page 323 of your textbook. Then, complete this conversation between two friends with the indicated words.

LAURIE: _____ **(1)**? Il y a des céréales ou je peux faire
                          (Are you hungry)

_____ **(2)** si tu préfères.
              (some toast)

SOPHIE: Non, merci. _____ **(3)** le matin.
                        (I'm never very hungry)

_____ **(4)** je prendrais bien du café s'il y en a.
       (However)

LAURIE: Oui, il y a du café, mais _____ **(5),** il n'y a plus de lait.
                            (I'm sorry)

SOPHIE: Ça ne fait rien *(That doesn't matter)*. Je préfère le café sans lait. Qu'est-ce que tu vas prendre?

LAURIE: Le matin, _____ **(6)** toujours du thé et quelquefois je
                 (I drink)

prends une tartine.

*D. Préférences.

Say whether the following people like the drink named **beaucoup, assez,** or **pas du tout.** Remember to use the definite article **(le, la, l', les)** with nouns after verbs indicating likes or preferences. Then say how often they drink it, using **en** with **souvent, quelquefois,** or **ne…jamais.**

    EXEMPLE   mon meilleur ami (ma meilleure amie) / le coca
                Mon meilleur ami (Ma meilleure amie) aime beaucoup le coca.
                Il (Elle) en boit souvent.

1. mes parents / le vin: _____

_____

2. moi, je / le jus d'orange: _____

_____

3. les Français / le café: _____

_____

4. mes amis et moi / l'eau minérale: _____

_____

5. mon meilleur ami (ma meilleure amie) / la bière: _____

_____

6. le professeur de français / le café: _____

E. Quantités. Answer the following questions about your morning eating habits, replacing the italicized words with **en.**

> **EXEMPLE** Buvez-vous beaucoup *de jus d'orange* le matin?
> **Oui, j'en bois beaucoup. / Non, je n'en bois pas (beaucoup).**

1. Buvez-vous souvent *du café* le matin?

   _____

2. Avez-vous pris *un café* ce matin?

   _____

3. Est-ce que vous allez prendre *du café* plus tard aujourd'hui?

   _____

4. Prenez-vous beaucoup *de sucre* quand vous mangez des céréales?

   _____

5. Mangez-vous souvent *des œufs*?

   _____

6. Avez-vous mangé *des œufs* ce matin?

   _____

F. Citations. Complete the following quotes by famous French and Belgian writers, journalists, philosophers, and artists by conjugating the **-ir** verbs in parentheses. Then number the quotes from **1** (your favorite) to **12** (your least favorite) to indicate which ones you prefer.

1. ____ Lire, c'est boire et manger. L'esprit qui ne lit pas _____ (maigrir) comme le

   corps qui ne mange pas. (Victor Hugo)

2. ____ Les écrivains *(writers)* ne _____ (se nourrir) pas de

   viandes ou de poulet, mais exclusivement d'éloges *(praise)*. (Henry de Montherlant)

3. ____ La difficulté de trouver l'aliment *(food)* _____ (grandir)

   en fonction de la pureté *(depending on the purity)* de la faim. / L'âme *(soul)*, à la différence du corps,

   _____ (se nourrir) de sa faim. (Gustave Thibon)

4. ____ La peur _____ (nourrir) l'imagination. (Joseph Joubert)

5. ____ L'esclave *(slave)* qui _____ (obéir),

   _____ (choisir) d'obéir. (Simone de Beauvoir)

6. ____ On ne _____ (choisir) pas ses parents,

   on ne _____ (choisir) pas sa famille. On ne

   _____ (se choisir) même pas soi-même *(oneself)*. (Philippe Geluck)

7. ____ La vie est faite d'illusions. Parmi *(Among)* ces illusions, certaines _____

   (réussir). Ce sont elles qui constituent la réalité. (Jacques Audiberti)

8. ____ Le plus souvent on _____ (réussir) non par *(not by)* ce qu'on

   fait, mais par ce qu'on ne fait pas. (Jules Tellier)

9. ____ L'important, ce n'est pas ce qu'on _____ (réussir), c'est ce

qu'on essaie. (Marcel Achard)

10. ____ Tout l'univers _____ (obéir) à l'amour; — Aimez, aimez, tout le

reste n'est rien. (Jean de La Fontaine)

11. ____ Un intellectuel, c'est d'abord quelqu'un qui _____ (réfléchir)

avant d'écrire et de parler, qui _____ (réfléchir) avant de réfléchir,

et qui _____ (réfléchir) même sur l'utilité de la réflexion avant la

réflexion proprement dite *(as such)*. (Bernard Pivot)

12. ____ Nous _____ (réfléchir) bien plus à l'emploi *(use)* de notre

argent renouvelable *(renewable),* qu'à celui de *(that of)* notre temps irremplaçable *(irreplaceable).*

(Jean-Louis Servan-Schreiber)

*G. Questions. Complete the following questions with the correct form of the logical verb in parentheses.
Then answer each question with a complete sentence.

1. Quand vous allez dîner au restaurant avec votre meilleur(e) ami(e), qui

_____ (finir, choisir) le restaurant généralement?

_____

2. Généralement, est-ce que vous _____ (finir, maigrir) le repas avec

un dessert?

_____

3. Si vous louez un film, est-ce que vous _____ (grossir, choisir) le plus

souvent un film d'amour, une comédie ou un film d'aventure?

_____

4. Et vos amis? Est-ce qu'ils _____ (grossir, choisir) un film étranger

quelquefois?

_____

5. Est-ce que vous _____ (obéir, réussir) à comprendre certaines phrases

quand vous regardez un film français en version originale?

_____

Partie auditive

6-33
A. Au petit déjeuner. When asked, say that you would like some of each of the items pictured, using the correct form of the partitive: **du, de la, de l', or des.** After a pause for you to respond, you will hear the correct answer. Verify your response and your pronunciation, and then repeat.

EXEMPLE
VOUS ENTENDEZ: Qu'est-ce que vous voulez?
VOUS DITES: **Je voudrais du café au lait.**
VOUS ENTENDEZ: Je voudrais du café au lait.
VOUS RÉPÉTEZ: **Je voudrais du café au lait.**

1   2   3   4

5   6   7   8

Now listen to a brief passage about French eating habits. Based on what you hear, identify three things that the French often eat in the morning and one thing they do not.

Le matin, les Français prennent souvent: Le matin, ils ne prennent pas:

1. _____   1. _____

2. _____

3. _____

6-34
B. Prononciation: Le verbe *boire*. Listen to a short passage comparing the types of drinks popular with Americans to those popular with the French. Then pause the recording. Imagine that a French person is speaking to an American. Complete each question or statement logically by selecting the appropriate choice in italics. Then, turn on the recording and verify your responses by repeating each sentence after the speaker. Pay particular attention to the pronunciation of the verb **boire.**

1. Le matin, je bois *du vin / du café.*

2. Est-ce que tu bois *du vin / du lait* le matin?

3. En France, on ne boit jamais *d'eau minérale / de lait* avec les repas.

4. Nous buvons souvent *du coca / du vin* avec un bon repas.

5. Vous buvez aussi *du vin / du coca* avec vos repas?

6. Les Français boivent quelquefois un café *avant / après* le dîner.

C. La bonne santé. Would people who pay attention to their health say that they eat or drink the things you hear mentioned? Answer affirmatively or negatively as a health-conscious person would, using the pronoun **en.** Then, as you hear the correct answer, select **OUI** or **NON** to indicate whether the response was affirmative or negative.

> **EXEMPLE** VOUS ENTENDEZ: Mangez-vous beaucoup de sucre?
> VOUS DITES: **Non, je n'en mange pas beaucoup.**
> VOUS INDIQUEZ: OUI _____ NON ✓

1. OUI _____ NON _____   3. OUI _____ NON _____   5. OUI _____ NON _____   7. OUI _____ NON _____

2. OUI _____ NON _____   4. OUI _____ NON _____   6. OUI _____ NON _____   8. OUI _____ NON _____

D. Prononciation: La lettre _s_ et les verbes en _-ir._ Pause the recording and review the _Prononciation_ section on page 326 of the textbook. Indicate how the **s**'s in these words are pronounced by writing **s** or **z** in each blank below them. Then turn on the recording. Listen and repeat these words.

cousin / coussin   poison / poisson   désert / dessert

je choisis / je réussis   j'ai choisi / j'ai réussi   ils choisissent / ils réussissent
— —   — —   — —

il choisit / ils choisissent   il obéit / ils obéissent   elle réussit / elles réussissent
                                                                      — —

elle grandit / elles grandissent il maigrit / ils maigrissent   elle réfléchit / elles réfléchissent
—   —

E. Les verbes en _-ir._ Rosalie is talking with Rose about her evenings out with André. Complete their conversation by filling in each blank with the verb that you hear.

ROSALIE: Quand nous sortons le soir, André _____ **(1)** le restaurant et moi, je

_____ **(2)** le film. Au restaurant, nous

_____ **(3)** un hors-d'œuvre et un plat principal. Après,

André _____ **(4)** son repas avec du fromage, mais moi je

préfère _____ **(5)** mon repas avec un dessert.

ROSE: Pourquoi ne _____ **(6)**-tu pas ton repas avec du fromage?

ROSALIE: Mon médecin préfère que je ne mange pas trop de matières grasses et je suis _(follow)_ ses conseils

(advice). De toute façon, j'_____ **(7)** un peu depuis que je

suis en France.

ROSE: Mais toi, tu _____ **(8)** toujours à rester en forme!

ROSALIE: Oui, je ne _____ **(9)** pas facilement, mais je

_____ **(10)** tout de même à rester en forme. D'abord, je fais

souvent de l'exercice et aussi je _____ **(11)** à ce que je mange.

 **COMPÉTENCE 4**

Choosing a healthy lifestyle

By the time you finish this **Compétence,** you should be able to say what you would change, if you could, to have a healthier lifestyle.

Partie écrite

A. Qu'est-ce qu'on devrait faire? What should one do or not do to accomplish the following goals? Complete each sentence with the logical action from the list.

manger peu de viande rouge

faire de l'aérobic

choisir des plats sains

arrêter de fumer

faire de la muscu

se promener à la campagne

faire du yoga ou de la méditation

boire beaucoup d'alcool

EXEMPLE Pour contrôler le stress, on devrait **faire du yoga ou de la méditation.**

1. Pour éviter les effets du tabac, on devrait _____.

2. Pour faire une randonnée, on devrait _____.

3. Pour améliorer *(to improve)* l'endurance cardio-vasculaire, on devrait _____.

4. Pour devenir plus fort, on devrait _____.

5. Pour manger des aliments *(foods)* avec beaucoup de vitamines, on devrait _____

_____.

6. Pour éviter les matières grasses, on devrait _____.

7. Pour oublier ses problèmes, on ne devrait pas _____.

*B. Une bonne santé. Answer the following questions about health with complete sentences.

1. À votre avis, que devrait-on faire pour être en bonne santé?

_____

_____

2. Quels aliments *(foods)* devrait-on éviter?

_____

_____

3. Mangez-vous souvent des plats sains et légers? des produits bio?

_____

_____

4. Est-ce que vous évitez le tabac et l'alcool?

_____

_____

5. Que faites-vous pour contrôler le stress? Faites-vous du yoga ou de la méditation?

_____

_____

6. Est-ce que vous vous sentez souvent fatigué(e)? Dormez-vous assez?

_____

_____

C. Conversation. Reread the conversation between Patricia and Rosalie on page 328 of your textbook. Then, complete this conversation between Nicolas and his brother with the indicated words.

NICOLAS: Tu as l'air _____ **(1)**.
          (tired)

LUCIEN: Oui, _____ **(2)** très bien. J'ai _____ **(3)**
          (I don't feel)   *(without doubt)*

mangé quelque chose qui m'a fait du mal.

NICOLAS: Tu as mangé _____ **(4)** à midi, non? C'était peut-
          (some shellfish)

être ça. _____ **(5)** qu' _____ **(6)**
          (Don't forget)   *(one should avoid)*

les huîtres en cette saison.

LUCIEN: Je mange des huîtres toute l'année, mais tu as sûrement raison.

NICOLAS: Tu _____ **(7)** rentrer à la maison.
          (would do better to)

D. Que feriez-vous? If you wanted to improve your health, would you do the following things? Put the verbs in the conditional.

> **EXEMPLE** dormir toute la journée
> **Non, je ne dormirais pas toute la journée.**

1. faire plus d'exercice: _____

2. éviter le stress: _____

3. boire beaucoup d'alcool: _____

4. aller à la salle de gym: _____

5. choisir des plats sains: _____

6. prendre des vitamines: _____

7. se coucher plus tôt: _____

8. manger beaucoup de sucre: _____

E. Soyons polis! You are eating with friends at a restaurant. Rewrite the following questions in the conditional so that they sound more polite.

1. Voulez-vous une table à l'intérieur ou sur la terrasse?

   _____

2. Avez-vous une autre table? _____

3. Est-ce que nous pouvons voir le menu? _____

4. Veux-tu manger des escargots? _____

5. Quel vin est bon avec ce plat? _____

6. Peux-tu me passer le sel? _____

F. Résultats. Would one have the indicated results if one ate or drank a lot of the illustrated items? Use a **si** (*if*) clause with the imperfect followed by a result clause in the conditional, as in the example.

   EXEMPLE   Si on mangeait beaucoup de frites, on ne maigrirait pas.

Exemple

manger... / maigrir

1

manger... / maigrir

2

manger... / éviter les matières grasses

3

boire... / rester en bonne santé

4

manger... / grossir

5

boire... / devenir plus fort

1. _____

   _____

2. _____

   _____

3. _____

   _____

4. _____

   _____

5. _____

   _____

Line art on this page: © Cengage Learning

G. Dans ces conditions. What would these people do in the following circumstances? Complete each sentence with the logical ending from the list, putting the verb in the conditional.

ne pas prendre beaucoup de dessert   boire de l'eau

mettre un pull   manger quelque chose

ne pas se marier   faire la sieste *(to take a nap)*

> **EXEMPLE**   Si nous avions faim, **nous mangerions quelque chose.**

1. Si les enfants avaient sommeil, ils _____.

2. Si nous avions soif, nous _____.

3. Si j'avais froid, je _____.

4. Si Rose voulait maigrir, elle _____.

5. Si Rosalie et André avaient peur du mariage, ils _____.

*H. Si… Say what you would do under the following circumstances. Complete each sentence with the indicated verb in the conditional.

> **EXEMPLE**   Si je sortais ce soir, **j'irais au cinéma.** (aller)

1. Si je sortais ce soir pour un dîner spécial, _____

_____. (aller)

2. Si j'invitais mon professeur de français chez moi pour dîner, _____

_____. (préparer)

3. Si j'avais plus de temps libre, _____

_____. (aimer)

4. Si je ne faisais pas mes devoirs en ce moment, _____

_____. (pouvoir)

---

*Journal. How would your life be if things were perfect? Write at least six sentences saying what changes there would be and what would stay the same as now (**comme maintenant**).

Si ma vie était parfaite… _____

_____

_____

_____

_____

_____

_____

_____

_____

_____

Partie auditive

A. Que veulent-ils faire? Listen to what changes these people are making in their lifestyle and fill in the missing words. Pause the recording between items to allow enough time to respond.

1. Henri essaie d'éviter _____, _____

    et _____.

2. Yannick fait _____ et prend

    _____.

3. Rosalie mange moins de _____ et plus de plats

    _____ et _____.

4. Rose _____, _____

    et _____ tous les jours.

5. André fait _____ tous les jours.

B. Prononciation: La consonne *r* et le conditionnel. Pause the recording and review the *Prononciation* section on page 331 of the textbook. Look at these sentences and decide whether people who want to improve their health would do these things. If they would, leave the sentence as it is. If they would not, place **ne... pas** in the blanks. Then turn on the recording and check your answers by repeating the statements after the speaker. Pay particular attention to the pronunciation of the endings of the verbs in the conditional.

a. Moi, je (j') _____ éviterais _____ le tabac.

b. Toi, tu _____ prendrais _____ de(s) repas copieux tous les jours.

c. Nous _____ irions _____ plus souvent à la salle de gym.

d. Vous _____ feriez _____ plus souvent de l'exercice.

e. Mes amis _____ mangeraient _____ beaucoup de matières grasses.

Now, listen to the beginning of a sentence and indicate which of the phrases above would logically finish it. Then, check your work as you hear the complete sentence.

EXEMPLE	VOUS ENTENDEZ:	S'ils faisaient attention au cholestérol...
	VOUS INDIQUEZ:	**e**
	VOUS ENTENDEZ:	S'ils faisaient attention au cholestérol, mes amis ne mangeraient pas beaucoup de matières grasses.

EXEMPLE ___*e*___   1. _____   2. _____   3. _____   4. _____

C. Résolutions. André has decided to improve his health. Here is what he told Rosalie he would do. Listen to each phrase and fill in the missing verb in the conditional.

J'ai dit à Rosalie…

1. que je _____ plus de fruits et de légumes.

2. que je _____ des plats plus sains.

3. que mes repas _____ moins copieux.

4. que nous _____ plus souvent à la salle de gym.

5. qu'on _____ de l'exercice ensemble tous les jours.

D. Rosalie et Rose préparent le repas. Listen as Rosalie (**mamie**) and Rose discuss the dinner they are preparing. Then pause the recording and complete these sentences according to what they say.

1. Pour prendre beaucoup de vitamines, on peut manger _____.

2. Comme exercice, Rosalie fait des promenades et Rose fait du _____ et de l' _____.

3. Rosalie voudrait diminuer *(to cut back)* _____.

4. Rose mange trop de _____.

E. Conseils. You are giving advice to a friend. Complete each sentence you hear with the logical ending. Then, as you hear the answer, identify the correct ending.

EXEMPLE   VOUS VOYEZ: tu dormirais mieux ____ / tu dormirais moins ____
VOUS ENTENDEZ: Si tu buvais moins de café…
VOUS DITES: **Si tu buvais moins de café, tu dormirais mieux.**
VOUS ENTENDEZ: Si tu buvais moins de café, tu dormirais mieux.
VOUS INDIQUEZ: tu dormirais mieux _✓_ / tu dormirais moins ____

1. tu te sentirais plus fatigué ____   tu te sentirais moins fatigué ____

2. tu maigrirais ____   tu grossirais ____

3. tu serais en mauvaise forme ____   tu serais plus fort ____

4. tu éviterais l'alcool ____   tu éviterais le tabac ____

5. tu te sentirais moins nerveux ____   tu te sentirais plus nerveux ____

6. tu oublierais mes conseils ____   tu ferais attention à mes conseils ____

*F. Et vous? Answer the questions with complete sentences.

1. _____

2. _____

3. _____

4. _____

5. _____

6. _____

En vacances

Chapitre **9**

COMPÉTENCE 1

Talking about vacation

By the time you finish this *Compétence,* you should be able to talk about future vacation plans.

Partie écrite

A. Où aiment-ils passer leurs vacances? Based on the illustrations, say where the indicated people like to spend their vacation and what they like to do there. Complete the sentences with the name of a place from the first box and the most logical pair of activities from the second box.

à la maison sur une île tropicale à la montagne dans une grande ville dans un pays étranger	se reposer et travailler dans le jardin courir sur la plage et bronzer visiter des sites historiques et goûter la cuisine locale faire du ski et admirer les paysages aller au théâtre et profiter des activités culturelles

EXEMPLE Mes parents aiment passer leurs vacances **à la maison.** Ils aiment **se reposer et travailler dans le jardin.**

1. Maryse aime passer ses vacances _____.

   Elle aime _____.

2. Éric et Thomas aiment passer leurs vacances _____.

   Ils aiment _____.

3. Mon frère aime passer ses vacances _____.

   Il aime _____.

4. Mes cousins aiment passer leurs vacances _____.

   Ils aiment _____.

Line art on this page: © Cengage Learning

B. Conversation. Reread the conversation between Lucas and Alex on page 350 of your textbook. Then, complete this conversation between two friends.

AHMAD: Je vais bientôt _____ **(1).**
(leave on vacation)

KARIMA: Et tu vas où?

AHMAD: _____ **(2)** aller _____ **(3).**
(I'm planning on / I'm counting on)   *(to the mountains)*

KARIMA: _____ **(4)!**
(What luck)

AHMAD: Et toi, qu'est-ce que tu vas faire?

KARIMA: Je vais passer 10 jours près de _____ **(5).** J'aime
(the sea)

_____ **(6)** sur la plage et _____ **(7)**
(to run)   *(taste)*

les spécialités de la région.

AHMAD: Génial. _____ **(8).**
(I hope you'll like it)

C. Voyage avec nous! Some friends are trying to convice you to go on vacation to the Antilles with them. Complete their statements with the correct *future tense* form of the verbs in parentheses. The first one has been done as an example.

Si tu viens en vacances avec nous, tu __verras__ **(1)** (voir) des choses

magnifiques. En Guadeloupe, on _____ **(2)**

(rencontrer) beaucoup de gens intéressants et on

_____ **(3)** (goûter) la cuisine créole. Le

paysage _____ **(4)** (être) beau aussi. On _____ **(5)**

(aller) au parc naturel et on _____ **(6)** (faire) du bateau dans l'eau

claire de la mer des Antilles. On _____ **(7)** (s'amuser) bien et tu

_____ **(8)** (aimer) beaucoup la Guadeloupe. Après notre séjour *(stay)*

en Guadeloupe, nous _____ **(9)** (aller) en Martinique.

Nous _____ **(10)** (arriver) en Martinique le 15 août. Nous

_____ **(11)** (être) à l'hôtel Bakoua jusqu'au 20 août, le jour où nous

_____ **(12)** (partir). Les enfants et Martine _____ **(13)**

(rentrer) de Guadeloupe le 25 août, mais moi, je _____ **(14)** (faire) un voyage à

Saint-Martin et à La Désirade. J'_____ **(15)** (aller) d'abord à Saint-Martin; ensuite je

_____ **(16)** (passer) 2 jours à La Désirade.

D. Dans ce cas... Review the use of the *present and future tenses* with clauses with **si** and **quand** on page 352 of the textbook. Then complete the following sentences in which Lucas talks about his plans with Anaïs for tomorrow with the correct form of the verb in parentheses. The first sentence has been done as an example.

> **EXEMPLE** Si Anaïs n'a pas trop de travail à faire demain, nous **passerons** (passer) la soirée ensemble. Quand elle **rentrera** (rentrer), nous sortirons.

1. Quand elle _____ (finir) son travail, elle viendra tout de suite chez moi.

2. Si j' _____ (avoir) le temps demain, je préparerai un bon petit dîner.

3. Quand elle arrivera chez moi, je _____ (servir) le dîner.

4. Après, s'il fait beau, nous _____ (faire) une promenade.

5. S'il _____ (faire) mauvais, nous irons au cinéma.

6. Quand elle _____ (devoir) rentrer, je la raccompagnerai chez elle.

E. Pour mieux lire: *Recognizing compound tenses.* Reread the explanation on recognizing compound tenses on page 354 of the textbook. Then select the appropriate English translation of the italicized parts of these sentences about Lucas's vacation.

_____ 1. Le 11 août, j'*aurai presque fini* mes vacances, mais je *ne serai pas encore rentré* à Paris.

    a. will almost have finished, will not have returned yet

    b. had almost finished, had not returned yet

    c. would have almost finished, would not have returned yet

_____ 2. J'*aurai passé* trois semaines en Guadeloupe et j'*aurai vu* des choses intéressantes.

    a. will have spent, will have seen

    b. had spent, had seen

    c. would have spent, would have seen

_____ 3. Si je *n'avais pas rencontré* Anaïs, mes vacances *auraient été* moins intéressantes.

    a. hadn't met, will have been

    b. hadn't met, would have been

    c. wouldn't have met, would have been

_____ 4. Si je *n'avais pas fait* une bêtise au parc naturel, nous *n'aurions jamais commencé* à parler.

    a. won't have done, would never have started

    b. hadn't done, would never have started

    c. hadn't done, had never started

F. Quelle aventure! Now reread Lucas's message to Alex on page 355 of the textbook and complete these sentences.

1. Lucas est allé faire l'esacalade de la _____, un énorme volcan en repos.

2. Il a pensé que le volcan allait exploser parce que la terre était toute _____ et il a vu des jets de _____ qui sortaient du sommet.

3. Il a commencé a crier aux autres touristes: «_____! _____!
Le volcan entre en éruption, il va exploser!»

4. Si Anaïs n'avait pas été parmi le groupe ils auraient tous commencé à _____, paniqués.

5. Elle leur a dit que c'était tout à fait _____.

6. Mais tout est bien qui _____ bien. Si Lucas n'avait pas fait cette bêtise, il n'aurait jamais fait la _____ de cette femme extraordinaire.

*G. Des vacances virtuelles. Will computers and virtual reality give us new vacation options in the future (**à l'avenir**)? Complete the questions with the given verbs in the *future tense.* Then, answer the questions.

1. À l'avenir, est-ce qu'on _____ (pouvoir) faire des voyages virtuels sans quitter la maison? Est-ce que la réalité virtuelle _____ (être) presque aussi réelle *(real)* que la réalité?

   _____

   _____

2. Si un jour on peut voyager dans le temps, _____-vous (faire) des voyages dans le temps?

   _____

   _____

3. Si un jour il y a un parc jurassique, est-ce que vous le _____ (visiter)?

   _____

4. Est-ce qu'on _____ (pouvoir) facilement visiter d'autres planètes à l'avenir?
   _____ -vous (faire) un voyage sur une autre planète un jour?

   _____

   _____

5. Est-ce qu'on _____ (avoir) plus de vacances à l'avenir parce que les ordinateurs _____ (faire) tout le travail ou est-ce qu'on _____ (devoir) travailler plus à l'avenir que maintenant?

   _____

   _____

Partie auditive

A. Que faire? Listen to what several people like to do on vacation. Label each picture with the name of the person who likes the illustrated activity.

| Pierre | Alain | Antoinette | Olivia | Daniel | Vincent |

a. _____

b. _____

c. _____

d. _____

e. _____

f. _____

Now replay the recording and listen again. This time, indicate where, according to the activities mentioned, the person named should spend his or her vacation.

1. ____ dans une grande ville / ____ à la mer

2. ____ dans un pays étranger / ____ à la montagne

3. ____ sur une île tropicale / ____ dans une grande ville

4. ____ à la montagne / ____ dans un pays exotique

5. ____ à la montagne / ____ dans une grande ville

6. ____ dans une grande ville / ____ à la mer

B. Prononciation: Le futur. First, listen to the sentences and fill in the missing verbs. Then listen again and repeat the sentences after the speaker to practice saying verbs in the *future tense.*

Je _____ un voyage en Guadeloupe cet été.

Tu _____ me chercher à l'aéroport.

Le voyage _____ assez long.

Nous _____ beaucoup de temps à la plage.

Ton amie Micheline et toi, vous _____ la région avec moi.

Les gens _____ très sympas.

C. Elle est dynamique! Anaïs is very active and prefers physical activities when she travels. You will hear two activities named. Complete the sentences to say which one she *will* do, using the *future tense*. Pause the recording as needed. You will then hear the correct answer. Verify your response and repeat.

EXEMPLE	VOUS ENTENDEZ:	rester à l'hôtel / faire une randonnée
	VOUS ÉCRIVEZ:	Elle **fera une randonnée.**
	VOUS ENTENDEZ:	Elle fera une randonnée.
	VOUS RÉPÉTEZ:	**Elle fera une randonnée.**

1. Elle _____.

2. Elle _____.

3. Elle _____.

4. Elle _____.

5. Elle _____.

6. Elle _____.

D. Les vacances de Lucas. Listen as Lucas talks to a friend about how his vacation will be. First, listen to the conversation at normal speed. Then, listen again and fill in the missing words as it is repeated at a slower speed.

_____ **(1)** pour la Guadeloupe le 20 juillet. Le voyage

_____ **(2)** plutôt long et _____ **(3)** trois semaines

là-bas. _____ **(4)** le 12 août. _____ **(5)** dans un

hôtel près de la plage. _____ **(6)** plein de choses: _____ **(7)**

à la plage, _____ **(8)** tous les sites et _____ **(9)**

la cuisine locale. Et toi? Où _____ **(10)** tes vacances?

_____ **(11)** un voyage?

*E. Et vous? A friend is asking you about your vacation travel plans this year. Answer your friend's questions in the *future tense,* explaining what you *will* do. If you do not have vacation plans yet, use your imagination.

1. _____

2. _____

3. _____

4. _____

5. _____

6. _____

7. _____

Preparing for a trip

By the time you finish this ***Compétence,*** you should be able to describe preparations for a trip and say with whom you stay in communication.

Partie écrite

A. Préparatifs. A friend will soon leave on a trip. What will he do? Fill in the blanks with the correct *future tense* form of the verb in parentheses. Then, number the activities in the order in which they *would* occur.

EXEMPLE   __2__ a. Il **partira** (partir) en voyage.
           __1__ b. Il **demandera** (demander) à sa voisine de donner à manger au chien.

© Cengage Learning

1. _____ **a.** Il _____ (dire) à sa famille où il ira.

    _____ **b.** Il _____ (décider) où aller.

2. _____ **a.** Il _____ (choisir) un vol *(flight)*.

    _____ **b.** Il _____ (acheter) son billet d'avion.

3. _____ **a.** Il _____ (réserver) une chambre.

    _____ **b.** Il _____ (s'informer) sur les hôtels.

4. _____ **a.** Il _____ (lire) un guide touristique.

    _____ **b.** Il _____ (faire) un itinéraire *(to plan an itinerary)*.

5. _____ **a.** Il _____ (faire) sa valise.

    _____ **b.** Il _____ (partir) pour l'aéroport.

6. _____ **a.** Il _____ (prendre) un taxi pour aller à son hôtel.

    _____ **b.** Il _____ (arriver) à l'hôtel.

B. Conversation. Reread the conversation between Catherine and Alex on page 357 of your textbook. Then, complete this e-mail from Alex to Lucas.

_____ **(1)** ton mail et devine quoi *(guess what)*! On a décidé de venir
     (I received)

te rejoindre en Guadeloupe. Nous aussi, nous voudrions _____
                                                           (to see the tropical scenery)

_____ **(2)** et _____ **(3)** du beau _____ **(4)**.
     (to take advantage)   *(climate)*

Catherine adore les fruits de mer et l'idée de _____ **(5)** la cuisine antillaise
                                          (to taste)

_____ **(6).** Moi, je voudrais faire la connaissance de la
   (pleases her [use **plaire**]*)*

Guadeloupéenne que _____ **(7)** là-bas.
                  (you met)

C. *Dire, lire* et *écrire*. Some friends are talking about what certain people they know say, read, and write. Complete what they say using the correct form of **lire, (s')écrire,** or **(se) dire** as indicated and the translations of the indicated words. *Use the present tense unless otherwise indicated.*

> **EXEMPLE** Moi, je **lis** (lire) beaucoup d'**histoires** *(stories)* d'aventure.

1. Dans ma famille, nous _____ (lire) beaucoup. Ma sœur _____ (lire)

   souvent des _____ *(novels)* d'amour et des _____ *(poems)*.

2. Mes parents _____ (lire) des articles dans le _____

   (newspaper) et des _____ *(magazines)*.

3. Vous _____ (lire) beaucoup dans votre famille? Et toi? Qu'est-ce que tu

   _____ (lire) le plus souvent? Qu'est-ce que tu _____

   lire [**passé composé**] récemment?

4. En cours de français, nous _____ (écrire) des _____

   (compositions) quelquefois et en fait *(in fact)*, nous _____ écrire [**passé**

   composé] une longue _____ composition hier.

5. Moi, j'_____ (écrire) mieux en anglais qu'en français. Et toi? Est-ce que tu

   _____ (écrire) bien en français?

6. Le week-end, les étudiants dans mon cours _____ (s'écrire) des mails quelquefois.

   Les autres étudiants et toi, est-ce que vous _____ (s'écrire) des mails quelquefois?

7. Quand j'arrive en cours de français, je _____ (dire) bonjour et quand le prof arrive

   en cours, il _____ (dire) bonjour aussi. Nous _____ (dire)

   tous bonjour au prof, bien sûr. Est-ce que tu _____ (dire) bonjour quand tu

   arrives en cours?

8. À la fin *(end)* du cours, les étudiants _____ (se dire) au revoir. Les autres étudiants

   et toi, est-ce que vous _____ (se dire) au revoir à la fin du cours? Qu'est-ce que tu

   _____ dire [**passé composé**] quand tu as quitté le cours aujourd'hui?

D. Le voyage de Lucas. Restate what Lucas does, using the verb in the initial sentence and a direct object pronoun **(le, la, l', les)** to replace the italicized noun. Then indicate with **a, b,** or **c** in the blank after your response whether he does the activity **a. avant le voyage, b. à son arrivée** *(arrival)*, or **c. à son retour** *(return)*.

> **EXEMPLE** Lucas fait *sa valise.* Lucas **la fait.** **a**

1. Il réserve *sa chambre d'hôtel.* Il _____. _____

2. Il achète *son billet* sur Internet. Il _____ sur Internet. _____

3. Il montre *son passeport.* Il _____. _____

4. Il montre *ses photos* à sa famille. Il _____ à sa famille. _____

Now continue with the following sentences, using an indirect object pronoun (**lui, leur**) to replace the italicized noun.

> **EXEMPLE** Lucas écrit une carte postale *à ses amis.* Lucas **leur écrit** une carte postale. **b**

1. Il dit *à ses parents* où il va. Il _____ où il va. _____

2. Il demande *à son voisin* de donner à manger à son chien. Il _____

   _____ de donner à manger à son chien. _____

3. Il téléphone *à ses parents* de Guadeloupe. Il _____

   de Guadeloupe. _____

4. Il téléphone *à sa sœur* pour dire qu'il est rentré. Il _____

   pour dire qu'il est rentré. _____

E. Votre temps libre.

Say whether you do or do not often do these things during your free time. Use a direct or an indirect object pronoun to replace each italicized noun.

> **EXEMPLE** inviter *vos amis* à la maison
>
> Je **les invite** souvent à la maison. / Je **ne les invite pas** souvent à la maison.

1. regarder *la télé:* Je _____ souvent.

2. faire *vos devoirs* devant la télé: Je _____ souvent devant la télé.

3. téléphoner *à votre meilleur(e) ami(e):* Je _____ souvent.

4. rendre visite *à vos amis:* Je _____ souvent visite.

5. écouter *votre iPod:* Je _____ souvent.

Review the position of the object pronouns on page 360 in your textbook and say whether or not you are going to do the things listed above tomorrow. Use the *immediate future.*

> **EXEMPLE** inviter *vos amis* à la maison
>
> **Je vais les inviter** à la maison demain. **/ Je ne vais pas les inviter** à la maison demain.

1. _____ demain.

2. _____ devant la télé demain.

3. _____ demain.

4. _____ visite demain.

5. _____ demain.

Now review the position of the object pronouns and the agreement of the past participle in the **passé composé** on page 360 in your textbook. Say whether or not you did the things listed above yesterday.

> **EXEMPLE** inviter *vos amis* à la maison
>
> **Je les ai invités** à la maison hier. / **Je ne les ai pas invités** à la maison hier.

1. _____ hier.

2. _____ devant la téle hier.

3. _____ hier.

4. _____ visite hier.

5. _____ hier.

*F. Et toi? Answer a friend's questions about your travel habits, replacing each italicized phrase with a direct or indirect object pronoun.

EXEMPLES Est-ce que tu prépares *tes voyages* bien à l'avance?
Oui, je les prépare bien à l'avance. / Non, je ne les prépare pas bien à l'avance.
Est-ce que tu dis *à tes parents* où tu vas?
Oui, je leur dis où je vais. / Non, je ne leur dis pas où je vais.

1. Est-ce que tu prépares *tes voyages* bien à l'avance?

_____

2. Fais-tu *ta valise* à l'avance ou au dernier moment?

_____

3. Dis-tu *à tes parents* où tu vas généralement quand tu pars en vacances?

_____

4. Demandes-tu *à ton voisin* de donner à manger à tes animaux?

_____

5. Est-ce que tu achètes *ton billet* sur Internet ou dans une agence de voyages?

_____

6. Où est-ce que tu as acheté *ton billet* la dernière fois que tu as voyagé?

_____

7. Est-ce que tu préfères réserver *ta chambre* sur Internet, par mail, par lettre ou par téléphone?

_____

8. La dernière fois que tu es descendu(e) à l'hôtel, comment as-tu trouvé *ta chambre*?

_____

9. Est-ce que tu as réservé *cette chambre* à l'avance?

_____

---

*Journal. Imagine that you will soon be leaving on vacation. Talk about who you will stay in touch with and how; saying, for example, how often you will telephone, write, or text him, her, or them. Use indirect object pronouns.

Je passerai mes vacances... Je resterai en contact avec...

_____

_____

_____

_____

_____

_____

_____

_____

_____

_____

Partie auditive

A. Avant le départ ou à l'arrivée? A tourist is preparing for a trip to France. Indicate whether each sentence you hear describes something she does **avant son départ** or **à son arrivée** at the airport in Paris.

1. _____ avant son départ   _____ à son arrivée

2. _____ avant son départ   _____ à son arrivée

3. _____ avant son départ   _____ à son arrivée

4. _____ avant son départ   _____ à son arrivée

5. _____ avant son départ   _____ à son arrivée

Now play this section again. Indicate which of the options would be the most logical thing for the tourist to do next. Repeat this section as needed, pausing the recording between items to allow enough time to respond.

1. Maintenant, elle devrait…   _____ **a.** montrer son passeport et passer la douane.

                                       _____ **b.** faire un itinéraire *(make an itinerary)*.

2. Maintenant, elle devrait…   _____ **a.** réserver son billet.

                                       _____ **b.** montrer son passeport et passer la douane.

3. Maintenant, elle devrait…   _____ **a.** faire ses valises.

                                       _____ **b.** montrer son passeport.

4. Maintenant, elle devrait…   _____ **a.** faire sa valise.

                                       _____ **b.** changer de l'argent.

5. Maintenant, elle devrait…   _____ **a.** acheter un plan *(map)* de la ville.

                                       _____ **b.** changer de l'argent.

B. Les verbes *dire, lire* et *écrire*. You will hear someone talk about the reading and writing habits of his family. First, listen to the passage at normal speed. Then, listen again and fill in the missing words as it is repeated at a slower speed.

Dans ma famille, nous _____ **(1)** beaucoup. Quand j'étais petit, je ne

_____ **(2)** pas beaucoup, mais maintenant je _____ **(3)** assez

souvent. Hier soir, j'_____ **(4)** un magazine et j'en _____ **(5)**

sans doute un autre ce soir. Mes parents _____ **(6)** souvent des romans. Ma sœur préfère

_____ **(7)** des poèmes. Tous ses amis _____ **(8)** qu'elle

_____ **(9)** bien. Moi, je ne _____ **(10)** rien parce que je

_____ **(11)** ses poèmes et jen' _____ **(12)**

que *(only)* des mails.

Nom _____ Date _____

C. Qu'est-ce que Lucas fait? Lucas is answering a friend's questions about how he generally prepares for a trip. Listen to the questions. After each one, pause the recording and complete Lucas's answer with the verb and a direct object pronoun (**le, la, l', les**). Then, turn on the recording and listen and repeat as you hear the correct answer.

EXEMPLE	VOUS ENTENDEZ:	D'habitude, tu achètes *ton billet* bien à l'avance?
	VOUS ÉCRIVEZ:	Oui, je **l'achète** bien à l'avance.
	VOUS ENTENDEZ:	Oui, je l'achète bien à l'avance.
	VOUS RÉPÉTEZ:	**Oui, je l'achète bien à l'avance.**

1. Oui, je _____ souvent sur Internet.

2. Oui, bien sûr, je _____ avant de partir en voyage.

3. Non, je ne _____ pas souvent à voyager avec moi.

4. Non, je ne _____ pas au dernier moment.

5. Oui, je _____ à mes parents.

Now Lucas is answering questions about his communication with others during his trip. After each one, pause the recording and complete Lucas's answer with the verb and an indirect object pronoun (**lui, leur**). Then, turn on the recording and listen and repeat as you hear the correct answer.

1. Oui, je _____ souvent des mails.

2. Oui, je _____ tous les jours.

3. Oui, je _____ souvent qu'elle est belle.

4. Non, je ne _____ pas souvent de cartes postales.

5. Oui, je _____ de ma vie à Paris.

*D. Et vous? Answer the questions you hear about your vacation trips and preparations. Use *the appropriate direct or indirect object pronoun* in your responses. Pause the recording between items to allow enough time to respond.

1. _____

2. _____

3. _____

4. _____

5. _____

 **COMPÉTENCE 3**

Buying your ticket

By the time you finish this *Compétence,* you should be able to make arrangements for a trip.

Partie écrite

A. Pour voyager. Complete each of these sentences with the logical expression from the box.

crédit	un passeport
son argent	bancaire
un billet d'avion	le numéro de votre vol
départ	les transports en commun

1. Pour faire preuve de *(to prove)* votre identité et de votre nationalité, il vous faut

   _____.

2. Pour prendre l'avion, on a besoin d'_____ et d'une carte

   d'embarquement *(boarding pass).*

3. Pour savoir à quelle heure votre vol partira, il faut savoir _____.

4. On peut aller à la banque pour changer _____.

5. On peut payer ses achats *(purchases)* par carte de _____ ou par carte

   _____.

6. Pour visiter la région, on peut louer une voiture ou on peut utiliser _____

   _____.

*B. Conversation. Reread the conversation between Lucas and the travel agent on page 362 of your textbook. Then, imagine that you are leaving on a trip. Complete this conversation to buy a round-trip plane ticket from Paris to the city of your choice.

Vous: Bonjour, monsieur. Je voudrais acheter un billet pour aller de Paris à

_____, s'il vous plaît.

L'AGENT DE VOYAGES: Très bien, monsieur/madame. Vous voulez un billet aller-retour ou un aller simple?

Vous: _____.

L'AGENT DE VOYAGES: À quelle date est-ce que vous voulez partir?

Vous: _____.

L'AGENT DE VOYAGES: Quand est-ce que vous voudriez rentrer?

VOUS: _____.

L'AGENT DE VOYAGES: Vous voulez un billet en première classe ou en classe économique?

VOUS: _____.

L'AGENT DE VOYAGES: Très bien. Voilà un vol possible. Ça vous convient?

VOUS: Oui, c'est parfait. Combien coûte le billet?

L'AGENT DE VOYAGES: C'est _____ euros.

VOUS: Bon. Alors, faites ma réservation. Voilà ma carte de crédit.

Now explain what you will do during this trip by writing sentences using the *form* of the following verbs.

> **EXEMPLE** aller à *[what city]*: **J'irai à Montréal / Miami…**

1. aller à *[what city]*: _____

2. voyager *[with whom]*: _____

3. partir *[when]*: _____

4. être en *[what class]*: _____

5. prendre *[what meals]* pendant le vol: _____

6. arriver à *[what time]*: _____

7. descendre / rester *[where]*: _____

8. rester *[how long]*: _____

9. rentrer *[when]*: _____

C. Lucas est prêt.
Lucas is talking to Alex about his trip. Fill in the blanks with the correct form of the verb **savoir** in the *present tense.* The first one has been done as an example.

ALEX: Tu _____ **sais** _____ **(1)** quand tu vas partir?

LUCAS: Oui, je _____ **(2)** la date et l'heure exacte de mon départ. J'ai téléphoné à ma sœur.

Elle _____ **(3)** quand elle doit m'amener *(to take me)* à l'aéroport.

ALEX: Vous _____ **(4)** de quel aéroport tu pars?

LUCAS: Bien sûr et nous _____ **(5)** aussi qu'il faut arriver à l'aéroport bien à l'avance.

Ne t'inquiète pas!

ALEX: Oui, mais les compagnies aériennes _____ **(6)** bien que tous les touristes ne

vont pas arriver à l'avance!

Now fill in the blanks in these sentences with the correct form of the verb **connaître** in the *present tense.* The first one has been done as an example.

1. J'ai demandé à ma sœur de m'amener à l'aéroport parce qu'elle _____ **connaît** _____ bien la route. Mes parents

la _____ moins bien.

2. J'ai lu plusieurs guides et je _____ assez bien l'histoire et la culture de la

Guadeloupe. Et toi, tu _____ la Guadeloupe?

3. Non, mais ma famille et moi, nous _____ d'autres îles caraïbes.

Ta famille et toi, quelles îles _____-vous?

D. *Connaître* ou *savoir*? Lucas's neighbor has just moved in, but he knows a lot about the neighborhood already. Fill in the blanks with **il sait** or **il connaît**.

> **EXEMPLE**   **Il sait** où tout se trouve *(is located)* dans le quartier et **il connaît** bien tous
> ses voisins.

1. _____ bien le quartier et _____ les meilleures routes

   pour aller en centre-ville.

2. _____ où il y a un bon restaurant et _____

   ce qu'ils servent chaque jour, mais _____ aussi faire la cuisine.

3. _____ tous ses voisins. _____ que certains de ses voisins

   sont américains, mais ce n'est pas un problème parce qu'_____ l'anglais.

4. _____ le numéro de téléphone de Lucas et _____ à

   quelle heure Lucas est chez lui d'habitude.

5. _____ bien les parcs du quartier et _____ si ses chiens

   sont permis *(permitted)* dans ces parcs.

E. Quel verbe? Lucas has problems the day of his departure. Complete the following passage with the correct forms of **savoir** or **connaître** in the *present tense*.

> **EXEMPLE**   Lucas ne **sait** pas quelle est la meilleure route pour arriver à l'aéroport parce qu'il ne
> **connaît** pas très bien cette partie de la ville.

Lucas a quelques problèmes le jour de son départ pour la Guadeloupe. D'abord, il ne

_____ **(1)** pas où il a laissé son billet et son passeport, mais son père

_____ **(2)** très bien son fils et les trouve tout de suite. Au dernier moment,

sa sœur ne peut pas l'amener *(take him)* à l'aéroport et il doit prendre un taxi. Le chauffeur de taxi ne

_____ **(3)** pas bien le quartier de Lucas et il se perd et arrive en retard *(late)*.

Ils ne _____ **(4)** pas si Lucas va arriver à l'aéroport à temps pour prendre

son avion. Arrivé à l'aéroport, Lucas ne _____ **(5)** pas où aller parce qu'il

ne _____ **(6)** pas l'aérogare *(terminal)*. Un employé de l'aéroport, qui

_____ **(7)** très bien les touristes, _____ **(8)** ce qu'il faut

faire pour l'aider et Lucas arrive à la porte d'embarquement *(departure gate)* juste à temps pour prendre son avion.

F. Entre amis. Lucas is answering questions about his relationship with his friend Alex. Complete his answers as he would, using the pronoun **me.**

> **EXEMPLE**   Il t'accompagne quelquefois en vacances?
> Oui, il **m'accompagne** quelquefois en vacances.

1. Il t'envoie souvent des textos? Oui, il _____ souvent des textos.

2. Il t'invite à sortir le week-end? Non, il _____ le week-end.

3. Il va te rendre visite ce soir? Oui, il _____ ce soir.

4. Il va t'aider avec ton travail? Non, il _____ avec mon travail.

5. Il t'a téléphoné récemment? Non, il _____ récemment.

6. Quand est-ce qu'il t'a vu récemment? Il _____ hier.

G. En cours. A student is answering questions about the interactions his French professor has with the other students and him. Complete what he says, using the pronoun **nous**.

> **EXEMPLE**   Votre professeur vous pose beaucoup de questions en cours?
> Oui, il **nous pose** beaucoup de questions.

1. Est-ce qu'il vous donne des devoirs tous les jours?

   Non, il _____ de devoirs tous les jours.

2. Il vous rend vos examens au début *(beginning)* ou à la fin *(end)* du cours?

   Il _____ nos examens au début du cours.

3. Quand vous posez des questions à votre professeur en anglais, est-ce qu'il vous répond en anglais ou en français?

   Il _____ toujours en français.

4. Il vous explique *(explains)* la leçon en anglais ou en français la plupart du temps?

   Il _____ la leçon en français la plupart du temps.

*H. Beaucoup de questions! The classmate who sits next to you is asking you these questions. Answer them using an indirect object pronoun **me, te, nous, vous, lui, leur.**

1. Quand tes parents partent en vacances, est-ce qu'ils *te* disent où ils vont?

   _____

2. Et toi? Quand tu pars en vacances, est-ce que tu dis *à tes parents* où tu vas?

   _____

3. Est-ce que tu écris des cartes postales *à ton meilleur ami (ta meilleure amie)*?

   _____

4. Est-ce que ton meilleur ami (ta meilleure amie) écrit des cartes postales *à tes autres amis et à toi* quand il/elle voyage?

   _____

5. La prochaine fois que tu partiras en vacances, est-ce que tu *m'*écriras? Est-ce que tu *m'*achèteras un cadeau *(gift)*?

   _____

   _____

Partie auditive

🔊 **A. Il faut...** You will hear lists of what one needs to have and to know to travel abroad. Fill in the missing
7-11 words. Pause the recording as needed.

1. Il faut avoir un billet, une carte _____, une carte

   _____ et _____.

2. Il faut savoir le numéro du _____, l'heure

   _____ et l'heure _____.

3. Il faut connaître _____ et

   _____ de la région,

   _____ et leur culture et

   _____ en commun.

🔊 **B. Lucas organise son voyage.** Listen as Lucas makes some inquiries and
7-12 arrangements for his trip. Pause the recording and indicate whether these statements
are true or false by selecting **vrai** or **faux.**

Lucas téléphone à l'agence de voyages.

1. Il y a encore de la place sur le vol du 20 juillet.   ___ VRAI   ___ FAUX

2. Lucas veut rester huit jours en Guadeloupe.   ___ VRAI   ___ FAUX

3. Lucas va rentrer le 22 août.   ___ VRAI   ___ FAUX

4. Lucas décide de faire ses réservations.   ___ VRAI   ___ FAUX

Now play this section again. Then pause the recording and complete these statements.

1. Le vol pour Pointe-à-Pitre part le _____ à ___h___.

2. Lucas va quitter Pointe-à-Pitre le _____ à 20h15.

   Il arrivera à Paris le lendemain à ___h___.

3. Le billet aller-retour coûte _____ €.

Nom _____ Date _____

C. Prononciation: Les verbes *savoir* et *connaître.* Pause the recording and complete each sentence with the appropriate form of either **savoir** or **connaître.** Then turn on the recording. Verify your answers and repeat the sentences after the speaker.

1. Je _____ une femme qui travaille en Guadeloupe, mais je ne

   _____ pas dans quelle ville elle habite.

2. Est-ce que tu la _____? Tu _____

   où elle travaille?

3. Elle ne te _____ pas, mais elle _____ qui tu es.

4. Nous _____ ce qu'il faut faire, mais nous ne

   _____ pas la région.

5. _____-vous la région? _____-vous où

   on peut acheter un guide?

6. Les gens d'ici _____ toute la région. Ils _____

   où tout se trouve *(is located).*

D. Entre amis. Lucas is asking Anaïs about her friend Olivia. After each question, pause the recording and complete Anaïs's response. Then turn on the recording and listen and repeat as you hear the correct answer.

EXEMPLE VOUS ENTENDEZ: Elle te téléphone tous les jours?
   VOUS COMPLÉTEZ: Non, elle **ne me téléphone pas** tous les jours.
   VOUS ENTENDEZ: Non, elle ne me téléphone pas tous les jours.
   VOUS RÉPÉTEZ: **Non, elle ne me téléphone pas tous les jours.**

1. Oui, elle _____ assez souvent.

2. Oui, elle _____ souvent un mail.

3. Non, elle _____ souvent de lettres.

4. Non, elle _____ toujours.

5. Non, elle _____ souvent de textos.

*E. Et ton meilleur ami? Another friend is asking about what your best male friend does for you. Answer the questions with complete sentences in French.

EXEMPLE Ton meilleur ami te comprend toujours?
   Oui, il me comprend toujours. / Non, il ne me comprend pas toujours.

1. _____

2. _____

3. _____

4. _____

5. _____

Nom _____ Date _____

Deciding where to go on a trip

By the time you finish this **Compétence,** you should be able to talk about where you went on vacation in the past and where you plan to go in the future.

Partie écrite

A. Quels pays aimeriez-vous visiter? Say which two places from the lists given below you would most like to visit for each region indicated.

l'Afrique: le Maroc, l'Algérie, l'Égypte, le Sénégal, la Côte d'Ivoire

l'Asie ou le Moyen-Orient: la Chine, Israël, le Japon, le Viêt Nam

l'Amérique du Nord, centrale et du Sud: les Antilles, le Canada, les États-Unis, le Mexique, l'Argentine, le Brésil, le Pérou, la Colombie, le Chili, la Guyane

l'Océanie: l'Australie, la Nouvelle-Calédonie, la Polynésie française

l'Europe: l'Allemagne, la Belgique, l'Espagne, la France, le Royaume-Uni, l'Irlande, l'Italie, la Russie, la Suisse, la Croatie, la Grèce

En Afrique, j'aimerais visiter _____ **(1)** et

_____ **(2).** En Asie ou au Moyen-Orient, je voudrais visiter

_____ **(3)** et _____ **(4).** En Amérique

du Nord ou en Amérique centrale, j'ai envie de visiter _____ **(5)**

et _____ **(6).** En Amérique du Sud, j'aimerais le mieux visiter

_____ **(7)** et _____ **(8).** En Océanie, je

préférerais visiter _____ **(9)** _____ **(10).**

En Europe, je voudrais visiter _____ **(11)** et _____ **(12).**

© Cengage Learning

B. Conversation. Reread the conversation between Anaïs and Lucas on page 369 of your textbook. Then, complete this conversation as indicated.

ANNICK: _____ **(1)** as-tu visités?
         (What foreign countries)

LIN: J'ai visité _____ **(2)** et _____ **(3).**
                    (Peru)   *(Mexico)*

        Et toi? Tu aimes voyager _____ **(4)**?
                                (in a foreign country / abroad)

ANNICK: Oui, beaucoup. L'année prochaine, _____ (5)

(I would like to visit)

l'Afrique. Je voudrais voir _____ (6) et

(Egypt)

_____ (7).

(Senegal)

C. Pays et continents. Review the use of articles with geographical places on page 370 of the textbook. Then, fill in the blank before the name of each place with the appropriate article (le, la, l', les).

EXEMPLE   En Océanie:

____l'____ Australie, ___la___ Nouvelle-Calédonie, ___la___ Polynésie française

1. En Afrique:

_____ Maroc, _____ Algérie, _____ Sénégal, _____ Côte d'Ivoire

2. En Asie et au Moyen-Orient:

_____ Chine, _____ Japon, _____ Viêt Nam

3. En Amérique du Nord et en Amérique centrale:

_____ Antilles, _____ Canada, _____ États-Unis, _____ Mexique

4. En Amérique du Sud:

_____ Argentine, _____ Pérou, _____ Colombie, _____ Chili, _____ Brésil, _____ Guyane

5. En Europe:

_____ Allemagne, _____ Belgique, _____ Espagne, _____ France, _____ Royaume-Uni,

_____ Suisse

Now list the names of the preceding countries or regions where French is spoken or where there is an important francophone cultural influence. Refer to the map in the front of your textbook if necessary.

la Nouvelle-Calédonie, la Polynésie française, _____

_____

D. Voyages et préférences. Fill in the blank before each place with the appropriate article (le, la, l', les). *If no article is needed, leave it blank.*

EXEMPLE   J'ai visité **le** Royaume-Uni où j'ai beaucoup aimé _____ Londres *(London)*.

1. J'aimerais visiter _____ France, surtout _____ Paris, _____ Lyon et _____ Côte d'Azur.

2. J'ai visité _____ Italie. J'ai beaucoup aimé _____ Rome.

3. En Asie, j'ai visité _____ Japon. J'aimerais voir _____ Chine aussi.

4. En Amérique, j'ai visité _____ États-Unis, _____ Canada et _____ Mexique. J'ai adoré _____

Montréal et _____ Californie.

E. Où? Review the chart on page 370 of the textbook on how to say *to* or *in* with geographical places. Say in which country from the choices given the following cities are located.

EXEMPLE   (Italie / France): Lyon est **en France.**

1. (Mexique / Argentine): Buenos Aires est _____.

2. (Chine / Viêt Nam): Beijing est _____.

3. (Côte d'Ivoire / Maroc): Casablanca est _____.

4. (Royaume-Uni / Allemagne): Berlin est _____.

5. (Australie / Nouvelle-Calédonie): Sydney est _____.

6. (Canada / États-Unis): Toronto est _____.

7. (Algérie / Sénégal): Dakar est _____.

F. Les voyages de Christian. Complete the paragraph with the appropriate preposition for each geographical place mentioned. The first one has been done as an example.

Christian habite **aux** États-Unis mais il a voyagé partout! L'année dernière il est allé _____ **(1)** Mexique,

_____ **(2)** Antilles et _____ **(3)** France! Il a habité _____ **(4)** Canada où il est allé à l'université de

Montréal. Après, il a voyagé partout _____ **(5)** Europe et il a passé quelques semaines _____ **(6)** Paris où

il a visité beaucoup de monuments historiques et de musées. Ensuite, il est allé _____ **(7)** Royaume-Uni,

_____ **(8)** Allemagne et _____ **(9)** Espagne. Mais finalement, il n'avait plus d'argent et il a dû revenir

_____ **(10)** États-Unis.

*G. Préférences. Complete the following questions with the correct prepositions. Then answer each question.

1. Est-ce que vous habitez _____ États-Unis, _____ Canada ou dans un autre pays?

   _____

2. Aimeriez-vous mieux passer vos vacances _____ Californie ou _____ Colorado?

   _____

3. Préféreriez-vous faire un voyage _____ Montréal, _____ Paris ou _____ Abidjan?

   _____

4. Est-ce que vous aimeriez mieux passer vos vacances _____ Asie ou _____ Afrique?

   _____

5. Êtes-vous allé(e) _____ Europe? Si oui, quels pays avez-vous visités?

   _____

H. Où vont-ils aller? A friend is talking about where various people are going on vacation. Complete these sentences saying to what country or region they *are going to go* and what they will do there using the expressions given in the *future tense*.

profiter des activités culturelles
visiter des sites historiques
faire du ski
aller à la plage

Espagne

EXEMPLE Mes parents vont aller **en Espagne.** Ils **visiteront des sites historiques.**

1. Mon meilleur ami va aller _____.

   Il _____.

France

2. Mes cousins vont aller _____.

   Ils _____.

Égypte

3. Mes amis et moi, nous allons aller _____.

   Nous _____.

Canada

4. Ma voisine va aller _____.

   Elle _____.

Antilles

Line art on this page: © Cengage Learning

---

*Journal. Describe an interesting vacation you would like to take. Name a place outside of your own country that you would like to visit and say what you would like to do there.

_____

_____

_____

_____

_____

_____

_____

Partie auditive

A. Où sont-ils? List the name of each place you hear under the name of its continent or region. The first one has been done as an example.

1. L'AFRIQUE

   _____

   _____

2. L'ASIE ET
   LE MOYEN-ORIENT

   _____

   _____

3. L'AMÉRIQUE DU NORD
   OU L'AMÉRIQUE CENTRALE
   _____le Canada_____

   _____

4. L'AMÉRIQUE DU SUD

   _____

   _____

5. L'OCÉANIE

   _____

   _____

6. L'EUROPE

   _____

   _____

B. Un tour du monde. You will hear a tourist describing his trip around the world. Number the places **1–8** on the map in the order that he goes to each one. The first one has been done as an example.

EXEMPLE VOUS ENTENDEZ: Je suis parti de Paris le 25 mai. D'abord, j'ai pris le train pour la Belgique où j'ai passé deux jours à Bruxelles…

VOUS MARQUEZ:

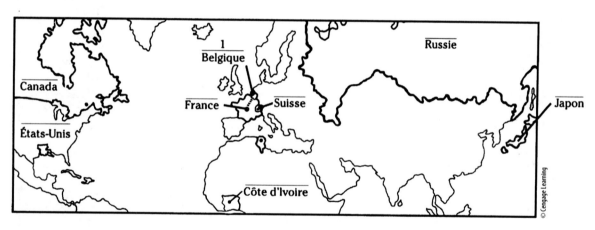

Now pause the recording and complete these sentences with the name of the appropriate country preceded by the correct preposition.

EXEMPLE Le 25 mai, il a pris le train de Paris à Bruxelles, _en Belgique_.

1. Le 28 mai, il a pris l'avion de Bruxelles à Montréal, _____.

2. Après, il a visité la Louisiane, _____.

3. Ensuite, il est allé à Tokyo, _____.

4. Après un séjour *(stay)* en Russie, il a pris le train pour Genève, _____.

5. Avant son retour à Paris, il a visité Abidjan, _____.

🔊 **C. Visitons le monde francophone!** A friend asks you to choose different places to visit. For each
7-18 choice, suggest the *francophone* location by completing the statements with the appropriate place and
preposition. You will then hear the correct response. Check your answer and repeat after the speaker.

EXEMPLE VOUS ENTENDEZ: On visite l'Égypte ou le Maroc?
VOUS COMPLÉTEZ: Allons **au Maroc**!
VOUS ENTENDEZ: Allons au Maroc!
VOUS RÉPÉTEZ: **Allons au Maroc**!

1. Allons _____!   4. Allons _____!

2. Allons _____!   5. Allons _____!

3. Allons _____!

🔊 **D. Qu'est-ce qu'ils deviendront?** What will become of the various characters you have met in the
7-19 different chapters of *Horizons*? Listen to what will happen to them and fill in the missing words.

1. **Chapitres 1 et 2:** Léa _____ à Nice,

   France, où elle _____ professeur d'anglais à l'université de

   Nice. David et elle _____.

2. **Chapitres 3 et 4:** Robert Martin _____ ses études à

   l'université Laval _____ Québec. Ensuite, il _____ à

   Lafayette où il _____ pour une grande société internationale.

3. **Chapitres 5 et 6:** Alice Pérez et sa famille _____ à

   San Antonio, _____ Texas, et elle _____ beaucoup de

   succès dans le commerce international.

4. **Chapitres 7 et 8:** Rosalie Toulouse et André Dupont _____

   le reste de leur vie _____ Normandie. Rosalie _____

   souvent _____ pour voir sa famille

   _____ Atlanta, _____ Géorgie.

5. **Chapitres 9 et 10:** Anaïs _____ voir Lucas _____ France.

   Ils _____ beaucoup de temps ensemble et ils

   _____ bien.

Line art on this page: © Cengage Learning

À l'hôtel

Chapitre 10

Deciding where to stay

By the time you finish this **Compétence,** you should be able to describe a stay at a hotel and make suggestions about travel.

Partie écrite

*A. Logements de vacances. Create sentences explaining where these people are staying on their next vacation and how they are going to pay their bill.

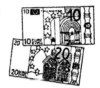

> EXEMPLE   Robert **descend dans une auberge de jeunesse.**
> **Il va régler la note en espèces.**

1. Georges et Cécile Duménage _____
   _____
   _____
   _____
   _____

2. M. et Mme Lefric _____
   _____
   _____
   _____
   _____

3. Moi, je _____
   _____
   _____
   _____
   _____
   _____

B. À l'hôtel. Reread the conversation between Lucas and the hotel receptionist on pages 386–387 of the textbook. Then, complete this conversation where another tourist is asking for a room.

La touriste: Bonjour, monsieur. Avez-vous _____ **(1)** pour ce soir?
                                                    (a single room)

L'hôtelier: Oui, nous avons _____ **(2)** avec
                               (a room)

_____ **(3)** et _____ **(4)** privés à 120 euros la nuit.
       (bathroom)   *(toilet)*

LA TOURISTE: Est-ce que _____ (5)?
(breakfast is included)

L'HÔTELIER: Non, il faut payer _____ (6) de 7 euros.
(an extra charge/supplement)

LA TOURISTE: Bon, c'est très bien. Je prends cette chambre.

L'HÔTELIER: Ah, attendez. Nous avons aussi une chambre avec _____ (7) et
(shower)

_____ (8) à 105 euros si vous préférez. C'est
(sink)

_____ (9) et il y a moins de _____ (10).
(courtyard side)   (noise)

LA TOURISTE: Oui, je préfère ça.

L'HÔTELIER: Très bien. Comment préférez-vous _____ (11),
(to pay the bill)

_____ (12), _____ (13)
(in cash)   (by credit card)

ou _____ (14)?
(by debit card)

LA TOURISTE: _____ (15).
(In cash)

L'HÔTELIER: Alors, vous avez la chambre numéro 12, _____ (16).
(at the end of the hallway)

Voici _____ (17).
(the key)

LA TOURISTE: Merci, monsieur.

L'HÔTELIER: Je vous en prie.

C. Règlements.

If you were staying at a hotel in a francophone country, would they tell you that one must or must not do the following things? Complete each sentence with **il faut** or **il ne faut pas**.

EXEMPLE Pour assurer que votre chambre soit *(is)* prête à votre arrivée, **il ne faut pas** arriver avant 14h00.

1. _____ quitter la chambre à 12h00 le jour de votre départ pour éviter des frais supplémentaires *(extra charges)*.

2. _____ payer un supplément de 18 euros par jour pour les animaux.

3. En cas d'incendie *(In case of fire)*, _____ prendre l'ascenseur.

4. _____ faire trop de bruit dans les couloirs.

5. _____ régler la note à votre départ.

6. _____ hésiter à contacter la réception si vous avez besoin de quelque chose.

D. Conseils. Based on what your friend says, give her suggestions by completing the statements with one of the choices given.

choisir une chambre côté cour / faire une réservation / changer d'hôtel / téléphoner à l'ambassade *(embassy)*
prendre l'ascenseur / régler la note par carte de crédit / demander une chambre à deux lits

EXEMPLE — Je préfère une chambre calme.
— Alors, il vaut mieux **choisir une chambre côté cour.**

1. — Le restaurant où on va dîner est très fréquenté *(busy)*.

— Alors, il vaut mieux _____.

2. — J'ai perdu mon passeport!

— Alors, il faut _____.

3. — Je ne dors pas bien quand je dois partager mon lit.

— Alors, il vaut mieux _____.

4. — Je n'aime pas du tout cet hôtel.

— Alors, il faut _____.

5. — Je n'ai pas assez d'argent pour payer l'hôtel.

— Alors, il faut _____.

6. — Ma chambre est au cinquième étage et j'ai beaucoup de bagages.

— Alors, il vaut mieux _____.

E. En voyage. Lucas has made two lists of things to do or not to do before and during a trip and has ordered each list according to how important it is to do the things mentioned. The first item in each list is the most important to do and the last one is the least important or should be avoided. Fill in the blank in each sentence with the appropriate expression from the box that precedes it.

il vaut mieux	il faut absolument	il ne faut pas	il n'est pas important de (d')

Avant de partir…

1. _____ réserver une chambre.

2. _____ acheter son billet bien à l'avance pour payer moins cher.

3. _____ préparer un itinéraire pour tout le voyage parce que
les projets changent toujours.

4. _____ oublier de demander à quelqu'un de donner à
manger aux animaux.

Pendant le voyage…

il est important de (d')	il n'est pas bon de (d')	il faut	il ne faut jamais

1. _____ faire attention à ses bagages et à son argent.

2. _____ avoir un bon guide.

3. _____ voyager avec beaucoup d'argent en espèces.

4. _____ laisser ses bagages sans surveillance à l'aéroport.

*F. De nouveaux étudiants. A group of new students has arrived at your school. Complete these statements with suggestions as to what they need to do to be successful.

1. Il faut _____.

2. Il ne faut pas _____.

3. Il vaut mieux _____.

4. C'est bien de (d') _____.

5. Il est essentiel de (d') _____.

*G. Et vous? Describe your last stay (or an imaginary stay) at a hotel by answering the following questions with complete sentences.

1. Dans quel hôtel êtes-vous descendu(e)? Aviez-vous une réservation quand vous êtes arrivé(e)?

_____

_____

2. Comment était votre chambre? Est-ce que c'était une chambre avec ou sans salle de bains ou douche? Est-ce qu'il y avait un grand lit ou deux lits?

_____

_____

_____

3. Est-ce qu'il y avait un mini-bar dans la chambre? Une télévision plasma ou LCD? Est-ce qu'il y avait le Wi-Fi gratuit?

_____

_____

_____

4. À quel étage était votre chambre? Est-ce qu'il y avait un ascenseur à l'hôtel? Que pouviez-vous voir de la fenêtre de votre chambre? Est-ce qu'il y avait un balcon?

_____

_____

_____

5. Est-ce qu'il y avait un restaurant à l'hôtel? Est-ce que vous avez pris vos repas dans votre chambre?

_____

_____

_____

6. Quel était le prix de votre chambre? Comment avez-vous réglé la note?

_____

_____

Partie auditive

A. Quel genre d'hôtel? You will hear short descriptions of several hotels. Indicate the category of each hotel by selecting **un hôtel pas cher** or **un hôtel de luxe.**

1. UN HÔTEL PAS CHER _____ UN HÔTEL DE LUXE _____

2. UN HÔTEL PAS CHER _____ UN HÔTEL DE LUXE _____

3. UN HÔTEL PAS CHER _____ UN HÔTEL DE LUXE _____

un hôtel pas cher   **un hôtel de luxe**

Repeat this section and listen to the description of each hotel again. Fill in the blanks with the information about each hotel.

L'Hôtel Carayou: Il y a _____ **(1)** chambres à l'hôtel. _____ **(2)** chambres sont avec salle de bains, toilettes séparées, téléphone, télévision, accès Internet Wi-Fi, mini-bar, radio et balcon donnant sur les jardins. L'hôtel se trouve *(is located)* _____ **(3).** Une chambre coûte _____ **(4)** euros la nuit.

L'Hôtel Amantine: Il y a _____ **(1)** chambres à l'hôtel. _____ **(2)** chambres sont avec salle de bains. L'hôtel se trouve _____ **(3).** Une chambre coûte _____ **(4)** euros la nuit.

L'Hôtel Diamant: Il y a _____ **(1)** chambres à l'hôtel. _____ **(2)** chambres sont avec salle de bains, balcon, cuisine équipée et téléphone. L'hôtel se trouve à _____ **(3)** minutes du centre-ville. Une chambre coûte _____ **(4)** euros la nuit.

B. Pour mieux comprendre: *Anticipating a response.* You will hear various tourists talking about hotels. Identify the sentence that would logically follow next. Then, check your work as you hear the statement again followed by the correct answer.

EXEMPLE   VOUS ENTENDEZ: L'ascenseur à côté de notre chambre fait trop de bruit. Je n'ai pas dormi du tout.
               VOUS INDIQUEZ: ____✓____ Il faut demander une autre chambre.
                              _____ Il faut revenir à cet hôtel la prochaine fois.
               VOUS ENTENDEZ: L'ascenseur à côté de notre chambre fait trop de bruit. Je n'ai pas dormi du tout. Il faut demander une autre chambre.

1. _____ Il faut demander une autre chambre.

    _____ Il faut revenir à cet hôtel la prochaine fois.

2. _____ Il faut chercher un autre hôtel.

    _____ Il faut réserver une deuxième nuit.

3. _____ Il faut payer par carte de crédit.

    _____ Il vaut mieux payer en espèces.

4. _____ Il est important de réserver bien à l'avance.

_____ Il n'est pas nécessaire de faire une réservation.

5. _____ Il vaut mieux demander une chambre côté rue.

_____ Il vaut mieux demander une chambre côté cour.

C. La chambre. Listen as a tourist talks about her hotel room. Then pause the recording and indicate whether these statements are true or false by selecting **vrai** or **faux**.

1. La chambre est grande.   VRAI _____   FAUX _____

2. La touriste ne va pas passer beaucoup de temps dans la chambre. VRAI _____   FAUX _____

3. Il y a une salle de bains, mais il n'y a pas de douche.   VRAI _____   FAUX _____

4. Il y a une belle vue sur la ville.   VRAI _____   FAUX _____

D. À l'hôtel. Listen to a conversation between two tourists about their hotel room and fill in the missing words. Pause the recording as needed in order to have enough time to respond.

ARIANE: Tu sais, je suis vraiment déçue *(disappointed)*! Regarde cette chambre! Nous payons

_____ (1) la nuit et _____ (2)

est toute petite.

SOPHIE: La prochaine fois, _____ (3) nous informer mieux que ça avant de choisir

un hôtel.

ARIANE: Tu as raison. Cette chambre n'est pas agréable du tout et en plus elle est côté rue et

_____ (4).

SOPHIE: Oui, _____ (5) demander une autre chambre pour

ce soir – quelque chose _____ (6). Pour pouvoir bien profiter

de notre séjour, _____ (7) bien dormir la nuit.

ARIANE: As-tu essayé _____ (8)? Ils ne sont vraiment pas très

confortables!

SOPHIE: Écoute, demain _____ (9).

ARIANE: Bonne idée. Alors, vaut-il mieux _____ (10) ce soir?

SOPHIE: Non, pas ce soir. J'ai _____ (11) et je peux la

_____ (12) demain matin.

ARIANE: Bon, d'accord. Et demain on cherche un autre hôtel!

COMPÉTENCE 2

Going to the doctor

By the time you finish this *Compétence,* you should be able to describe how you feel when you are ill and give recommendations about what to do.

Partie écrite

A. Le corps. Label the following body parts in French. Use the definite article with each body part (**le, la, l, les**).

1. _____
2. _____
3. _____
4. _____
5. _____
6. _____
7. _____
8. _____
9. _____
10. _____
11. _____
12. _____
13. _____
14. _____

B. Où ont-ils mal? Say what body part probably hurts.

dents	gorge	jambes	nez
tête	yeux	ventre	

EXEMPLE Je tousse beaucoup. J'ai mal à **la gorge.**

1. J'éternue beaucoup. J'ai des allergies.

    J'ai mal au _____.

2. J'ai trop mangé et j'ai envie de vomir.

    J'ai mal au _____.

3. J'ai fait un marathon ce matin.

    J'ai mal aux _____.

4. J'ai bu trop de bière hier soir. Ce matin, j'ai mal à la _____.

5. Je dois aller chez le dentiste parce que j'ai mal aux _____.

6. Je vais chez l'oculiste *(eye doctor)* parce que j'ai mal aux _____.

(Figure: labeled human body diagram with numbers 1–14. Number 10 is marked [the back]. © Cengage Learning)

C. Conversation. Reread the conversation between Lucas and the doctor on page 392 of your textbook. Then, complete this conversation between another patient and the doctor with the indicated words.

Le médecin: Bonjour, madame. _____ **(1)**?
                                                     (What's wrong)

Mme Garnier: _____ **(2).** _____ **(3)**
                         (I feel bad)   *(I have the shivers)*

                 et _____ **(4)** tout le temps.
                                 (my head hurts)

Le médecin: Vous avez une forte fièvre *(fever)* aussi. Je pense que c'est _____ **(5).**
                                                                                    (the flu)

Mme Garnier: Qu'est-ce que je dois faire?

Le médecin: Voici _____ **(6).** Il faut que vous preniez ces
                             (a prescription)

                 médicaments _____ **(7)** et _____ **(8)**
                                 (three times per day)   *(it's essential)*

                 que vous vous reposiez.

D. Il faut se soigner! Suggest something to help the following people feel better by completing each recommendation with the logical phrase from the list. Put the verb in the *subjunctive*.

manger des plats plus légers le soir   changer de lunettes

boire moins d'alcool   porter des gants *(gloves)* la prochaine fois

prendre de l'aspirine   arrêter de fumer

acheter de nouvelles chaussures   utiliser de la crème solaire la prochaine fois

> **EXEMPLE**   — J'ai toujours mal aux yeux.
> — Il faut que vous **changiez de lunettes.**

1. — J'ai souvent mal aux pieds à la fin de la journée.

   — Il faut que vous _____.

2. — Mon mari a toujours mal à la gorge et il tousse beaucoup.

   — Il faut qu'il _____.

3. — Mon fils est sorti avec ses amis hier soir et il a mal à la tête ce matin.

   — Il faut qu'il _____

   et qu'il _____.

4. — J'ai souvent une indigestion et mal au ventre quand je me couche.

   — Il faut que vous _____.

5. — Ma fille a passé la journée à la plage. Maintenant, elle a un mauvais coup de soleil *(sunburn)*.

   — Il faut qu'elle _____.

6. — J'ai travaillé dans le jardin ce matin et maintenant, j'ai mal aux mains à cause des rosiers *(rose bushes)*.

   — Il faut que vous _____.

E. Chez le médecin. Imagine the doctor's reactions to these remarks by his patients. Complete the statements with the logical phrase in parentheses. Put the verb in the subjunctive.

    EXEMPLE   Nous sommes souvent très fatigués. (rentrer tard, se coucher plus tôt)
                     Il faut que vous **vous couchiez plus tôt.**
                     Il ne faut pas que vous **rentriez tard.**

1. Mes enfants sont souvent très fatigués. (sortir tous les soirs, prendre des vitamines)

    Il faut qu'ils _____.

    Il ne faut pas qu'ils _____.

2. Ma femme est très stressée. (se reposer, réfléchir trop à ses problèmes)

    Il faut qu'elle _____.

    Il ne faut pas qu'elle _____.

3. Mon fils a grossi récemment. (choisir des plats légers, manger beaucoup)

    Il faut qu'il _____.

    Il ne faut pas qu'il _____.

4. Je suis enceinte. (fumer, dormir assez)

    Il faut que vous _____.

    Il ne faut pas que vous _____.

5. Mon mari a besoin de faire plus attention à sa santé. (boire trop d'alcool, maigrir un peu)

    Il faut qu'il _____.

    Il ne faut pas qu'il _____.

F. Une bonne santé. Give a friend who wants to improve his health advice by completing the following statements with the logical ending from each pair. Remember to use the subjunctive.

    EXEMPLE   (être toujours nerveux / boire moins de café)
                     Il vaut mieux que tu **boives moins de café.**
                     Il n'est pas bon que tu **sois toujours nerveux.**

1. (faire attention à ce que tu manges / manger trop de sucre)

    Il faut que tu _____.

    Il ne faut pas que tu _____.

2. (savoir combien de calories il y a dans chaque plat / prendre des plats avec trop de calories)

    Il est important que tu _____.

    Il n'est pas bon que tu _____.

3. (maigrir trop vite / perdre quelques kilos)

    C'est bien que tu _____.

    Il est mauvais que tu _____.

4. (faire de l'exercice / aller tous les jours à la salle de gym)

Il faut que tu _____.

Il n'est pas nécessaire que tu _____.

5. (pouvoir te reposer de temps en temps, être trop stressé)

Il faut que tu _____.

Il ne faut pas que tu _____.

G. Dans l'avion. You are training to be a flight attendant and you are going over the regulations. Complete each sentence logically with **il faut** or **il ne faut pas** in the first blank and the subjunctive of the verb in parentheses in the second one.

> **EXEMPLE** **Il faut** que le dossier du siège *(seatback)* de chaque passager **soit** (être) en position verticale au décollage et à l'atterrissage *(on take-off and landing).*

1. _____ que chaque passager _____ (avoir)

une carte d'embarquement *(boarding pass)* pour monter dans l'avion.

2. _____ que les passagers _____ (savoir)

utiliser les masques à oxygène en cas de dépressurisation de la cabine.

3. _____ que tous les bagages à main *(carry-on luggage)*

_____ (être) dans les compartiments à bagages ou sous le siège *(seat)*

situé devant les passagers.

4. _____ que les passagers _____ (fumer)

dans les toilettes.

*Journal. Remember the last time you were sick and imagine that you have come down with the same illness again. Write a conversation between you and the doctor in which you describe your symptoms and the doctor tells you what you need to do. Be sure to use the subjunctive as needed.

_____

_____

_____

_____

_____

_____

_____

_____

_____

_____

Partie auditive

A. Le corps. Repeat each part of the body you hear and put the corresponding number in the appropriate blank.

EXEMPLE	VOUS ENTENDEZ:	les dents
	VOUS RÉPÉTEZ:	**les dents**
	VOUS METTEZ:	

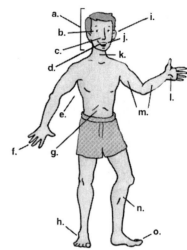

LE CORPS

a. _____   i. _____

b. _____   j. _____

c. _____   k. _____

d. _Exemple_   l. _____

e. _____   m. _____

f. _____   n. _____

g. _____   o. _____

h. _____

B. J'ai mal partout! Where do the following people hurt? Repeat each sentence you hear and put the corresponding number with the appropriate illustration.

EXEMPLE	VOUS ENTENDEZ:	Il a mal à la main.
	VOUS RÉPÉTEZ:	**Il a mal à la main.**
	VOUS INDIQUEZ:	

a. _____   b. _____   c. _Exemple_   d. _____

e. _____   f. _____   g. _____   h. _____

C. Pour avoir la santé. A doctor is explaining to a patient how to feel better and have more energy. Repeat each sentence and indicate whether the doctor is expressing what should be done (**oui**) or what shouldn't be done (**non**) by putting the number of each statement and **oui** or **non** in the blank for the corresponding illustration.

EXEMPLE VOUS ENTENDEZ: Il vaut mieux que vous évitiez les matières grasses.

  VOUS RÉPÉTEZ: **Il vaut mieux que vous évitiez les matières grasses.**

  VOUS INDIQUEZ:

a. _____ b. _____ c. _____

d. **Exemple: oui** e. _____ f. _____

D. Que faut-il faire? Imagine you are a doctor. Listen to what each of your patients says, then use **il faut que vous** and the most logical solution from each pair below to recommend what each patient should do. You will then hear the correct response. Check your answer and indicate the correct option.

EXEMPLE VOUS VOYEZ: aller chez le dentiste _____ / boire moins de café _____

  VOUS ENTENDEZ: J'ai souvent mal à la tête et je dors mal.

  VOUS DITES: **Il faut que vous buviez moins de café.**

  VOUS ENTENDEZ: Il faut que vous buviez moins de café.

  VOUS INDIQUEZ: aller chez le dentiste _____ / boire moins de café ✓__

1. acheter d'autres chaussures _____ / boire moins d'alcool _____

2. écrire moins _____ / changer de lunettes _____

3. dormir plus _____ / manger moins rapidement _____

4. fumer moins _____ / boire moins d'eau _____

5. nager plus souvent _____ / boire moins de café _____

6. travailler moins _____ / aller chez le dentiste _____

*E. Et vous? Answer the following questions with complete sentences.

1. _____

2. _____

3. _____

4. _____

Line art on this page: © Cengage Learning

Nom _____ Date _____

Running errands on a trip

By the time you finish this *Compétence,* you should be able to talk about running errands on a trip and say what you want yourself and others to do.

Partie écrite

A. Pourquoi? Lucas is saying where he and Anaïs went and why. Complete his statements.

| **Exemple** | **1** | **2** | **3** | **4** | **5** |

acheter de l'aspirine
changer de l'argent
retirer de l'argent

envoyer des cartes postales et acheter des timbres
acheter un journal et une carte téléphonique
acheter un cadeau

EXEMPLE   Anaïs est allée **au distributeur de billets** pour **retirer de l'argent.**

1. Je suis allé _____ pour _____.

2. Anaïs est allée _____ pour _____.

3. Anaïs est allée _____ pour _____

_____.

4. Je suis allé _____ pour _____

_____.

5. Je suis allé _____ pour

_____

B. Conversation. Reread the conversation between Anaïs and Lucas on page 398 of the textbook. Then, complete this conversation where two female friends are making plans for one's visit.

AURÉLIE: _____ **(1)** tu viennes me voir. Quand vas-tu arriver?
            (I'm happy that, I'm glad that)

FLORENCE: Je pars lundi matin.

AURÉLIE: À quelle heure est-ce que je devrais _____ **(2)** à l'aéroport?
            (to go pick you up)

FLORENCE: Non, ne viens pas _____ **(3).** Je peux prendre
            (to pick me up)

_____ **(4).** Je ne veux pas que tu perdes ton temps à
            (the shuttle)

l'aéroport si l'avion arrive _____ **(5).**
            (late)

AURÉLIE: Mais non, _____ **(6)**! L'avion arrive à quelle heure?
(I insist)

FLORENCE: À 18:15 heures.

AURÉLIE: _____ **(7)**, nous pouvons aller dîner
(If you don't have other plans)

en ville. _____ **(8)** un bon petit restaurant pas loin de l'aéroport.
(I know)

FLORENCE: Bonne idée! J'aurai faim _____ **(9)**.
(after my flight)

AURÉLIE: _____ **(10)**. À lundi, alors.
(Perfect)

FLORENCE: Oui, au revoir, à lundi.

C. Réactions. How would you respond if a travel companion with whom you were planning to spend the day told you the following things? Begin each response with the logical expression in parentheses and do not forget to use the *subjunctive*.

    EXEMPLE   Je n'aime pas du tout ma chambre. (C'est dommage que… / Je suis content[e] que…)
               C'est dommage que tu n'aimes pas du tout ta chambre.

1. Le restaurant à l'hôtel est excellent. (Je suis content[e] que… / C'est dommage que…)

   _____

2. Il y a trop de bruit la nuit. (Je suis heureux [heureuse] que… / Je regrette que…)

   _____

3. Je ne peux pas bien dormir. (Je suis désolé[e] que… / Je suis content[e] que…)

   _____

4. Je suis fatigué(e). (C'est dommage que… / Je suis content[e] que…)

   _____

5. Je n'ai pas envie de sortir. (Je suis heureux [heureuse] que… / Je regrette que…)

   _____

6. Je veux passer toute la journée à l'hôtel. (Je suis surpris[e] que… / Je suis content[e] que…)

   _____

7. Je commence à me sentir mieux. (Je suis désolé[e] que… / Je suis heureux [heureuse] que…)

   _____

8. Je t'invite au restaurant ce soir. (Je regrette que… / Je suis content[e] que…)

   _____

D. Quel temps fait-il? The weather can often change vacation plans. Give your feelings about the weather, using the French equivalent of each expression from page 400 of the textbook.

  EXEMPLE **Je suis surpris(e) qu'il fasse mauvais.**

faire froid   faire chaud   faire du soleil   pleuvoir   faire mauvais

Exemple   **1.** *It's too bad that...*   **2.** *I'm sorry that...*   **3.** *I'm happy that...*   **4.** *I regret that...*
I'm surprised that...

1. _____

2. _____

3. _____

4. _____

*E. L'idéal. What traits do you require in your ideal partner? Complete each sentence with the phrase from the list that best expresses your feelings and the subjunctive of the verb in parentheses.

   Je veux que...   Je préfère que...   Il n'est pas important que...   Je ne veux pas que...

   EXEMPLE   **Il n'est pas important qu'**il/elle **soit** (être) riche.

1. _____ il/elle _____ (vouloir) avoir
   des enfants.

2. _____ il/elle _____ (avoir) déjà
   beaucoup d'enfants.

3. _____ il/elle _____ (pouvoir) sortir avec
   moi tous les soirs.

4. _____ il/elle _____ (gagner) beaucoup
   d'argent.

5. _____ il/elle _____ (savoir) parler une
   autre langue.

6. _____ il/elle _____ (être) plus ou moins
   du même âge que moi.

7. _____ il/elle _____ (finir) ses études
   universitaires.

8. _____ il/elle _____ (faire) des études
   supérieures *(postgraduate).*

9. _____ il/elle _____ (avoir) un bon sens
   de l'humour.

10. _____ il/elle _____ (s'intéresser) aux
    mêmes choses que moi.

F. Un voyage. One friend is making plans with another to go on a trip. Complete the following sentences with the verbs in parentheses, using either the infinitive or the subjunctive.

EXEMPLE   Je voudrais **aller** (aller) en Guadeloupe et je voudrais que tu y **ailles** (aller) avec moi.

1. Je veux que tu _____ (choisir) l'hôtel, mais je ne veux pas _____ (payer) trop cher.

2. Je voudrais _____ (être) dans un hôtel près de la plage et je préfère que l'hôtel _____ (ne pas être) trop grand.

3. J'aimerais _____ (partir) le matin, mais je ne veux pas que notre vol _____ (partir) trop tôt.

4. En avion, je préfère _____ (dormir) et je ne veux pas que les autres passagers à côté de moi _____ (faire) beaucoup de bruit.

5. Je veux que tu me _____ (dire) ce que tu veux _____ (faire) en Guadeloupe parce que je veux _____ (préparer) un itinéraire détaillé avant de partir.

6. Je veux que ce voyage _____ (être) facile et je ne veux pas _____ (avoir) de problèmes.

7. Je veux que tu _____ (prendre) beaucoup de photos avec ton nouvel appareil photo *(camera)* parce que j'aimerais _____ (faire) un album de photos.

8. Je suis content que tu _____ (faire) ce voyage avec moi parce que je ne veux pas le _____ (faire) tout seul.

*G. Et vous? Answer the following questions about traveling with complete sentences.

1. Où voudriez-vous passer vos prochaines vacances? Aimez-vous avoir un itinéraire détaillé quand vous voyagez ou préférez-vous faire des projets au jour le jour *(day by day)*?

    _____

    _____

2. Préférez-vous être dans un hôtel moins cher mais loin du centre-ville ou préférez-vous que l'hôtel soit près de tout, même si *(even if)* vous devez payer plus cher?

    _____

    _____

3. Préférez-vous avoir une chambre non-fumeur *(non-smoking)* ou préférez-vous pouvoir fumer?

    _____

4. Aimez-vous mieux que le petit déjeuner soit compris dans le prix de votre chambre ou préférez-vous ne pas prendre le petit déjeuner à l'hôtel? Si vous visitez un autre pays, aimez-vous goûter des plats exotiques ou préférez-vous que la cuisine ne soit pas trop différente de chez vous?

    _____

    _____

    _____

Partie auditive

A. Des courses. You will hear what errands Lucas and Anaïs ran today. Repeat what you hear, then put the number of the sentence with the corresponding illustration.

EXEMPLE   VOUS ENTENDEZ: Lucas est allé à une boutique de cadeaux.
VOUS RÉPÉTEZ: **Lucas est allé à une boutique de cadeaux.**
VOUS INDIQUEZ:

a. _____

b. _____

c. _____

d. _____

e. _____

f.   _Exemple_

B. Des touristes en vacances. You will hear several tourists say what they need to do today. Based on what they say, tell them where they need to go, using **il faut.** After a pause for you to respond, you will hear the correct response. Fill in the missing words in the sentences as you listen.

EXEMPLE   VOUS ENTENDEZ: J'ai besoin d'acheter un journal.
VOUS RÉPONDEZ: **Pour acheter un journal, il faut que vous alliez au kiosque.**
VOUS ENTENDEZ: Pour acheter un journal, il faut que vous alliez au kiosque.
VOUS ÉCRIVEZ: Pour **acheter un journal,** il faut que vous alliez au kiosque.

1. Pour _____, il faut que vous alliez au bureau de poste.

2. Pour _____, il faut que vous alliez au bureau de poste.

3. Pour _____, il faut que vous alliez à la boutique de cadeaux.

4. Pour _____, il faut que vous alliez au distributeur de billets ou à la banque.

5. Pour _____, il faut que vous alliez au bureau de change ou à la banque.

7-31

C. Qui va le faire? Lucas's parents are leaving on vacation and his mother is talking to her husband, Lucien, about who is going to do what. Based on the lists shown, does she tell him that she wants him to do each thing named or that she prefers to do it herself? Play the role of Lucas's mother. Note that she forgets to mention two of the listed items.

Moi
acheter un guide
lire le guide
préparer l'itinéraire
réserver une chambre
faire les valises

Lucien
acheter un journal
préparer la voiture pour le voyage
dire aux voisins la date de notre départ
acheter une carte téléphonique
aller chercher tes médicaments à la pharmacie

© Cengage Learning

EXEMPLES	VOUS ENTENDEZ:	acheter un journal
	VOUS RÉPONDEZ:	**Je veux que tu achètes un journal.**
	VOUS ENTENDEZ:	Je veux que tu achètes un journal.
	VOUS ENTENDEZ:	acheter un guide
	VOUS RÉPONDEZ:	**Je préfère acheter un guide moi-même** *(myself).*
	VOUS ENTENDEZ:	Je préfère acheter un guide moi-même.

Later, Lucas's mother remembers the two items she forgot to mention. Complete the following statements with what she says.

1. Je veux que tu _____.

2. Je préfère _____ moi-même.

7-32

D. L'arrivée. Pause the recording and review the conversation on page 398 of the textbook. A friend of Anaïs's, Salima, is coming to visit her. Turn on the recording and listen to their conversation. You will hear their conversation twice. The first time, just listen at normal speed. Then listen as it is repeated at a slower speed, with pauses for you to fill in the missing words. Play this section again as needed.

ANAÏS: Comme je suis contente _____

_____ **(1)** chez moi. Tu arrives quand?

SALIMA: Jeudi matin _____ **(2).**

ANAÏS: Tu veux _____ **(3)** à l'aéroport?

SALIMA: C'est gentil, mais je ne veux pas _____ **(4)**

à l'aéroport si jamais *(in case)* _____ **(5).**

Il y a _____ **(6)**, non?

ANAÏS: Non, non, j'_____ **(7).** Mais je préfère _____ **(8)**

juste devant la sortie principale. Comme ça, je n'aurai pas besoin de trouver un parking.

Disons vers _____ **(9)?**

SALIMA: C'est parfait. À jeudi, alors.

ANAÏS: Oui, à très bientôt.

Giving directions

By the time you finish this *Compétence,* you should be able to give and follow directions in French.

Partie écrite

A. En ville. Complete the following sentences with a logical preposition according to the illustration. You are standing in the street, facing the **Hôtel Molière.**

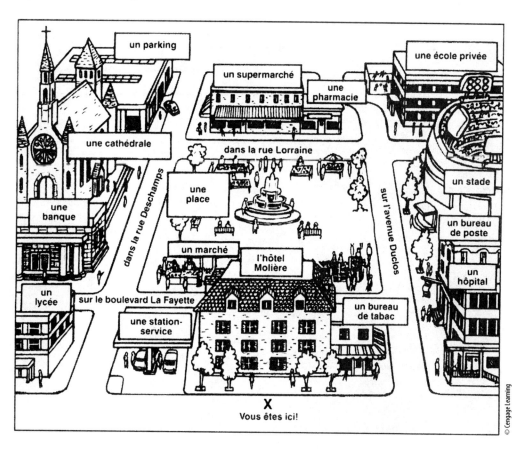

à côté / à gauche / à droite / en face / entre / au bout / au coin

1. La station-service est _____ de l'hôtel Molière et le bureau
   de tabac *(tobacco shop)* est _____ de l'hôtel.

2. Il y a un bureau de poste _____ de l'hôpital.

3. Le stade est _____ le bureau de poste et l'école privée.

4. Il y a un parking _____ de la rue Lorraine et de la rue Deschamps.

5. _____ du parking, de l'autre côté de la rue Deschamps, il y
   a un supermarché.

6. _____ de l'avenue Duclos, il y a une école privée.

*B. Pour aller à... You are standing in the street, facing the **Hôtel Molière** in the illustration in ***A. En ville.*** Give directions to the following places.

EXEMPLE   le parking:
**Montez la rue Deschamps et continuez tout droit jusqu'au
bout de la rue. Le parking est à gauche au coin de la rue
Lorraine et de la rue Deschamps.**

1. le supermarché: _____

_____

_____

2. le stade: _____

_____

_____

3. la pharmacie: _____

_____

_____

C. Conversation. Reread the conversation between Anaïs and the employee at the tourist office on page 407 of the textbook. Then, complete this conversation where another tourist is asking for directions.

L'EMPLOYÉ: Bonjour, madame, _____ **(1)?**
                                       (may I help you)

LA TOURISTE: Oui, s'il vous plaît, monsieur, _____ **(2)**
                                            (could you explain to me)

comment aller à la gare routière *(bus station)?*

L'EMPLOYÉ: Bien sûr, madame, c'est très simple. C'est tout près.

_____ **(3)** la rue Provence _____ **(4)**
       (Go up)   *(until, up to)*

la rue Duplessis et _____ **(5).**
                                (turn left)

LA TOURISTE: _____ **(6)** la rue Provence et
                     (I go up)

_____ **(7)?**
                (I turn left)

L'EMPLOYÉ: Oui, c'est ça. _____ **(8)** et la gare routière sera
                                  (Continue straight)

_____ **(9)** la rue Dubouchage.
       (on your right, just after)

LA TOURISTE: _____ **(10),** monsieur.
                     (I thank you)

L'EMPLOYÉ: Je vous en prie, madame.

D. Un safari. A group of tourists is receiving instructions before leaving on a safari in Africa. Give logical commands telling them to do or not to do the following things using a direct object pronoun (**le, la, l', les**), an indirect object pronoun (**lui, leur**), **y,** or **en** for the italicized words.

> **EXEMPLES**   oublier *votre passeport:* **Ne l'oubliez pas.**
> garder *(to keep) votre passeport* avec vous: **Gardez-le avec vous.**

1. boire *de l'eau du robinet (tap water):* _____

2. acheter *de l'eau* en bouteille: _____

3. obéir *au guide* pendant le safari: _____

4. perdre *le guide* de vue: _____

5. aller *dans la jungle* tout seul: _____

6. toucher *les animaux:* _____

7. donner à manger *aux animaux:* _____

8. donner un pourboire *(tip) au guide:* _____

9. oublier *le pourboire:* _____

E. Et toi? Tell a friend who is leaving on vacation to do or not to do the following things by changing the statements in the subjunctive to commands.

> **EXEMPLES**   Il ne faut pas que tu t'ennuies!
> **Ne t'ennuie pas!**
>
> Je veux que tu m'écrives.
> **Écris-moi!**

1. Je veux que tu t'amuses!

   _____

2. Je veux que tu me montres tes photos après!

   _____

3. Il ne faut pas que tu me demandes de l'argent pour le voyage!

   _____

4. Il ne faut pas que tu te perdes!

   _____

5. Je veux que tu m'invites la prochaine fois!

   _____

6. Je voudrais que tu me téléphones quand tu arriveras!

   _____

7. J'aimerais que tu m'achètes un souvenir!

   _____

8. Je ne veux pas que tu m'oublies!

   _____

F. Faisons-le ensemble! Complete these short conversations in which you tell a friend with whom you are leaving on vacation to do the following things. Your friend says he/she doesn't feel like it, so you suggest doing them together. Replace the italicized words with a direct object pronoun (**le, la, l', les**), an indirect object pronoun (**lui, leur**), or with **y** or **en** in the second and third sentences of each item. Follow the example.

> **EXEMPLE** faire *les valises*
> — **Fais** les valises!
> — Je n'ai pas envie de **les faire.**
> — Alors, **faisons-les** ensemble!

1. choisir *l'hôtel*

   — _____ l'hôtel!

   — Je n'ai pas envie de _____!

   — Alors, _____ ensemble!

2. aller *à la banque*

   — _____ à la banque!

   — Je n'ai pas envie d'_____!

   — Alors, _____ ensemble!

3. acheter *de nouveaux vêtements pour le voyage*

   — _____ de nouveaux vêtements pour le voyage!

   — Je n'ai pas envie d'_____!

   — Alors, _____ ensemble!

4. téléphoner *à l'agent de voyages*

   — _____ à l'agent de voyages!

   — Je n'ai pas envie de _____!

   — Alors, _____ ensemble!

---

*Journal. You are inviting some classmates to your place after class. Write precise directions telling how to get there from the university.

_____

_____

_____

_____

_____

_____

_____

_____

_____

_____

Partie auditive

7-33

A. Des indications. Imagine that you are at the hotel on the **boulevard Angoulvant**. (Look for the X on the following map.) Listen to the directions and determine where you end up. In the list below, put the number of the directions given next to the place you end up. Directions will be given to only two of the destinations.

EXEMPLE   VOUS ENTENDEZ: Sortez de l'hôtel et tournez à droite. Descendez le boulevard Angoulvant jusqu'à l'avenue Terrasson de Fougères. Tournez à gauche et continuez tout droit. Traversez le boulevard Clozel et ça va être sur votre gauche.

VOUS INDIQUEZ: **Exemple *by* bureau de poste**

Assemblée nationale _____

Cathédrale St-Paul _____

Place Climbié _____

Bureau de poste _Exemple_

Palais de Justice _____

Restaurant Climbié _____

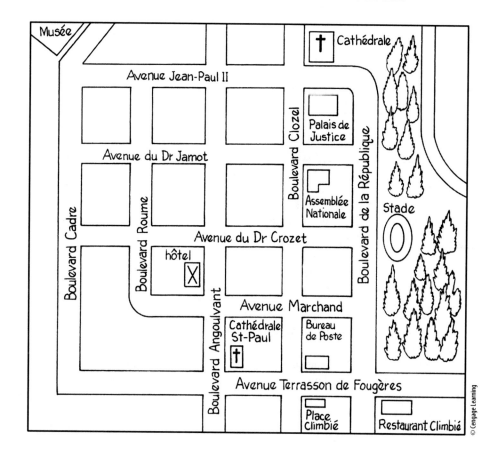

Now play this section again and fill in the missing words in each set of directions. Pause the recording as needed.

1. Sortez de l'hôtel et _____ sur le boulevard Angoulvant.

Au premier coin, _____ sur l'avenue du Dr Crozet.

Ensuite, _____ sur le boulevard Clozel

et ça va être _____.

2. Sortez de l'hôtel et _____ sur le boulevard Angoulvant.

_____ l'avenue Jean-Paul II.

Là, _____. _____

le boulevard Clozel et ça va être _____.

B. En voyage. You are traveling with a friend who always puts everything off as long as possible. What does your friend say to do in each case? Answer with a **nous**-form command and a direct object pronoun. You will then hear the correct response. As you listen, complete the sentences with the missing words.

EXEMPLE	VOUS ENTENDEZ:	On réserve la chambre d'hôtel avant de partir ou on la cherche après notre arrivée?
	VOUS DITES:	**Cherchons-la après notre arrivée!**
	VOUS ENTENDEZ:	Cherchons-la après notre arrivée!
	VOUS COMPLÉTEZ:	**Cherchons-la** après notre arrivée!

1. _____ au restaurant!

2. _____ demain matin!

3. _____ plus tard!

4. _____ plus tard!

5. _____ plus tard dans une banque!

6. _____ demain matin!

C. À la réception. The clerk at your hotel's front desk is asking if you want the following things done for you. Answer affirmatively or negatively with a **vous**-form command, as in the examples. You will then hear the correct response. As you listen, fill in the missing words in each sentence.

EXEMPLE 1	VOUS VOYEZ:	Oui, _____ ma chambre, s'il vous plaît.
	VOUS ENTENDEZ:	On vous montre votre chambre?
	VOUS DITES:	**Oui, montrez-moi ma chambre, s'il vous plaît.**
	VOUS ENTENDEZ:	Oui, montrez-moi ma chambre, s'il vous plaît.
	VOUS ÉCRIVEZ:	Oui, **montrez-moi** ma chambre, s'il vous plaît.
EXEMPLE 2	VOUS VOYEZ:	Non merci, _____ le petit déjeuner dans ma chambre.
	VOUS ENTENDEZ:	On vous sert le petit déjeuner dans votre chambre?
	VOUS DITES:	**Non merci, ne me servez pas le petit déjeuner dans ma chambre.**
	VOUS ENTENDEZ:	Non merci, ne me servez pas le petit déjeuner dans ma chambre.
	VOUS ÉCRIVEZ:	Non merci, **ne me servez pas** le petit déjeuner dans ma chambre.

1. Oui, _____ une autre clé, s'il vous plaît.

2. Non merci, _____ demain matin.

3. Oui, _____ avec les bagages, s'il vous plaît.

4. Non merci, _____ le dîner dans ma chambre.

5. Oui, _____ le nom d'un bon restaurant, s'il vous plaît.

6. Oui, _____ comment aller à ce restaurant, s'il vous plaît.

7. Non merci, _____ demain matin.

CPSIA information can be obtained
at www.ICGtesting.com
Printed in the USA
FFOW01n2030071217
43947398-43042FF